Authority
in
Protestant
Theology

BOOKS BY ROBERT CLYDE JOHNSON
Published by The Westminster Press

The Meaning of Christ
  (*Layman's Theological Library*)
Authority in Protestant Theology

Authority
in
Protestant
Theology

ROBERT CLYDE JOHNSON

Philadelphia
THE WESTMINSTER PRESS

© W. L. JENKINS MCMLIX

Library of Congress Catalog Card No. 59–9824

To Elizabeth and Catherine

two of a kind

✠

Contents

Preface

T HE analytical quest recounted in these pages began more than ten years ago in a parish. It was provoked initially by the burden of preaching. Doubtless every minister who has experienced the unrivaled privilege, and the terrifying responsibility, of speaking to a people week by week, month by month, of the reconciliation and redemption wrought by God in Jesus Christ, has reflected at one time or another on the deeper sense in which the New Testament category " burden " is peculiarly appropriate to preaching.

When one is installed in a pulpit and assumes the pastoral care of a people, the question of theological orientation immediately ceases to be a matter of dialectical gymnastics. It suddenly becomes, in a literal sense, a matter of life and death. With the passage of time, a minister becomes increasingly conscious of the mysterious, enigmatic, redemptive efficacy of the Word of God. He discovers that there is a power in preaching that surpasses even the most exaggerated potentiality which he may attribute to the words that he speaks from the pulpit. Concurrently and inescapably, however, he also becomes slowly aware of the fact that he may thwart the Word of God. He discovers that he can nullify the cross of Christ, and inflict paralysis upon a church, by unfaithfulness in the pulpit.

It is with this discovery that the deeper element of fear and trembling pervades the preaching office. It likewise is just at this point that the question of theological authority rudely intrudes itself. The problem lies beneath the level of all questions regarding psychological sincerity, and the gravity of motive, as important as these may be. The constraint may be quite clear and compelling. But how is one to know what must be said here and now? . . . by what authority?

I am one of many who have Martin Luther to thank for the most penetrating insight that came to me as I struggled with this problem during the first years of my ministry. It was the releasing realization that our theology and our preaching, no less than the moral side of our lives, are justified by faith. This permits the Christian liberty, of which Paul and the Reformers had so much to say, to become directly relevant to theological reflection and immediately applicable to the preaching ministry.

It was my experience, which merely confirmed the contention of the Reformers, that this radically rehabilitates the preaching office. It contributes an inexplicable synthesis of reliance and freedom, which simply is not available if we imagine that the ultimate effectiveness of our words is commensurate with, and contingent upon, the limited ability and the questionable content that we take with us into the pulpit. Here even the burden of preaching becomes a part of the " light burden " of which our Lord spoke. This undoubtedly is the primary prerequisite of Christian preaching.

It also was Luther who reminded us, however, that if we have taken our stand under justifying grace, and availed ourselves of the surety and freedom that the gift of faith makes possible, this will intensify rather than mitigate the urgency of obedience. This is why an application of the doctrine of grace and justification to the ministry, which could be the most desperate need of American Protestantism at the moment, will deepen rather than weaken the compulsion to be faithful in the pulpit.

We find that it does not solve the formative theological problem of preaching. It merely quickens it. It regenerates concern, and it drives the minister back to a re-examination of the footing and the orientation of his ministry. When this occurs, he cannot avoid facing the complex question of authority. This is why we should view the scattered but recurrent indications that the American church is beginning to face this issue once more, after having more or less circumvented it for half a century, as evidence of latent health and hope.

Robert Clyde Johnson

Western Theological Seminary
Pittsburgh, Pennsylvania

Prologue

IT WAS Sören Kierkegaard who turned to theological use the homey observation that you cannot sew without a knot in the thread. Protestants have always been more uneasily aware of the theological implications of this statement than Christians of other traditions. The very genius of Protestantism prohibits it from giving the question of theological authority a simple, static, or final answer, and forces it to reopen the matter as a new issue with each major development in the dynamic movement of theological thought. There are those who wish that this were not so; and there will always be those who will attempt to prevent its being so; but in the very nature of the case it must be so if Protestantism is to remain faithful to its formative motif. This is why P. T. Forsyth could remark that the question of authority in its religious form is the last as well as the first issue of life. It is the previous question of theology, the question that has been answered if an answer is ventured to any other theological question. But even the answer that we give to this previous question is in every sense a human answer, and as such it must be examined and tested, and re-examined and retested in every generation.

When the question is cast in its most elemental form, it is simply this: By what authority is one theological statement or doctrine preferred over another? In every approach to theology a critical tool is implied and employed. It is present in a preliminary way in the selection of the material to be utilized and the rejection of the material to be ignored; and it is employed in a final way in the choice that a theologian inevitably must make between conflicting doctrines

11

and between one formulation or statement of a doctrine and another. Whenever it is assumed that one theological affirmation is true and another false, or that one is more nearly true than another, a principle of theological authority has been utilized. It may have been employed explicitly or implicitly, consciously or unconsciously, but its presence in the theological process is inescapable.

When we refer to this question as theology's previous question, this is in no sense to say that because of its logical priority it must be accepted as the most important, or even as a chronologically prior, issue of theology. Here Prof. Karl Barth's provocative, fundamental protest against theological prolegomena is well taken.[1] The entire history of Protestant thought vividly illustrates that it is fatal to abstract this question in any way, either under the illusion that it can be answered prior to the decisions that are materially determinative for a theological system, or as though the issue could be settled without regard to the entire content of the Christian faith. This has been attempted in various periods, and as we shall see, the results have invariably been disastrous. Perhaps the most important lessons that can be learned from a survey of the winding path that has been followed in the development of Protestant theology are that the question of theological authority is one that must be answered in view of the whole, and that any answer that is not consistent with the necessary orientation and the essential content of Christian theology is *ipso jure* unacceptable.

This does not prohibit our singling out this issue for special attention, however, just as a serious affirmation of the doctrine of the Trinity in no sense prohibits all future consideration of the specific problems of Christology. And it would appear that the contradiction of the present situation, which is apparent both in clerical and in lay circles in American Protestantism, strongly suggests the need for a new, open discussion of the matter. The last major work addressed to this subject, if we do not catalogue Barth's *Doctrine of the Word of God* as such, was formulated as the nineteenth century gave way to the twentieth, and prior to even the earliest signs of the breakdown of the synthesis that had been erected on the basis of Schleiermacher's radical reorientation of Protestant theology. In sharp contrast, a professor in one of the leading theological seminaries in this country remarked recently that among present-day theological students this is the one issue that commands the most attention and is approached with the deepest concern.[2] We can easily understand why it was kept carefully submerged in the first half of the century; but the time is long past when it should have been permitted to emerge, and the conversation that surrounded it in all previous periods resumed in public.

Certainly it is to be regretted that many, if not most, Protestant laymen in America today are largely unconscious of the fact that there is an alternative between blind acceptance of a heteronomous norm, and an autonomous rejection of any theological authority whatsoever. When they speak to the subject, or indirectly reveal their unspoken presuppositions, they almost invariably reflect a feeling that this is the choice which must be made: either we must embrace the Bible in an unquestioning, superstitious way, as a theological textbook which contains answers to all questions for those who are persistent enough to search them out; or we must concur with the vague conviction of a "right of private judgment" under the illusion that this was the gift of the Reformation. Prof. A. E. Taylor once recounted a conversation between a Roman Catholic theologian and an outsider who insisted that he could discern no real difference between the theological position of Rome and that of a well-known Anglo-Catholic. The Roman theologian is reported to have replied: "We are at the opposite pole from X. He holds every doctrine that we hold, but he holds them all for the entirely irrelevant reason that he thinks them true."[3] The representative Protestant theology of the mid-twentieth century may be heterogeneous in the extreme, but it clearly represents a third alternative; and we cannot avoid the judgment that while we permit the opinion to prevail in the church that a choice must be made between subscription to the Christian faith as a body of belief that must be accepted *on dit,* and the obligation to accumulate a collection of *Privatmeinungen,* personal opinions with little or no basis beyond private bias, we are without excuse. For this reason, if for no other, we need to bring this issue into the open.

This study is an analytical attempt to determine the present status of the problem as a background for conversation, recognizing that this can be done only by tracing it from its inception in the Reformation into the present. One of the most disconcerting facets of the current situation is an almost universal confusion in the use of the terminology required to discuss the matter. The words "norm" and "criterion" are frequently used interchangeably, and often as synonyms; and if they are intended to imply differing connotations or nuances, the difference is infrequently explicit. An attempt has been made to circumvent this confusion by assigning specific meanings to these central terms, and adhering arbitrarily to their use in the specified sense except where the context clearly indicates otherwise.

Norm is a singular term derived from the Latin *norma,* the word that was used for the carpenter's square which assured right angles. A right angle is always ninety degrees, and thus the *norma* invariably was ninety degrees. The word has retained this connotation of permanence, inflexibility, and exclusiveness. A theological norm is assumed to be absolute or, by its very nature, to exclude the acceptance of other theological norms. The theologians of late Protestant orthodoxy were employing the term accurately when they spoke, within the context of the *sola Scriptura* principle, of the Bible as the "singular norm" of theology (*autopistos* and *axiopistos,* per se and in se, self-authenticating in and of itself, bearing its own *certitudo* or authority).[4] Their intention was to attribute autonomy to Scripture as the singular, exclusive authority over theology, and thus they were etymologically correct in describing it as the theological *norma.*

A criterion, from the Greek *kritērion,* is a functional critical instrument or authority. This term was first used to designate the judge who presided and passed sentence in a court of law. The authority of a judge is not absolute but derivative and mediate; and his authority does not reside in his person but in his office, commission, or status. He functions under the norm that is embodied in the law or in the sovereign of the state; and he is not a singular authority, for the presence of other judges and superior authorities within the province or state is assumed. These connotations are present in the use of the word "criterion." It is assumed that theological criteria do not necessarily exclude one another. Several criteria may be employed within the same system, or a criterion that is materially the same may assume differing forms within different loci. The authority of a criterion is not absolute but derivative and mediate; and because they are of this nature, theological criteria are necessarily under the superior authority of a theological norm.

The word *discrimen,* which is used frequently, is intended to designate a configuration of criteria that are in some way organically related to one another as reciprocal coefficients. Calvin's doctrine of the Word and the Spirit may be cited as a classic example of a theological *discrimen.* It requires the *testimonium Spiritus Sancti,* or that the Holy Spirit " attest " the written word of Scripture, in order for it to be authoritative and useful for theological purposes. It also requires that the word of Scripture be utilized to " test " the Holy Spirit, or to " test the spirits to see whether they are of God " (I John 4:1). Within this doctrine both Scripture and the testimony of the Holy Spirit are criteria, but they are organically and inseparably related as reciprocal coefficients. It is this type of configuration of criteria which the technical term *discrimen* is intended to designate.

The original lines that circumscribe the Protestant approach to the question of theological authority were drawn in the sixteenth century. But there are two background factors, inherited by the Reformation, which have not always been given the weight that they demand in an examination of the complex approach of Luther and Calvin to this question. They are peculiarly important to an understanding of the significance of the insistence, common to the Reformers, upon the *sensus literalis* and *simplex intelligentia* of the Bible, the simple, single-level, " literal " comprehension and interpretation of the Biblical text. One is the almost universal acceptance of the allegorical method of Biblical interpretation during and in the centuries just preceding the Reformation. The other is the verbal assent that was accorded, parallel to the use of allegory, to " literalism " in the exegetical approach to the Bible. These two factors, for our purposes, may be associated primarily with Origen and Nicholas of Lyra, who both symbolize and were dominant in creating the basic issue that the Reformers encountered in the area of authority.

Origen could look back across a long history of the use of the allegorical interpretive method, both by Jewish rabbis and by Greek philosophy; and he was heavily influenced by Philo and the Septuagint as he fashioned a systematic rationale for this type of exegesis for Christian theology.[5] He began with the axiomatic assumption that the Bible is divine, or " of God " ; and, appealing to the authority of the words of Paul in I Thess. 5:23, he moved on to an identification of the body, soul, and spirit of the Biblical text. Origen did not dismiss the bodily or historical, and the spiritual or moral meanings, which he assumed to be present in the Bible, but he did assign them an inferior status for theological purposes. He conceded that many Biblical passages demand their use, and that the majority of believers, who cannot be expected to rise above " simplicity " in their comprehension of the Scriptures, need and must be guided by them. He argued, however, that others, and certainly those to whom the church commits its theological task, should find the word of Scripture a " pattern," a " shadow," or an " allegory " of " heavenly things." This demanded that the theologian " trace out the meaning of the Spirit of God, which is perhaps lying profoundly buried "; and it required that he remember in doing so that a Biblical passage quite often is " pointing in another direction than the ordinary usage of speech would indicate." Origen insisted that it is through this use of the spiritual, figurative, or allegorical approach that the theologian becomes " a sharer in the knowledge of the Spirit, and a partaker in the divine counsel." [6]

The ascendency that this assumption of the necessity for a *multiplex intelligentia* of Scripture enjoyed for more than a thousand years is well known.[7] One church historian has remarked of Origen that " even those who attacked him most vigorously were often influenced by his thought," so that " his influence on medieval allegorists though indirect is incalculable." [8] The motivation of Origen can be defended and justified, for a literalistic simple-mindedness that made utter nonsense of the Scriptures was threatening to grip the church and had to be combated. But what must be seen for our purposes is that whatever value we may place on Origen's contribution for his own time, it was his systematization of the allegorical method that opened the door to the unbelievable accumulation of doctrines, traditions, and practices that Luther confronted and was forced to combat in his reformation efforts. Farrar's remark was undoubtedly too strong, but it frames the problem that the Reformers faced: " Scholasticism treated the letter of Scripture, even in its plainest histories, as an enigma which veiled the latest afterthoughts of theology." [9] Another writer has remarked that the Biblical studies that underlay pre-Reformation theology were "like straining milk through a coal sack." [10] Fortunately a much saner view is now being taken of the whole matter, but it leaves the basic datum for our problem undisturbed. Scripture, church, and tradition comprised the explicit triad of authority; but with the use of this *multiplex* approach it was always possible to show that the Biblical text conformed neatly with prevailing doctrine and practice. When we view Luther's problem before this background, we recognize immediately that his efforts to recall the church to the faith that he had rediscovered through the Bible would have failed utterly had he not been able to undermine the widespread confidence in this interpretive method.

The figure who symbolizes the first successful effort to control this complex approach is Nicholas of Lyra, a Franciscan Biblical scholar and a professor at the Sorbonne in the fourteenth century. He had predecessors who were both more conservative and, from a scholarly point of view, much more important than he; but his *Postillae,* which appears to have been the first Biblical commentary ever printed, became a rather popular manual of exegesis in the late Middle Ages and was known to Luther. Nicholas of Lyra did not break theologically with the reigning doctrine of hermeneutics. But inspired by his own inquiries into the Hebrew text of the Old Testament, which had been reintroduced in the thirteenth century, he argued strongly that the allegorical, mystical, or spiritual interpretation had been abused to the degree that it had distorted and hidden the necessary "literal," or the obvious, historical meaning of the Biblical text. He then proposed a fresh approach to the whole matter, within which the allegorical meaning would follow upon, and be accountable to, the natural, historical, or literal meaning of a passage. His influence proved to be neither strong nor widespread; but by one of those happy accidents of history Luther became familiar with his work, and thus the seed of reform that he planted reaped a belated but abundant harvest. Together with Origen, he symbolizes the complexity of the situation that Luther faced as he slowly identified the practical problem that confronted his reformation endeavors.

PART ONE

The Reformation

CHAPTER I

Martin Luther

IF WE remark that Luther was the freest and most creative theologian of the Reformation, the statement is so manifestly true that it conveys clear overtones of redundancy. He possessed an almost unerring ability to ignore the nonessential and penetrate directly to the heart of the theological matter at hand. It was this uncanny reductive skill which permitted the extricating simplification with which he broke through the medieval synthesis and gave us Protestantism. This penetrating critical faculty proved to be at the same time, however, the source of profound theological dilemmas. We should not permit either the old or the new temptation to absolutize the Reformers to obscure the fact that their legacy is complicated and in part confused. It may be that this was inevitable because of the historical and theological roles that they were called to play; but in any event it is true and particularly true of Luther. Read rightly, he will always be exasperating to anyone who prefers neat theological formulas to creative theological power.

The deduction that should be drawn from this obvious fact is that when our approach to Luther is motivated primarily by a compulsion to systematize, we both cloud his contribution and read him incorrectly. Harnack has remarked that he " romped in the church like a child at home." [1] " He simply was not indwelt by the irresistible desire of the thinker who strives for theoretical clarity. In fact he had an instinctive disgust for, and an innate mistrust of, every spirit who, guided merely by knowledge, boldly corrected errors." [2] Luther himself said, as he pondered his theology in retrospect the year before his death, that his writings had been so much determined by "the confusion of events" that they were "a sort of crude and disorganized chaos" in which even their author was hard pressed to find any system or order.[3]

This perception must not be abnormally exaggerated, as it is when Luther's faculty for subsuming doctrine is overlooked,[4] or when it is suggested that he coveted inconsistency or had no feeling for the interrelation of theological affirmations. Even Harnack's more tempered deduction — that "the attempt to analyze seems to entangle us in insoluble contradictions," which suggests that it would be better if we could content ourselves with some sort of empathetic recapitulation of Luther's "mood" or "attitude" [5] — is undoubtedly an oversimplification prompted by distinctively nineteenth-century presuppositions. But the basic characteristics of Luther's thought which provoked this suggestion are highly important, and they indicate an integral attribute of his theology which must be taken seriously.

Karl Barth has given us a clue that can be valuable in our reading of Luther. He makes an important, if "relative," distinction between nonsystematic and systematic theologians, or between what he calls "irregular dogmaticians" and "regular dogmaticians." The characteristic that separates the two is said to be "completeness." [6] The irregular dogmatician is one who does not place a primacy of emphasis upon systematic completeness and consequently is very little preoccupied with, or hampered by, problems of consistency in construction and exactness of terminology. Barth is careful to say that neither irregular dogmatics, nor regular dogmatics, is preferable to the other. Either may be, in turn, merely the theological product of a "tired age"; and properly pursued, each is, in turn, necessary to the ongoing life of the church. The point that he wishes to make lies elsewhere. It is that these are two distinctly different types of theological approach, and that we must not fail to notice and take into account the difference that separates them.

With this distinction in mind, we may observe that Luther was, as Barth has remarked, "characteristically" and "candidly" the classic example of the irregular dogmatician.[7] Writing from an earlier, different, Ritschlian point of view, Reinhold Seeberg made substantially the same observation: "The rediscovered gospel bore within itself the hidden impulse for the construction of new theological formulas, and with lavish hand, and almost recklessly, Luther dashed them from his pen. But the reformation of the theology which he effected was not directed by any thought of a complete revision of the traditional dogmatic system." [8]

When we acknowledge the truth that is suggested by this summary characterization, we have conceded that we can only becloud the issue by demanding systematic " completeness " of Luther. If we call him to account because he assumes one theological posture within one context, and then appears to assume a different posture elsewhere; or if we fret because a term or concept bears one meaning in one place, and then appears to communicate a quite different meaning elsewhere — when we permit the understandable perplexity that this creates to delimit his contribution, we unnecessarily and unjustifiably complicate the matter. Nor should we fail to notice that the opposite may be said to be just as true. Whenever we insist upon finding carefully balanced doctrines in Luther where he himself made no pretense of having such, we create untold confusion and shackle his contribution to the theological thought of our time.

These are more or less elementary observations upon which most contemporary students of Luther are in essential agreement, at least in theoretical and methodological principle. They take on a disproportionate degree of importance, however, when they are applied to the problem under consideration; and our decision to abide by them, or not to abide by them, proves to be a determinative factor. For we discover that Luther's answer to the question of theological authority — even if it is not, as Harnack insisted, a " flagrant contradiction " [9] — is at best disconcertingly dichotomous. He appealed directly to the Bible, insisting with considerable feeling that it must be the "touchstone," " ruler," " plumb line," or " Lydian stone " of all Christian doctrine; [10] and that, as such, it must be read and interpreted in its "literal sense" (*sensus literalis* or *buchstabischer Sinn*). He also approached and dealt with the Scriptures with a remarkably free, critical temperament, with no hesitation whatsoever about questioning and sifting Biblical materials, and taking with complete seriousness levels of meaning and truth in the Bible. These two facts, each equally lucid and indisputable in Luther's writings, and each demanding to be taken with equal seriousness, plot the dimensions of the problem that confronts us when we attempt to designate the *discrimen* of his theology.

1. LUTHER'S PRACTICAL PROJECT

It would appear that Luther rather stumbled into the question of theological authority, not fully aware at the outset of the complexities involved in the answer that he found himself compelled to give. There is a marked absence of evidence that he struggled with the question as such before the appearance of the Ninety-five Theses in October, 1517. The theses themselves, hopefully designed to question and correct abuses, reveal no open or hidden challenge of the accepted authority of the church, which was becoming increasingly centered in the pope. Many years later, in 1545, he remarked, "When I first took up this cause, I was so inebriated, so drunk on papal doctrine, that I would have been fully prepared, if I had had the power, to kill (or at least to help kill, and have killed) anyone who denied or refused obedience to even a single syllable of the pope." [11]

In his writings that appeared during the year following the formulation of the theses, the broad issue has begun to take form for him; but it seems clear that he still had no conscious intention of raising the specific question of theological authority. He says as much in a letter to Staupitz; [12] and in the covering letter that he sent to Rome with his " Resolutions " he acknowledges without reserve or qualification the " apostolic authority " of the " supreme pontiff," and confesses that in the voice of the pope he recognizes and accepts the " voice of Christ." [13]

There are, in brief, conclusive strands of evidence that suggest that this question actually was not first raised as a public issue by Luther, but by his " threatening friends," principally Eck, Tetzel, and Cajetan. The evidence also indicates that the form in which Luther immediately answered the question was essentially practical, and decidedly polemical, provoked from him by the recurring attacks of these " friends." Precisely when the answer first appeared is a subject open to conjecture and debate; but we do know that he was quite clear on the matter by 1519. In a letter written in January of that year, he says, "We are simply forced to fly for refuge to that solid rock of Scripture, and not to believe anything, no matter what, that speaks, commands, or does anything without this authority." [14] And when the *Letter to the Christian Nobility* appeared in June of the same year, he had progressed to the point of leveling this criterion directly at Rome. "Where the pope acts against the Scriptures, we have an obligation to stand by the Scriptures, to correct and constrain him." [15] It was this early clarity which he reached on the matter that opened the way for the classic works of 1520.

This early answer was framed to meet an ultrapractical situation in which Luther found himself quickly embroiled. We find him, from the very beginning, making a sharp differentiation between "God's Word" (*Gottes Wort*) and the "doctrine of man" or "teaching of men" (*Menschenlehre*), or between the "gospel," on the one hand, and the vast assortment of laws, customs, traditions, and questionable theological claims, on the other. It would appear that the initial impetus to make this functional and polemical distinction and the confidence with which he wielded it were themselves derived from the Scriptures (cf. Mark 7:6-13; Rom. 16:17; Col., ch. 2), although this is not certain.

We find this crucial differentiation made freely and repeatedly, and in almost every conceivable context. [16] The seed of it is in the Ninety-five Theses, where one of the principal charges that he brings against those whom he criticizes is that they "preach man." [17] In *The Babylonian Captivity* (1520), it has crystallized as a part, if not essentially the sum and substance, of his attack upon the "miserable captivity" of the Roman curia. "The Word of God is incomparably superior to the church," he says; and "here certainly is something the church has the power to do: distinguish the Word of God from the words of men." [18] By 1522 the expressions "doctrines of men," "teaching of man," and "words of man," ordinarily juxtaposed to "God's Word," have become familiar and recurring concepts, and he entitles a treatise: *On Avoiding the Doctrines of Men, and an Answer to the Texts Wielded to Defend the Doctrines of Men.* [19]

This was the context within which Luther confronted the problem of theological authority, the practical necessity to distinguish and separate, with more than subjective arbitrariness or mere human

authority, *Gottes Wort* and *Menschenlehre*. It is obvious that this
task demanded a keen-edged criterion, a sharp tool that could cut
the legitimate theology free from the questionable theology in the
maze of Scholastic teaching that he brought under scrutiny. The
criterion that he seized upon, and wielded vigorously, is neither
difficult to discover nor held apologetically. It is explicit; and it is
championed vehemently. " It ought to be God's Word alone that
teaches us," he said; and " he is a liar who adds anything to the
words of God." [20] This permitted him to frame the issue in a decisive, clearcut way:

> We do not condemn the doctrines of men simply because
> they are the doctrines of men — for we would be glad to suffer
> them — but because they are against the gospel and the Scrip-
> tures. The Scriptures free men's consciences, and forbid that
> they become ensnared with the doctrines of men. We cannot
> harmonize this discord between the Scriptures and the doc-
> trines of men. . . . They are by nature opposed to one an-
> other, like water and fire, like heaven and earth. . . . Because
> the Scriptures and the doctrines of men contradict one another,
> one must lie and the other be true. Let us see to which they
> ascribe the lie.[21]

One of the clearest examples of this strong advocacy and use of
the Scriptures as the functional theological authority is found in
Luther's ultrapolemical writings of 1520 and 1521 against Hierony-
mus Emser, the " Leipzig goat." Emser had subtly criticized Luther,
and his treatise had borne his coat of arms, elaborately adorned with
the head of a long-horned goat. Luther's most spirited reply carries
the title, *Answer to the Superchristian, Superspiritual and Super-
ingenious Book of Goat Emser of Leipzig;* and his salutation reads,
" Dear Goat: butt me not." [22]

The encompassing purpose for which Luther is writing is not only
clear, but may even be said to be blatant. He asks, somewhat
heatedly: " How often must I scream at you thick, ignorant papists
to come with Scripture? Scripture, Scripture, Scripture. Do you not
hear, you deaf goat and dumb ass? " [23] " Paul wrote, ' scrutinize all
teaching, and retain that which is good,' " he observes. And he asks,

" If we would prove, as Paul says, what shall we take as a touch-stone [*Probierstein*], other than the Scriptures? " [24] This is his sin-gular position: " I will and must be subdued with Scripture, not with the uncertain life and doctrines of men, however holy they may be." [25]

The " touchstone " is then applied, in turn, to the church fathers, to all customs that the church has appended, and to the question of the sacraments. We must read the fathers " with discretion," he in-sists, accepting their teaching only when " they quote clear texts and explain Scripture with clearer Scripture." [26] We are obliged to fol-low them " only as they lead us to the Scriptures, as they were led," because " we must remain with the Scriptures alone." [27] Precisely the same is said of the accretion of customs, articles of faith, and sacraments. " No custom can change anything in the Scriptures," and " no holy father has the authority to formulate and advance an article of faith or sacrament that the Scriptures have not ordered and set forth." [28]

Obviously the criterion that Luther here employs is in no sense ambiguous or subtle. He simply demands that both the inclusive and the exclusive limits of Christian doctrine be fixed by direct appeal to the content of Scripture, and *only* by use of the Scrip-tures.[29] " We have no obligation to believe, except what God has commanded us in the Scriptures to believe, to which no one may add, and from which no one may subtract." And " other than the Scrip-tures nothing shall be taught." [30] When he is defending this position in another context, he remarks that all who do not so conform their theology to the Scriptures ought to be punished as blasphemers; and that, if we lack the authority to prescribe such punishment, the least that we can do is " hiss in unison " as the holy fathers did when the Arians reported at the Council of Nicaea.[31]

This insistence that Scripture is the *principium* and criterion of doctrine obviously calls into question a traditional characterization of the essential difference between Luther and Calvin. It has fre-quently been said that Luther permitted the inclusion of anything that illuminated and did not contradict Biblical material, while Calvin excluded whatever could not be found in the Scriptures. Transposed into ethics, this was the origin of the popular notion that

Luther permitted whatever was not prohibited by the Bible, while Calvin, and Puritanism, prohibited whatever was not expressly permitted by the Scriptures. As we shall see presently, this popular way of formulating the matter does indicate a broad difference of attitude and emphasis between Luther and Calvin in the area of authority; but the fact of the matter is that in formal statement *each* insisted that the Bible defines *both* the inclusive and the exclusive limits of doctrine. In actual practice Calvin, as did Luther, made continuous and free use of the fathers. Moreover, Luther as well as Calvin drew upon Scholastic theology much more than has ordinarily been recognized and granted. And although many of Luther's statements on the authority of Scripture are more naked than Calvin's, they are not naïve. Years later, in 1545, he remarked: " While it is true that in the things that pertain to God one should teach nothing other than the Scriptures, this only means that one should teach nothing different. We cannot hold that one should not make use of additional words, or words other than those in the Scriptures." [32] Actually the theoretical principle of Luther and Calvin, at this point, is essentially the same. The Bible is the formal criterion both in an inclusive and an exclusive sense. The difference emerges only when we turn to the questions of the systematic formulation of the *discrimen* and of pragmatic approach.

Luther makes no attempt to justify his criterion within this context, and relatively little attempt elsewhere to defend it. He seems to have assumed that it is, or that it should be, self-evident to any Christian. However, the hermeneutical question does rear its head briefly, and it is given a clear and almost curt answer. " We must merely illumine Scripture with Scripture. The right method is to put Scripture beside Scripture, properly and correctly." [33] By " properly and correctly " he means primarily three things. He insists, first, that texts and passages must not be used indiscriminately, but with a keen sense of their " natural " relevance, avoiding the temptation to practice eisegesis by dragging in confusing, irrelevant material. He is quite explicit, if not completely definitive or methodologically clear, on this point; and he quickly became indignant and sarcastic when it was violated. " I have until now held that when one would prove something with the Scriptures, the Scriptures must really be relevant to the point. But now I learn that it is enough to throw the texts together in any crazy way, whether they agree or not — and, if this is to be the way, I can prove from the Scriptures that bad beer is better than good wine." [34]

He insists, secondly, that if we are to illuminate Scripture with Scripture " properly and correctly," we must look to " the sense of the words," regarding them as " the speech of God " or " the words of God," and interpreting them in their " literal " sense. [35] This, as was suggested earlier, is the spearhead that he employed in his frontal attack upon figuremongering, the allegorical hermeneutics inherited from Origen, with the consequent assumption of a *multiplex intelligentia* of the Biblical text. Luther pointedly remarks: " They were right who formerly have prohibited the books of Origen. He looked too much to the spiritual sense, which was unnecessary, and allowed the necessary written sense to fade away. This submerges what is written, and never makes one fundamentally a good theologian. Only the single, proper, original sense, the sense in which it is written, makes good theologians. The Holy Spirit is the simplest writer and speaker in heaven and earth. Therefore his words can have no more than a singular and simple sense, which we call the written or literally spoken sense." [36] Also: " There are strong reasons for my feeling, and especially that violence should not be done to the form of the words of God, by man or angel. But wherever possible their simplest meanings are to be preserved; and, unless it is otherwise manifest from the context, they are to be understood in their proper, written sense, so that we do not give our adversaries occasion to evade all the Scriptures. It was because of this that Origen was formerly, and rightly, repudiated, because he changed the trees and everything else written of paradise into allegories and was contemptuous of the grammatical meaning." [37]

There is perhaps no other, single locus in the voluminous tomes of Luther where he insists with more passion on a " literal " interpretation of Scripture. But even here it is obvious that what he intends is intrinsically different from the Protestant interpretive method that emerged under the name of " literalism " in the seventeenth and eighteenth centuries, a vestige of which — metamorphosed and hardened by rationalism — survives today. Pages are devoted to

an analysis and refutation of Origen's *multiplex intelligentia,* with its
" spiritual method," [38] making it quite clear that by " literal " Luther
means " nonallegorical," " nonpneumatic," or " non-Origenistic." It
is interesting that at one point he turns aside to observe that
" literal " is not a very satisfactory term, either in German or in
Latin, for what he is insisting upon, and that it would be better if it
were called the " lingual or spoken sense," or the " grammatical,
historical sense." [39] It is of no little significance that we should find
this (almost parenthetical) observation appearing within the context
of the Emser writings, where we also find Luther's most vehement
insistence that the Bible, interpreted " literally," must be the singular
criterion of theology.

The third requisite for proper and correct hermeneutics that is
noted is that Christ must be the *telos* toward which interpretation
moves. This is the echo, in the area of theological authority, of the
centrality of the " theology of the cross " (*theologia crucis*), which
has been the principal emphasis of the recent wave of Luther studies.
It is important to recognize that Luther meant more by this, as a
hermeneutical principle, than that we should orient Biblical interpretation by the New Testament and seek " types " in the Old Testament, although each of these was a part of his personal exegetic
practices. His larger point was intrinsically soteriological as well as
Christological.

It is quite true, as we shall see in more detail below, that Luther
insisted that the gospel is incipiently present in the Old Testament,
and that in a real sense Christ is present and may be known throughout the Scriptures. This claim is the context of his familiar statement
that the law and prophets are the " swaddling-clothes " and " man-
ger " in which Christ lies.[40] But his hermeneutical concern is much
broader than this contention, as it consistently overreaches the contours of revelation per se. It embraces even an insistence that the
" letter of the law " should be interpreted, *as law,* to the end that the
" benefits " of Christ may be known.[41] His most consuming concern is symbolized by the fact that he recommended the letter to the
Romans as the best introduction to the Old Testament! [42] He insists
that *all* Biblical interpretation, to be Christian interpretation, must
be soteriologically motivated and directed.

This is the most unique and telling strain that permeates Luther's approach to the Bible, and the one that has most frequently been lost — both by those who have abnormally exaggerated and unjustifiably warped his concern for the " literal " sense of Scripture and by many who have not. Just as in the broader sense he avoids a dichotomy of revelation and redemption, so he avoids a bifurcation of hermeneutics and soteriology, and subsumes soteriology under hermeneutics, or hermeneutics under soteriology, as the occasion may require. And for Luther it is first and foremost in this sense that Christ is, and should be, the center of the circle of Biblical interpretation. This is why it is so utterly amazing, and genuinely perplexing, that it could ever have been assumed that he was concerned for " correct doctrine " for the sake of correct doctrine.

2. LUTHER's FREEDOM

So much is clear. It permits us — or, if need be, forces us — to conclude that Luther utilized the text of the Bible in a direct and singular way as the criterion of Christian doctrine, and that the sharpening and clarification that this approach received in practical and polemical contexts places the question of its use beyond dispute. This is only one side of the coin, however; and if we fail to see more than this, we misrepresent his complex reply to the question of theological authority, which clearly cannot be identified with the *sola Scriptura* principle of later orthodoxy.

It is no less evident that Luther transcended every type of slavery to the written text of Scripture, and neither viewed nor used the Bible in an axiomatic, legalistic, or rationalistic way. Without attempting to thrust a systematic doctrine upon him, we can observe this freedom and transcendence in action, even as he regards himself as being guided by and bound to the Bible as the " touchstone," by a brief analysis of another consistent differentiation which he employed from first to last.

Just as Luther frequently made a clear-cut distinction between *Gottes Wort* and *Menschenlehre,* the differentiation that has been suggested as the one that framed the problem of theological authority for him, so he distinguished throughout his writings between " law " and " the gospel." It not only may be said that this distinction recurs, but it is quite possible that there is no differentiation that appears more often in his writings.

When we attempt to trace the indications and implications that this recurring distinction may have for the problem of theological authority, we must be careful to notice that Luther did not regard " law " and " the gospel " as synonymous with " Old Testament " and " New Testament." The assumption that he did so regard them has sometimes been used as a device for screening the dilemmas in his position — by insisting that he placed the two Testaments on different levels and thus could not have been entirely serious in his insistence that the Bible per se must be employed as the theological criterion. His distinction between the Testaments, as it bears upon the question of authority, is not basically a qualitative one. It is a functional distinction; and it carries no suggestion that the New Testament is the superior authority, or is in some sense the *real* Word of God.

Luther is quite clear on this; but, inasmuch as innumerable secondary works are not so clear on the matter, it needs to be examined more closely. In his 1523 introduction to the Old Testament, he says: " Understand that this book is a book of laws, where we learn what one should do, and refrain from doing; and at the same time examples and stories indicate how these laws are kept or broken. In the same way the New Testament is a book of gospel or grace, and teaches where one is to lay hold of what is required to fulfill the law. But, even so, in the New Testament, side by side with the teaching of grace, many other teachings are also given which are laws and commandments — to govern the flesh, since in this life the spirit is not perfected and thus grace alone cannot reign. There also are in the Old Testament, side by side with the laws, some promises and declarations of grace, with which the holy fathers and prophets who were under the law were preserved, as we are, under the faith of Christ." [43]

When " law " and " gospel " are differentiated in this manner, it is clear that each spans both Testaments — in such an embracing way, in fact, that there is the suggestion of a doctrine of the unity of the Bible, and one that has not as yet been developed in the recent spate of theories on Scriptural unity. Luther even includes " law " in our "knowledge of Christ," although he carefully distinguishes it from a " correct " knowledge of the gospel. " Christ in the Gospels, and in addition St. Peter and St. Paul, give many commandments and doctrines and expound the law, which one ought to reckon as all of the other works and benefits of Christ," he says. But " even so, to know his works and historical life is not yet a correct knowledge of the gospel, for here you do not yet know that he has conquered sin, death, and the devil." [44]

We also must be careful not to assume that the term " law," as Luther, following Paul, uses it in this differentiation, is synonymous with " laws " or with the Mosaic law. It has a meaning much deeper and broader than can be encompassed by external prohibitions or laws, whether these be written or oral, human or divine. " You must not here understand the little word ' law ' in a human sense," he says, " as a teaching about works we should do or refrain from doing. With human laws one performs the law sufficiently with works, whether the heart is in them or not. God judges according to the bottom of the heart. Therefore his law also claims the bottom of the heart, and cannot be satisfied with works." [45]

When we understand " law " in this infinitely more encompassing sense as the depth demand of God or the embodiment of the demand of God upon the human life and "heart," it then will be recognized that when Old Testament interpretation is subsumed under the law-gospel distinction, all the books of the Old Testament, even the highest level of the Prophets, become from this point of view essentially " law." They join with " Moses " in bringing the demand of God upon the human heart, and thus they function to lead (or drive) us to Christ the Savior. He asks: " What are the other books, the prophets and histories? I reply that they are nothing other than what Moses is, for they all carry on the office of Moses. . . . They hold fast so that through the law the people will be kept in a proper understanding of their own incapacity; and thus they drive them to Christ, as Moses did." [46]

Moreover, we may now see why Luther could, and did, emphasize that the New Testament contains " law." Wherever the effort is made to bring the demand of God to bear upon the human heart, whether it be in the Decalogue and Prophets, in the Sermon on the

Mount as Jesus fulfills his office of "lawgiver,"[47] or in the New Testament letters, this is "law." We likewise may recognize why, for Luther, this demand of God, or "law," whether it comes through Moses, a prophet, a historian, Christ himself, or the letter of James, is a full and essential part of *Gottes Wort.*

When we "know Christ," we see that "law" is necessary and indispensable in a twofold sense, or that it has a double " use " (*usus,* as in Calvin) or dual function as " Word of God." The first is to " curb the godless."[48] The second is called its " proper office " (*officium proprium*) or its " theological or spiritual use."[49] Here it functions to " reveal to man his sin, blindness, wretchedness, impiety, his ignorance, hatred, and contempt of God, and the death, hell, judgment, and wrath of God which he fully deserves."[50] This " leads," or if need be, " drives," us to Christ. " Therefore the proper office of the law is to lead us out of our tabernacles, that is out of our peace and self-reliance, place us before God, and reveal his wrath to us."[51] " This, therefore, is the most glorious use of the law, namely, that so far as it influences us, just so far is one humbled and aroused to thirst for Christ."[52]

It should at least be noted that Luther also spoke of another " use " of the law in Christian life. It broadly corresponds to Calvin's " third use," " third office," or " special use " of the law.[53] It matters not how much we " grow in sanctification " and " become a new creature in Christ," Luther says, " we must have the law not only because it tells us in a legal way what we are obligated to do, but also that we may see in it how far the Holy Spirit has brought us with his work of sanctification."[54]

Even apart from this " third use," however — which, of course, many have denied was of any appreciable importance to him — when we remember Luther's strong, overarching emphasis upon the situation of the Christian as *simul peccator et justus,* it is readily evident that for him " law " is in an integral and indispensable sense a part of the " Word of God." He states flatly, " It is not possible for anyone to hear the gospel, and allow himself to be made alive by the grace of the Spirit, who will not first permit himself to hear the law and be put to death by its letter."[55] The law " leads us to Christ " not only in an initial but also in a continuing sense; and it is only as we are so led to Christ and taught by him that we can recognize as *good* the " good news " of God's mercy which constitutes " the gospel." And, in turn, it is only when we so recognize "the gospel" to be something intrinsically and qualitatively different from "law" that the *discrimen* of theology can be properly utilized and " correct doctrine " formulated. Luther states this both negatively and positively: " Unless gospel is truly and plainly separated from law, it is not possible to hold fast to sound Christian doctrine." Hence, " whoever can correctly separate gospel from law should thank God, and know that he is a real theologian." [56]

It requires only the most cursory acquaintance with the theology of Luther to know that the importance of this distinction was tremendous and all-embracing for him. It is one of the foremost examples of his ability to subsume the quintessence of Christian doctrine under any one of its major heads — the methodology with which, while remaining an " irregular dogmatician," he preserved a genuine organic unity in his theology. Viewed from one side (*in loco justificationis*), the law-gospel differentiation is simply the insight of justification by faith *sola* (i.e., and not by " works of the law "). Looked at from another side (the Christological), it is the knowledge of Christ as Savior which comes only as " the gospel " that God has given through him is sharply distinguished from " law." It is only when we have recognized this subsumed content that we may account for the fact that this differentiation was so crucial for Luther, and explain why it consistently occupied a place in the very heart of his theology.

Luther's use of the law-gospel distinction both symbolizes and illustrates his virtually uninhibited theological freedom — a freedom that has not always been recognized, even in the present " Luther renaissance," and that has even more seldom been seen to be intrinsic to his methodology. It was a freedom born of the Biblical message and brought back to the Bible when he approached it for theological purposes. The contemporary theologian (of the American movement that is now in the midst of a studied attempt to become known as " evangelical theology ") who is battling for a twentieth-century type of Biblical " literalism " on the assumption that this is " the historic Protestant method " is both honest and accurate when he feels it necessary to record, in small print in a brief footnote, that " Luther had some rather loose views on the Bible and inspiration." [57] From his point of view, this is ever so true. Luther drives for a *radical* separation of the two parts of the " Word of God," convinced that the cause of Christendom is hopelessly paralyzed where they are not carefully separated; and this consuming project of diastasis prompts a critical freedom in his use of the Bible that is amazing even in these days.

When we view them within this broader context of the law-gospel differentiation, we recognize immediately that many of Luther's most troublesome (and, at the same time, helpful) statements about Biblical material — which otherwise appear to be a " flagrant contradiction " of his insistence that Scripture is the criterion — are in reality functional theological criticism *within* the Bible, practiced in the service of the law-gospel distinction. In fact, the best-known and most bothersome of these statements, the disparaging remarks about The Letter of James found in his Biblical prefaces, furnish one of the best examples of the nature and limits of Luther's " Biblical criticism."

3. Luther's Legacy

When we return to the question of the Bible as the theological criterion, with the approach illustrated by the law-gospel distinction in hand, we have no difficulty recognizing and acknowledging that generally when Luther refers to the Bible as the " Word of God " or " God's Word," it is the entire Bible, both the Old and New Testaments, to which he has reference, irrespective of whether its particular parts contain " law " or " gospel." This acknowledgment then permits a clarification of this most confused stratum of the problem of theological authority in Luther studies, the claims that repeatedly have been made on the basis of his blunt observations about James. This is a burned-over area; but it needs to be reopened because Luther scholars, through the nineteenth century and to the present, have so frequently filled it with more significance than it can support.

The most recent full study of the question of authority in Luther may be cited as an example of the perplexity that Luther's statements pose. The broad suggestion that is made is that Luther assumed that certain parts of the New Testament were not, or did not contain, the " Word of God." The clinching point made in support of this suggestion revolves about the well-known quotation from the preface to James and Jude, which is sandwiched between the assumptions that are italicized:

> Now comes the clearest and most definite statement in the whole of Luther's writings *about the relationship between the Word of God and the books of the New Testament:* " The task of a true apostle is that he preach about Christ's sufferings, resurrection, and office, and lay the foundation of this faith, as Christ himself says in John xviii [*sic*], ' ye shall bear witness of me '; and all genuine holy books agree in this respect, that they all preach Christ and treat of him. Moreover, one applies the true touchstone for judging all books, if one sees whether they treat of Christ or not, since all Scripture shows forth Christ (Romans iii), and Paul wishes to know nothing save Christ (I Corinthians ii). That which does not teach Christ is not apostolic, even if Paul or Peter is the teacher; again, that which preaches Christ is apostolic, even if Judas, Annas, Pilate, and Herod do the preaching."

We conclude therefore that from 1520 onwards Luther was very liable to speak and write in his unguarded moments as if he identified the text of the Bible with the Word of God; but that when he applied himself carefully to the study of the Bible and published the results of that study he concluded that within the New Testament the books were each to be tested by the criterion: does it preach the gospel of justification or not? with the corollary that *those about which the answer " No " had to be given were not to be regarded as part of the Word of God.*[58]

A hasty rereading will confirm that Luther says nothing whatsoever within this context about whether the letter of James is part of the " Word of God." The point that he is debating is expressly stated: whether this epistle is or is not an " apostolic writing." Moreover, the question of the content of the " Word of God " is not

mentioned in the entire preface; and the passage that is quoted is
preceded by Luther's clear statement about the letter: "I praise it
and deem it good, because it sets up no doctrine of men [*Menschenlehre*] and drives hard the law of God." [59]

The ambiguity that has persisted around this passage, and the
renowned remark that James is "a right strawy epistle," is appreci-
ably mitigated if we recall the *Menschenlehre-Gottes Wort* project
and the crucial law-gospel distinction, and remember that for Luther
both law and gospel are found within the entire Bible and included
within "God's Word." He observes that James primarily contains
"law," or that its value resides in the fact that it "drives hard the
law of God." This prompts several correlative observations. The
letter becomes highly suspect from the point of view of "gospel"
or as an "apostolic" book, because the function of an apostle is to
witness to Christ. He states flatly, although as a "personal opinion,"
that it is "not the writing of an apostle." [60] And he can observe that
when it is placed beside the "chief books" of the New Testament
(the Gospel and letters of John, the letters of Paul, especially Romans, Galatians, and Ephesians, and the first letter of Peter), it becomes obvious that it "has nothing of the nature of gospel in it."
Hence he remarks that from the point of view of "the gospel" it is
"a right strawy epistle *compared to them*." [61] (These words [*gegen
sie*] are not in italics in the original, although in retrospect the opinion could be ventured that it would have been well had they been.)

It would seem obvious that these observations — read in context
and in the light of Luther's underlying *Menschenlehre-Gottes Wort*
and law-gospel projects, which he succinctly outlines once more in
the first paragraphs on the first pages of the 1522–1523 prefaces to
the Old and New Testaments — in no way disqualify James as
"Word of God" any more than Moses' preoccupation with the law
disqualifies "his books" as "Word of God." We know from other
passages that Luther did regard the question of the original inclusion
of James in the New Testament canon as a highly debatable one
because of what he felt to be a total absence of "the gospel" in it.
In the same way, he found the position of Hebrews (and Jude and
Revelation) debatable, and insisted that it is not an apostolic writing
and has a lot of "wood, straw, and hay" strewn through it. But he

conceded much to it by way of " law," remarking that it is " an exceedingly fine epistle " which " beautifully and copiously expounds the Old Testament." [62] In like manner, James could remain for him " a good book " because it contains no *Menschenlehre* and " drives hard God's law." The question of whether it is or is not *Gottes Wort* is not even raised. It need not be, because while " law " is neither " apostolic " nor " evangelical," and must not be confused with " the gospel," it *is* an integral, indispensable, and invaluable part of " God's Word."

The matter is less neat elsewhere, even where James is discussed — or especially where James is discussed.[63] But this is sufficient to suggest that many of the difficulties that we face when we encounter the provocative statements that Luther made about various parts of the Biblical literature are of our own devising and often spring from a failure to recognize his subsumptive methodology as an " irregular dogmatician " and a consequent urge to systematize what he left unsystematized. When we submit to this compulsion, the temptation is always with us to read him within our twentieth-century, rather than within his sixteenth-century, *Sitz im Leben;* and this transposes his queries and observations into modern questions and claims of a historical-critical nature. It may be self-evident, but apparently it is not always easy to remember, that the conclusions of Luther's " Biblical criticism," as well as the assumptions about the authority of the Bible that they presupposed, were formulated before the nineteenth century and therefore are pre-historical–critical assumptions and conclusions. The naked suggestion, explicit or unconsciously implied, that he was in some sense " the freest of Biblical critics " can only confuse the issue and mislead us.

If we grant freely that Luther's " criticism " was not historical criticism in any modern, nineteenth- or twentieth-century sense, and repress the urge to claim him for this cause, we are no longer diverted from recognizing that his " Biblical criticism " was essentially a theological criticism. It was rooted in, and co-ordinate with, his newly discovered evangelical freedom, which brought with it an intrinsic theological freedom. This is why it was, in intention at least, a freedom exercised *within* the Bible, not a freedom derived from presuppositions about development and causality in history and brought to the Bible. Luther had his predispositions; but their basic affinities were with Scholastic and fifteenth- sixteenth-century assumptions, and not with the historical-critical approach that has become *habitus* in us today. And seriously acknowledging this fact would, in turn, force the acknowledgment that while it is quite true that he did not identify the " Word of God " with the Scripture in an exclusive way, as recent studies have reiterated,[64] he did identify them both in a functional and in a subsumptive way. Once more, the freedom that he achieved with his use of a " theology of the Word " was arrived at theologically, not under a compulsion to combat " orthodoxy " and " fundamentalist " assumptions and open the Scriptures to a historical-critical approach.

Luther's larger doctrine of the Word of God actually was so flexible that he had no difficulty subsuming within it whatever particular area of theology happened to be his immediate concern. When he approaches from the side of Christology, Christ is subsumed. " Christ himself is the Word." [65] And " in all Scripture there is nothing other than Christ." [66] When he approaches from the side of the doctrine of God, the Godhead is subsumed. *Gottes Wort,* he says, " brings with it the entire essence of the divine nature " so that " whoever has the Word has the entire Godhead." [67] When he approaches from the side of the question of the church, the church is subsumed. " What the church says is not the Word of God, but the Word of God says what the church will be. The church does not make the Word, but is made by the Word." [68]

This tells us a great deal about Luther's theological methodology, and it reveals how utterly foreign " literalism " in the late orthodox or in the modern sense necessarily would have been to him. But, to Luther's mind, none of this in any way, or in any sense, freed Christianity from its principle of theological authority wherein the Bible is the " touchstone." " Christ is of no benefit to you," he says, " and you cannot know anything about him, unless God put him into words, that you may hear and learn to know him." [69] And although he clearly says otherwise elsewhere, in this context he could even insist that " there is no other testimony on earth to Christian truth than the Holy Scriptures." [70] Nor does the position of the " later " or " old Luther " differ basically from that of the " earlier " or "young Luther" on this particular question.[71] It was the "old Luther" who wrote the following: "Dear Lord God, if the Christian faith were to depend on men, and be grounded on words of men, what need do we have for the Holy Scriptures, or why has God given them?" "The Scriptures must remain master and judge" (*Meister und Richter*).[72]

It would appear that we should allow the matter to rest here, conceding that Luther's legacy in this area is insolubly *duplex,* or that even in its final form it is the product of "irregular dogmatics," and thus resisting the temptation to thrust upon him a systematic "solution," either to the problems raised on the right by later orthodoxy, or to the peculiar problems that we today face on the left. In addition to the specific perceptions and emphases that have been discussed, broadly speaking he bequeathed two gifts that certainly must be preserved. He oriented Protestant theology, in an inescapable way, under a Bible that was theologically authoritative. And he exemplified a theological freedom that made him almost completely immune to the temptation to employ the Bible in a normative or in a legalistic way. It is easily understandable how orthodoxy could have utilized the openness of his position to claim him for the twofold, material-formal principle of authority, the formulation that opened the door to a normative, nonhistorical, propositional use of the Bible. This could, or can, be accomplished, however, only by an indefensible systematization of what Luther left intrinsically unsystematized in this direction. His legacy had a part in preparing the way for this answer; but this was not his answer.

CHAPTER II

John Calvin

WHEN we turn from Luther to Calvin, or from the first to the second wave of the Reformation, we move from the complicated to the complex. The added layers of complexity are created primarily by two problems not found in Luther. The first derives from the fact that in Calvin we are dealing with Protestantism's classic " regular dogmatician "; and this terminology of Barth would appear to be a somewhat more satisfactory designation both for Calvin's intent, and for his accomplishment, than either of the two common descriptive terms, Biblical theologian or systematic theologian. For while it is true that Calvin formally defined his project as an effort to organize and state the theology of the Bible, in no sense did he slavishly limit himself to Biblical sources and categories, or even to specifically Biblical problems. Nor can the popular nineteenth- and early twentieth-century charge be substantiated, that he was driven by a compulsion for " systematic " logical consistency to the extent of quitting the ground of Biblical presuppositions when it was necessary to do so to resolve antinomies. We are led to this conclusion only when we read the *Institutes* under the refracted light of Reformed orthodoxy. Calvin did, however, strive mightily through the accumulative editions of the *Institutes* for dogmatic " completeness," and this entailed the development of a complete, formal statement of a principle of theological authority. The primal problem issues from a recognition that this final, formal treatment is not obviously consonant and co-ordinate with his total system.

The second level of complexity is created by the position that the main body of this statement occupies in the *Institutes*. It is inserted somewhat parenthetically into Book One, following his so-called *theologia naturalis,* and before his treatment of the " knowledge of God the Creator " which is derived from the Scriptures.[1] This is an understandable and logical location, understandable because the question of authority had become one of the foremost issues as the Reformation progressed, and logical because it permitted a discussion of the question of the authority of the Bible prior to any systematic use of its contents. However, theologically it proved to be questionable, and by Calvin's own admission the doctrine of authority that he formulated cannot be abstracted in the way that this location suggests. " It never seriously affects us," he reiterates, " till it is confirmed by the Spirit in our hearts." [2] And he expressly says: " I pass over many things at present, because this subject will present itself for discussion again in another place. Only let it be known here, that that alone is true faith which the Spirit of God seals in our hearts." [3] This immediately and intrinsically correlates the question with a context that is not developed, as such, within Book One, where Calvin is concerned primarily with the problem of the certification of Scripture, not with the question of its assimilation and use either for redemptive or for theological purposes.

Oddly enough, this placement of the statement proved in a real sense to be the most troublesome enigma connected with it.[4] It seemed to permit the use of Calvin's *discrimen* in an extrapolation-abstraction way, allowing it to be relocated as the essential element of " prolegomena " (in the *de Scriptura sacra* or *de Scriptura sancta* sections of the systems of orthodoxy), and utilized without an intrinsic relationship to the redemptive work of God in Jesus Christ. That Calvin did not intend this seems quite clear. But it also is clear that the organization of his system, in the final and so-called definitive edition of the *Institutes,* permitted it; and this odd permissive happenstance became a crucial factor in the later development of Protestant theology.

The materials with which Calvin labored were not qualitatively different from those used by Luther. As did Luther, he carried forward fundamental presuppositions from the Middle Ages; and he continued the running battle with the *multiplex* exegetic assumptions of Scholasticism. The principal difference between the two great Reformers in this area, which is not nearly so great as has often been assumed, resides in Calvin's desire for " completeness," which led him in a definite and definitive way beyond Luther. We shall examine this systematic doctrine, raising intermittently the questions of the intention that underlay it and of its affinity with the contentions of Luther. Its dominant lines are clear and simple, however ambiguous and troublesome its implications and involvements may seem to be.

Calvin's final *discrimen* can be succinctly stated, although to be understood it must be examined in specifics. He insists, with Luther, that the Bible as the " source " (*principium*) of all legitimate dogmatic material is at the same time the " Lydian stone," " rule," or " correct and certain criterion " of Christian doctrine:[5]

> This, moreover, is a governing principle: that to enjoy the light of true religion we must begin with the doctrine of heaven. Nor may anyone know even the slightest taste of correct, sound doctrine unless he has been a disciple of Scripture. True understanding emerges from this source [*principium*], where we reverently embrace this witness to himself which God has chosen to give.[6]

In Calvin's system, even as it is developed within Book One, this is never permitted to stand alone. Luther referred to the Holy Spirit as " the simplest writer and speaker in heaven and earth," [7] and insisted that " the Spirit is required for an understanding of the whole Scripture, and in the same way for an understanding of every part of it." [8] But Luther developed no " regular " *discrimen,* or no consistent interrelation of these affirmations. Calvin wedded them inseparably, and then proceeded to chart the various strands of thought to which their conjuncture gave birth. The result was a systematic doctrine of " Word and Spirit," the rudiments of which were to become definitive for the vast majority of Protestants for more than two centuries. For purposes of clarification, and in order that his movements beyond Luther may be more accurately identified, we shall run the risk that has so frequently proved fatal to Calvin's formulation and look at each of these two sides separately before bringing them together.

1. THE AUTHORITY OF THE SCRIPTURES

Calvin assumes that every man has implanted in his essential nature not only a " sense of the deity," under which the works of God in creation and providence may be known, but even a " seed of religion." [9] This is to say that God has made himself known to man chronologically prior to, and outside of, the Bible; and that he continues to do so, to the degree that all are " without excuse." [10] Calvin insists, however, that the " depravity " or " inherited corruption " of man, with its distortion of every facet of his existence, is so complete that this knowledge is perverted, " partly by ignorance, partly by wickedness," with the result that it inevitably leads man not to God, but into idolatry.[11] Thus, although this " natural knowledge of God " still serves the pretheological function of placing man under just condemnation, in and of itself it proves to be as inadequate to serve efficaciously in a theological role as to serve a soteriological purpose.[12] Sinful man, because of his sin, is wholly incapable of " certain, sound, or distinct " knowledge of God — not because it is not available to him, but because he is sinful. Calvin expresses this conviction rather vividly in one of his Biblical commentaries: " Man, with all his acuteness, is as stupid of obtaining for himself a knowledge of the mysteries of God as an ass is unqualified for understanding musical harmonies." [13]

It is seen to be an act of sheer, gratuitous mercy, therefore, when God makes himself known to man in the midst of this sinful existence. He does so by an " adaptation " or an " accommodation " to man's condition; and this is one of the primal noetic categories of Calvin's theology. God, accommodating himself, " not only uses mute teachers, but even opens his own sacred mouth," giving us through the Scriptures " his sacred Word." [14] It is this gratuitous act which makes " correct " theology possible for fallen man; and, except as he stands under this act, his theology — as well as his worship — inevitably veers toward idolatry.

Calvin contends that, because of its " self-authenticating " nature, this written Word necessarily will be recognized by the Christian as the intended *principium* and criterion of all Christian doctrine. The theologian will see and acknowledge that Scripture embraces all that it is theologically necessary for him to know, and thus he will accept it as "the doctrine of the living God." [15] "God shutteth out whatsoever is added to the Holy Scripture," he says, "and showeth that it shall not be reckoned or received by him." [16] The necessary deduction is: "Nothing is safe, therefore, except to banish everything that depends upon the audacity of human perception, and adhere only to what is communicated by the Scripture." [17] Here God has not only given all the essential answers, but has even posed the proper questions. He has, in brief, delivered in the Bible "the whole summary of heavenly doctrines." [18]

It is important to recognize that, for Calvin, this was not merely an epistemological and methodological affirmation, and that it was in no sense a purely arbitrary contention. The effort that has sometimes been made to label his doctrine of the authority of the Bible as abstract and somewhat obstinate, and to picture it as a dominantly polemical expedient, formulated to further his practical reformatory interests, merely reveals a failure to interpret his *discrimen* within the full context of his theology. His diagnosis of man's situation, when it was yoked with his consuming concern for "assurance" or "certainty," actually made this view of the role of the Bible in theology necessary.

He reinterpreted the doctrine of the "image of God," denying that it could be identified in a singular way with human reason, and differentiated from a "likeness" or *similitudo* that was lost in the Fall. And although it is quite true that he concedes that the *imago Dei* was not "utterly annihilated" in the Fall, he insists that it was so distorted that what remains, including human reason, is a "horrible deformity." [19] This makes it completely necessary that, in its essential substance, Christian doctrine should be spelled out for man by God, if theology is to embrace the element of "surety." Otherwise the ultimate questions of human existence and destiny would be left depending for their answers upon the "mutable" mind of man, upon his "fallen reason." This Calvin — with his strong predilection for "assurance" and "certainty" — regarded as an impossible situation for faith:

> For we know that our faith would have too weak a foundation if we had only the authority of men. We would be, then,

always shaky unless our spirits were raised above the world and were founded in God, knowing that it is from him that this Word of salvation has proceeded which is daily preached to us. And that is why this account has been set down for us in writing, so that whenever we read or hear the Word of God, this comes before us, that men have not invented what is contained in the Old and New Testaments, but God by a visible sign has testified, even as there was need, that men were organs solely of his Holy Spirit.[20]

Here the Bible has become in a quite real sense, and by virtue both of its origin and of its content, a theological depository, the *principium* from which all Christian doctrine must be drawn, and the *discrimen* to which all doctrine that purports to be Christian must be referred. Calvin often applied the traditional category "rule" (*regula*) to it. And an illustration of the seriousness with which he propounded this principle is found in the fact that he even regarded Jesus to have been bound, although in a kenotic sort of way, by this same "rule":

He had even received and imposed on himself the same law, in order that no one might refuse to submit to it. "My doctrine," he says, "is not mine, but his that sent me." He who was always the eternal and only counselor of the Father, and was constituted by the Father the Lord and Master of all, yet because he sustained the office of a teacher, prescribed, by his own example, the rule [*regula*] which all ministers ought to follow in their teaching.[21]

This, then, sketches the outer limits of theological authority, both in a negative and in a positive sense. It means, put negatively, that man's knowledge of God is, as it were, "fixed" or "prescribed" (*praescripta*) in the written Word. The doctrine of authority under which theology functions must presuppose, as its minimal datum, that "the human mind is unable, through its imbecility, to attain any knowledge of God without the assistance of his sacred Word." [22] This necessitates the unhesitant verdict that "persons who, abandoning the Scripture, imagine to themselves some other way of approaching to God, must be considered as not so much misled by error as actuated by frenzy." [23] Hence, at the outset and to the end, the theologian must recognize that the only theologically safe way is to confine himself within the boundaries set by the Scriptures:

> If we only consider that the Word of the Lord is the only way to lead us to an investigation of all that ought to be believed concerning him, and the only light to enlighten us to behold all that ought to be seen of him, this consideration will easily restrain and preserve us from all presumption. For we shall know that when we have exceeded the limits of the Word, we shall get into a devious and darksome course, in which errors, slips, and falls will often be inevitable.[24]

It means, on the other hand, when it is formulated positively, that clear and consistent knowledge of God, and thus trustworthy and efficacious theological material, is available and is assured to the church and the theologian. Because of God's gracious accommodation, essential theological presuppositions and principles, worthy of life-and-death confidence, have once-for-all been given to man. We are, and we remain, in the blindness of our historical existence, " as persons who are old, or whose eyes are by any means become dim." But God, in his mercy, has accommodated himself to this " accidental " situation, giving us the Scriptures as a " lens " or as " spectacles." And when we level our theological gaze through this " lens," we have " a clear view of the true God." [25]

The conclusion, for the question of criterion, is unclouded; and Calvin both advances it unambiguously and defends it without qualification:

> Let this, therefore, be a firm axiom [*axioma*]: nothing should be permitted in the church as the Word of God except what is, first, in the Law and Prophets, and, secondly, in the writings of the apostles; and that there is no correct mode of teaching except within the prescribed limits [*praescripto*] and under the rule of this Word.[26]

2. The First Noetic Office of the Holy Spirit

This " firm axiom " is intrinsically and inseparably wedded, by Calvin, to the action of the Holy Spirit. The relationship of the

Spirit to the Bible as the written Word of God is said to be a two-fold one, or the Spirit has two noetic " offices " in conjunction with the Word. It was through the Holy Spirit that God became, as it were, the " author " of the Bible. And it is through the " testimony of the Holy Spirit," and only through this *testimonium Spiritus Sancti,* that the Bible becomes the Word of God for the church as it exists within history, for the individual Christian in his given situation, or for the Christian theologian as he formulates his theology.

The first of these relationships affirms what may be called a " finished work " of the Holy Spirit; and thus it offers us, in a sense, a " guarantee " that the Bible is the Word of God. This is a thesis that we did not find developed explicitly in Luther. Calvin insisted that the Bible *is* the Word of God, independently and objectively, or prior to and apart from its being known and received as the Word of God. Although this is not allowed to stand alone, in so far as the functioning of Scripture as the criterion in the theology of the church is concerned, this facet of his view of the work of the Holy Spirit needs to be kept in mind. It constitutes an element of sheer " out-thereness " in his thought, which was to become a stepping-stone to the establishment of the Bible as an objective norm by seventeenth- and eighteenth-century orthodoxy.

It should immediately be recognized, however — and the consequences are disastrous when it is not — that the inner logic of Calvin's system prohibits this " finished work " of the Spirit from having any chronologically prior value, in and of itself, for the theological project; and thus it is impossible for us to use it as the foundation of a doctrine of authority. When he places a correct use of Scripture, by the individual or by the church, under the necessity of the testimony of the Holy Spirit, Calvin thereby brackets this " guarantee " with the knowledge of God in creation. It has value for theology proper only in a retroactive and corroborative way. This forces us to say that, in reality, this first noetic office of the Spirit guarantees the authority of Scripture only to those who no longer have any essential need of the guarantee — because its authority has already been " confirmed by the Spirit." Calvin says of the " persuasion " that the Bible is theologically authoritative: " They who have been inwardly taught by the Spirit feel an entire acquiescence in the

Scripture, and that it is self-authenticated, carrying with it its own evidence. . . . It is such a persuasion, therefore, as requires no reasons; such a knowledge as is supported by the highest reason, in which, indeed, the mind rests with greater security and constancy than in any reasons." [27] This observation alone casts a shadow of suspicion across any doctrine of authority that is erected primarily on Calvin's " dictation theory of inspiration."

This recognition does not, however, annul or obliterate, or even mitigate, Calvin's initial point; and it was his thought within the area of the first of these noetic offices of the Spirit that opened the door to one of Protestantism's most troublesome problems. He insisted that the Holy Spirit was, not simply in a purposeful but in a quite direct and instrumental fashion, the " author" of the Bible. Although he readily acknowledged that the Word of God comes to us "through the ministry of men," he reiterated that in a deeper sense "we have received it from God's own mouth." [28] " God designed by the apostles and prophets to speak to us," and we must acknowledge that as each spoke his mouth was veritably " the mouth of the only true God." [29] Therefore, he says: " Let us always remember that the Holy Scripture will never be of any service to us, unless we are persuaded that God is the author of it." [30]

If this assertion had something of the flavor of a figure of speech in Luther, in Calvin it has assumed the proportions of dogma. It is quite true that his words on this subject frequently have been asked to support too much weight, in what Rabaud called " the cold intellects of certain doctors of Protestant Scholasticism." [31] It is also true that sufficient consideration has seldom been given to the historical context within which this view was formulated. Nevertheless, it appears quite certain — recent denials of the fact notwithstanding — that Calvin ascribed the verbal, conceptual substance of the original Biblical documents to God, acting through the Holy Spirit.[32]

This conviction is expounded copiously and in a thoroughly systematic way in the *Institutes,* and is assumed in the commentaries. " It was his will that his Word should be committed to writing," Calvin says; [33] and so, having given the law through Moses,[34] the priests were ordered to teach " only out of the mouth of the Lord," or they were commanded to " teach nothing extraneous, or different from that system of doctrine which the Lord had comprised in the law." [35] In the Prophets "God published new oracles"; [36] but inasmuch as the prophets too were speaking "out of the mouth of the Lord," their teaching was in reality only a further and deeper interpretation of the law. Nevertheless, "because it pleased God that there should be a more evident and copious doctrine, for the better satisfaction of weak consciences, he directed the prophecies also to be committed to writing." [37] Then came "the histories," and these were recorded "under the dictation of the Holy Spirit." [38] Finally, when God had sent his Son, the New Testament was written by "the apostles," who are described as "certain and authentic amanuenses of the Holy Spirit." [39]

The historical context of the deep concern that Calvin had for this "final guarantee" of the authority of the Bible should be recognized. He was preoccupied with two projects of major proportions. To his mind the "most pernicious error" that had been floating on the surface of Scholastic theology was the notion that the authority of the church was necessary to certify the authority of the Bible. He regarded this as the dogma primarily responsible for opening the door to the accretion of questionable theological doctrines that had obscured the gospel, a fact obvious in the epithets that he hurled at it — "cavil," an "absurdity," an "impious fiction," "contempt of the Holy Spirit." [40] It thus was the first dogma that had to be undermined if the way were to be prepared for a reformed faith; and it was Calvin's concern to discredit this assumption which led him to place so heavy an emphasis upon the noetic office of the Spirit as "author" of the Scriptures. This was the context of his contention that the Bible is *autopistos,* so that here "self-authenticating" basically means not requiring authentication by the church.

His other major concern was to join with Luther in the full-scale war upon the "folly and wickedness" of the "pneumatic," "spiritual," or Origenistic hermeneutical method. Calvin's so-called "formal principle" forbids that anything should be included in theology that was not, in essential substance, there beforehand in Scripture, or that "has man mixed with it." [41] The kinship of this principle with Luther's *Menschenlehre-Gottes Wort* project is apparent. But Calvin was less content to rely upon polemics; and thus he became increasingly conscious that if this project were to be carried through effectively, theology had to be grounded in systematic Biblical exegesis. He recognized also, and immediately, that this could occur only if exegesis proceeded on the basis of a hermeneutical method with the inherent possibility of repelling eisegesis; and that this, in turn, would remain impossible until the accepted practice of allegorizing had been discredited. This led him to champion, with genuine reforming passion and conviction, the *sensus literalis* for which Luther had been fighting.

Commenting on Paul's use of *allēgoreō* in Gal. 4:24, Calvin remarks:

> Because he says, " this is an allegory," Origen — and many others with him — seized the occasion to corrupt the Scripture in diverse ways, with inferences far removed from its true and natural sense. For they falsely concluded that the literal sense was too inferior and contemptible, and that it was therefore necessary for them to seek the loftier secrets hidden under the bark of the letter, which can only be extracted by forging allegories. This they did readily; for the world has always preferred, and always will prefer, subtle speculations to firm, solid doctrine. In time the most acute forging was accepted and approved, so that not only was the person who simply amused himself interpreting Scripture not restrained, but the greatest praise was conferred upon him. . . . Undoubtedly this [subtle transfiguration of the inviolable Word of God] was an invention of Satan, to diminish the authority of the Scriptures. . . . And the Lord God avenged this profanation with just judgment when he permitted the pure meaning to be buried under corrupt and false glosses.[42]

When we realize that Calvin's motivating concern was identical with that of Luther, to destroy this traditional assumption of a *multiplex* meaning in Scripture, we have no difficulty recognizing that, within the context of his sixteenth-century project, the word " literal " did not encompass the connotations that it later acquired in the more rationalistic atmosphere of the seventeenth- and eighteenth-centuries, or that it conveys today. It clearly was intended in the sense of anti-Origenistic, or nonallegorical. " The true meaning of Scripture," he insisted, " is the *natural* and *obvious* meaning." [43]

We should not overlook, and fail to appreciate, the value that this concentration upon the first noetic office of the Spirit had for the reform of theology and the permanent orientation of Protestant doctrine. A striking example is found in Calvin's relational emphasis, his preoccupation with the *Deus pro nobis,* the " God-for-us." It was his deep conviction that God has, in the Scriptures, staked out the proper territory of Christian theology, even to the point of posing the proper questions, that motivated his determination to turn his back upon speculation about the " essence " of God and confine himself to the Biblical ground of a " practical " or redemptive concern. He censured the preoccupation with the question, What is God? (*Quid sit Deus*), insisting that the question that God has posed for us in sending the Mediator, and testifying to him in Scripture, is, What kind of God is God? (*Qualis sit Deus*).[44]

If Calvin was not so sensitive as we might wish to the Docetic seeds that his concern planted in the Protestant view of the authority of the Bible, and if it seems to us today that he had too little feeling for the *Sitz im Leben* of the Biblical documents, and the problems involved in acknowledging the historical nature of their origin and transmission, it should be recognized that this was because he lived before the eighteenth century. It avails us little, and robs us of the possibility of profiting fully from their saving reorientation of theology, when we demand that the Reformers answer questions that were not to be asked for some two hundred years. Their consuming concern was to reorient Christian doctrine under a theological *discrimen* that would wed it to the Biblical revelation. They created many problems in doing so; but they did so.

3. The Second Noetic Office of the Holy Spirit

If we disregard the subsequent development of the matter, and look only to Calvin, we are forced to take with total seriousness his reiteration that the Word and the Spirit are inseparable in constituting the *discrimen* that must reign over Christian doctrine. It was the development of this second noetic office of the Spirit which first gave Protestantism a systematic doctrine of theological authority. It is one of the real anomalies in the history of doctrine that it should have been Calvin, among the Reformers, who was primarily responsible for opening the door to the kind of rationalistic-axiomatic use of the Bible that subsequently appeared in Protestantism, when it was this same Calvin who emphasized, and re-emphasized, more than any other among the Reformers, that the Word becomes authoritative as, and *only* as, it is joined with the *testimonium Spiritus Sancti*.

Although " the majesty of God " is " displayed " for all in the Scriptures, he said, " yet none but those who have been enlightened by the Holy Spirit have eyes to perceive what ought, indeed, to have been visible to all." [45] This conjuncture of Word and Spirit within the theological *discrimen* was for him a *nexus inviolabilis,* " an inviolable union." [46] He had no hesitancy whatsoever in charging the theologian who breaks it with " detestable sacrilege." [47] This is why we not only may but must say that in its classic contours or in its original intention the theological authority of Calvinism was a vital, dynamic, and intrinsically existential one. The French Calvinist, Lecerf, revealed a deep feeling for Calvin when he persisted with the point that " for the Calvinist, the supreme religious authority is *living*." [48] This is inescapably true, in so far as the Calvinist follows Calvin. In fact, it is so true that as competent a Reformation scholar as Auguste Sabatier could conclude that Calvin's ultimate authority actually was " subjective " and " experiential." [49] This is, as we shall see, a highly questionable nineteenth-century conclusion; but it is instructive that the possibility could have been advanced and defended.

" The Spirit goes before the church, to enlighten her in understanding the Word," Calvin says, " while the Word itself is like the Lydian stone, by which she tests all doctrines." [50] Thus, while the authority of the Bible was, functionally speaking, virtually absolute for Calvin, its authority was completely qualified by the necessity of the presence of the Spirit. Just as Scripture could become an instrument of redemption only by the action of the Spirit, so it could become theologically authoritative only under a personal relationship to the sovereign God through the personal presence of his Holy Spirit. And this not only permits but forces us to conclude that whenever and wherever this personal, vital dimension is lost, Calvin's doctrine of theological authority has been forsaken. Only those

" who have been inwardly taught by the Spirit " have the possibility of utilizing the Bible authoritatively, for only they can " feel an entire acquiescence in the Scripture." [51]

Theologically speaking, it was necessary for Calvin to assert this " inviolable union " because he located the basic problem of human existence in the " heart " of man, not in the mind — " the diffidence of the heart being greater than the blindness of the mind." [52] His analysis is primarily in terms of sin, rebellion, and idolatry, not in Socratic or noetic terms.[53] He concedes that man can read and, in a sense, understand the Bible, and even hear the promises of God and accept them in a rational or intellectual way, apart from the presence of the Spirit. The point is, rather, that man cannot *believe* these promises, or that the Word of God cannot in fact become the Word of God to him, and for him, except through the testimony of the Spirit. " Our mind must be illuminated, and our heart established by some exterior power, in order for the Word of God to obtain full credit with us." [54]

Here human reason is neither set aside nor disparaged. But it is pronounced impotent for any ultimate soteriological, and for any efficient and acceptable theological, purpose — except as it is " illumined " by the presence of the Spirit. " The Spirit acts as a seal, to seal on our hearts the very promises, the certainty of which has previously been impressed on our minds, and serves as an earnest to confirm and establish them." [55] Hence the Christian theologian, together with the theologically unlettered Christian, will recognize that " the testimony of the Spirit is superior to all reason. For as God alone is a sufficient witness of himself in his own Word, so also the Word will never gain credit in the hearts of men, till it be confirmed by the internal testimony of the Spirit. It is necessary, therefore, that the same Spirit, who spake by the mouths of the prophets, should penetrate into our hearts, to convince us that they faithfully delivered the oracles which were divinely instructed to them." [56] At this point the Westminster Confession of Faith is completely true to Calvin, in insisting that the relationship of the church and the individual Christian to the Bible has an indispensable personal and vital dimension: " Our full persuasion and assurance of the infallible truth and divine authority thereof is from the inward work of the Holy Spirit, bearing witness by and with the Word in our hearts." [57]

The other side of this doctrine was an even more daring, and is today a far more controversial, assertion; but it was this conclusion which gave the *discrimen* its inestimable pragmatic value in the sixteenth and seventeenth centuries, against both Rome and the left wing of Protestantism which was threatening to disrupt and destroy the gains of the Reformation. This is the contention that, under this "inviolable union" of Word and Spirit, the written Word may and must be used to "examine" the Spirit. "For Calvin, it is in the Scripture that the Holy Spirit speaks," remarked Lecerf.[58] Hence no theological "truth" is in fact true, or may be believed to be inspired and certified by the Holy Spirit, unless its substance is to be found within the pages of the Scriptures. Just as the Spirit must at all times *attest* the written Word, so the written Word must at all times *test* the Spirit, or be functionally related to the testimony of the Spirit in the sense of "calling him back for the trial of examination." [59] This, Calvin insisted, is not only as it should be, but as it must be; for this is the relationship that God has established in sending the same Spirit who "dictated" the written Word to serve as the "earnest" or "seal," to "confirm" its truth in our hearts. "The Lord has joined, in a reciprocal union, the certainty of his Word and Spirit: so that our minds are indwelt by a firm and reverent respect for the Word, when by the light of the Spirit we are enabled to see in it the countenance of God; and, in turn, with no fear of hallucination we embrace the Spirit, as we recognize him in his image, that is in the Word. So it is." [60]

If we recoil somewhat from this suggestion that the Holy Spirit is, as it were, limited or circumscribed by the Bible, or that the *revelationis fines,* the limits of revelation or the boundaries of the truth to which the Spirit may testify, are prescribed by a book, Calvin refers us back to the first article of his doctrine. If the Holy Spirit truly was the "author" of the Scriptures, or if in actuality the written Word is his *imago,* then to "test" the testimony of the Spirit by the content of the Scripture is in reality only to examine the truth of the Holy Spirit by the truth of the Holy Spirit. And, Calvin asks, "while he is compared with himself, and considered in himself, who will assert that he is thereby injured? This is calling him back for the trial of examination. I confess that it is. But it is the way that he has chosen for the confirmation of his majesty among us." [61] This "examination" Calvin believed not only permissible, but theologically obligatory. The question with which he countered objections is, even yet, quite pertinent: "For, as Satan transforms himself into an angel of light, what authority will the Spirit have with us, unless we can distinguish him by the most certain criterion?" [62]

4. Calvin and Calvinism

Until quite recently Protestant theologians have generally tended to identify Calvinism and Calvin; and, although to a lesser degree, the interpretation of Luther has inevitably been colored by later developments of Lutheran orthodoxy. This was, and undoubtedly will continue to be, inevitable to some degree, inasmuch as the Reformed and Lutheran traditions gave rise to confessional churches. The assumption that this is, as such, a corruption of the Reformation is a rather foolish one. It roots in part in a subtle canonization of the Reformers and a consequent implication that their theology had no need of further development, and in part in a failure to recognize and appreciate the aspects of grandeur in late sixteenth- and seventeenth-century Protestant theology. Neither of these assumptions will stand examination, although it is doubtful that we are quite ready to see and concede this in the midst of the excitement of the current revival of "pure" Reformation thought.

It remains important, nevertheless; and it is particularly important in the area of theological authority to be able to separate and distinguish the thought of the Reformation proper from its later developments. The theological revolution that occurred in the nineteenth century rendered many post-Reformation developments completely untenable and useless to the contemporary church. Consequently, a failure to distinguish sixteenth-century doctrines from extensions upon them in later orthodoxy results in an unwarranted and unnecessary eclipse of the Reformers. Many ministers in American Protestantism today, even in the confessional traditions, have very little knowledge of (and even less interest in) Reformation theology; and this is in large part because of a lingering distaste for "Protestant Scholasticism," or for "orthodoxy," together with a failure to recognize that in innumerable areas Luther and Calvin simply were not "orthodox." It is, to a great degree, this recognition of a clear breach between the Protestant theology of the sixteenth century and that of the seventeenth and eighteenth centuries, which has given rise to the recent "Luther renaissance" and the movement that now is known as "Neo-Calvinism." From one point of view each of these is a concentrated attempt to disentangle the Reformers and the accretions from orthodoxy in order that Reformation insights that were later fashioned into dogmas that are unacceptable today may be cut free and once more put into service for the church.

We have noted several of these subsequent developments as they affected the area of authority. They clustered about the principle that the Bible is the "exclusive" or, in the words of the great Reformed theologian of orthodoxy, J. H. Heidegger, "the single norm of faith." [63] It is apparent from our look at Luther and Calvin that this was a quite logical extension of one side of the thought of each; but it also is clear that they did not, themselves, erect this extension. As one writer has expressed it, they "left doors open which they did not enter"; [64] and these doors overlooked paths that, when followed to the end, led to conclusions that were at some distance from the territory within which the Reformers labored, and upon which they built their conclusions.

Early orthodox theology, even as it was moving beyond the Reformers, included levels of profundity that saved it from many of the untenable contentions of later developments. These levels derived primarily from its serious attempt to preserve a Christocentric hermeneutical method, with its doctrine of the *fundamentum Scripturae,* the foundation of Scripture, which centered in the covenant. These *de fundamento* sections in the orthodox systems insisted that "in one word, Christ is taught in the whole of Scripture, and he alone is to be sought in it"; [65] and this permitted theologians, even as they were insisting that the Bible is the single *principium* and the singular *norma* of theology, to distinguish between "essential" and "derivative," or "fundamental" and "nonfundamental," doctrinal levels in the Biblical literature.[66] Although the controversy was never settled (and attempts by self-styled "fundamentalists" are even yet being made to renew it) as to just what constitutes this canon within the canon, or which are the "necessary" and "fundamental," and which the "nonfundamental" articles, this distinction defied and delayed for a time the encroachments of rigidity and preserved a genuine openness in early orthodoxy.

It was inevitable, however, that the ground of the Reformers should eventually be evacuated when orthodoxy moved the acute accent from the second to the first noetic office of the Holy Spirit in Calvin's doctrine. Although every attempt was made to guard against it, the Spirit unavoidably was reassigned to a subsidiary position in the functional presuppositions of the principle of authority. When the emphasis had been shifted to the question of the certification of Scripture, it was necessarily assumed that the "finished work" of the Holy Spirit was his major work in the area of authority; and immediately the vital and dynamic orientation of the *discrimen* of the Reformers was threatened. This is why a virtual identity of the concepts "Word of God" and "Holy Scripture" could develop without apparent uneasiness, and the naked contention that the Bible *is* the Word of God could become the reigning tenet. If the weight of emphasis is shifted to the conviction that it was God who spoke in the Bible, away from the recognition that "it is God who speaks in it," then Calvin's "principal proof," which is "from the person of God who speaks" (*a Dei loquentis persona*), ceases to be the *principal* "proof."

This shift occurred slowly in early orthodoxy and was far more implicit than explicit. When it had been made, however, it permitted the very error that Calvin had warned most strongly against, as it was no longer possible to preserve the "inviolable union" of Word and Spirit in the full sense that he intended. As Karl Barth has observed, the church soon found itself in the role of a widow left with her deceased husband's legacy. Logically, the next step was to confer a status of autonomy upon the assertion that Scripture carries *certitudo,* authority and certainty, in itself. When this step had been taken, it then was essential, in the words of the father of the Federal Theology, "that every word, as being contained in letters which were sacred as signs, should be accepted and held as the word of the Holy Spirit." [67] Now it was necessary to add a section on "the attributes of Holy Scripture"; to assert that the writers were "preserved on all sides from any error of mind, memory, language, and pen " (the Leiden Synopsis, III: 7); to debate whether a quotation from the devil carries the same normative authority as " a word from the Lord "; to dispute as to whether heresies could be countered and anathematized that were not expressly named in the Bible; and finally to insist that the vowel points of the Masoretic text were " dictated." It is not even surprising to find a distinction between the " strict literal sense " and a " figurative literal sense "; but perhaps the outer edge was reached when the traditional Origenistic *multiplex* assumption of analogical, tropological, and allegorical meanings was reinstated, now as a designation of the forms of the *sensus literalis.*

There exists today, and in a real sense for the first time, the possibility of banishing the confusion that emanated from this development in orthodoxy. The concentrated effort to do so that was made during the nineteenth century failed, as we shall see, because the Protestant theologians who freed themselves from the presuppositions of later orthodoxy were unable to accept the original premise of the Reformation, that the Biblical literature must play the formative role in theology. This premise has been reasserted and re-established in the twentieth century, with the result that a reaffirmation of the essential elements of the Reformation principle of authority could be made within our twentieth-century theological milieu. Whether this is actually the direction in which Protestant theology is moving is the question that must occupy us, after we have charted the new *Fragestellung,* the altered setting of the question that emerged from nineteenth-century developments.

PART TWO

The Nineteenth Century

The Nineteenth-Century Revolt

T HE nineteenth century proved to be the great era of intellectual miscegenation in the Western world; and we may regard the odd confusion of noises thrown off by the turmoil either as the death rattle of an old order or as the birth pangs of a new. Protestant theology shared in this epochal transition, and one consequence was an almost violent shift of the footing under the discussion of theological authority. It was, summarily speaking, a shift from the far right to the far left, or from the area encompassed by the post-Reformation dogmas of Biblical authority, where late orthodoxy had managed to circumscribe the conversation, to the vast, unfenced prairies of " religious experience."

For better and for worse, this epoch-marking shift produced three immediate, crucial results which altered the Protestant view of authority. It emancipated the Bible, permitting a growing sense of the significance of history and the science of historical criticism to develop virtually unimpeded by the earlier theories of verbal inspiration and textual inerrancy.[1] Secondly, it opened the way for a creative rediscovery of the existential dimension of the Reformation *discrimen,* the side of the thought of Luther and Calvin that had lost its original status and its inherent vitality in the systems of late orthodoxy. And, thirdly, it threatened, and to all practical intents and purposes annulled, the wedding of theology to the Biblical revelation that had been consummated in the Reformation.

The way was prepared for these alterations in the structure of the question by the shift in philosophical thought, and particularly by the negative conclusions of Kant's first *Critique,* to which we shall return in another context.[2] In the more immediate sense, Schleiermacher represented in theology what Kant had effected in philosophy;[3] and it was primarily the theology of Schleiermacher's *Glaubenslehre* that gave form and content to the swiftly developing tendencies that were to force a fresh, universal Protestant pondering of the problem. In one, quite definite sense, all contemporary Protestant theology, in so far as it is not merely sterile repristination, is a conversation with Schleiermacher — and this is true even where it is most vehemently denied that it is true. We must not permit the fact that at the moment most theologians pose as disputants in the debate with Schleiermacher to divert us from recognizing that this is a family quarrel. We cannot even understand the intensity of the quarrel unless we listen from within, under a consciousness of the blood kinship that continues to exist even as we are disavowing it. Karl Barth's candid observation is completely true: " No one can say today whether we have actually overcome him as yet; or whether, with all of our loud, fundamental protest against him, we are not still at bottom children of his century." [4] To fail to see and acknowledge this basic kinship leads unerringly to a misreading of current theology.

1. Friedrich Schleiermacher

Admittedly the relationship is subtle. The subtlety is created by the fact that Schleiermacher's influence has been primarily formal rather than material. The particular reformulations of doctrine that he attempted have been largely rejected and forsaken. But his identification mark has remained on Protestant theology, like the watermark on a postage stamp, because of the reorientation that he helped to effect, and continues to symbolize, at the levels of authority and methodology. The legacy of his influence on the question of authority is not conceded as openly and often as it should be, and principally because it has been customary to regard his system as " nonnormative " theology. It is quite true, of course, that he created and contributed Protestantism's classic inductive system; but it is not true that his theology is nonnormative in the pure phenomenologist sense in which we tend to understand this assertion today. And it is necessary for us to recognize and concede this fact before an accurate estimate of his influence may be made, and his fingerprints identified on current systems.

Schleiermacher defined theology as "the science which brings together the doctrine which is effectual in the fellowship of a Christian church at a given time."[5] But doctrine is defined as "the portrayal of human states of mind"; and Christian doctrines are described as "verbal interpretations of pious Christian states of mind."[6] This implies that theology deals exclusively with transcendental materials: "There is only one kind of doctrine. Perfect or imperfect, it originates in the religious consciousness itself and the direct expression of it."[7] Thus the Christian theologian is assigned the task of systematic, inductive analysis of "religious consciousness" as it has appeared, and appears, in a Christian form.

If we accept these statements at face value, and reflect on them apart from other considerations, it is not difficult to understand how many of the nineteenth-century theologians who took Schleiermacher seriously could have regarded theology as a descriptive discipline in the pure sense. Taken alone, these formal definitions suggest a methodology that involves the theologian in nothing more than a research project in the psychology and history of piety. This explains why it was so often assumed that Schleiermacher had created a system of doctrine in which there not only was no preestablished norm brought to the theological task, but no judgments made in either conscious or unconscious subservience to an a priori authority. This certainly appears to be true when we judge him by the orientation of late orthodoxy; but if we examine his theology closely from the point of view of the question of theological authority, and utilize the cardinal advantage of distance, we see immediately that this assumption of nonnormativeness must be qualified.

This is so for at least three reasons. First, and foremost, is the fact that Schleiermacher clearly acknowledges, and carefully delineates, a *discrimen* for his theology and does so within his prolegomenon and not as a hidden part of his system. Our principal task will be to analyze this functional theological authority. For the moment we need only notice that he explicitly states that it serves to "discern whether any particular aspects of religious consciousness are Christian or not, and whether the Christian element is strongly and clearly, or vaguely, expressed in them." [8] Entirely apart from its content, the formal fact of the presence of this *discrimen* in the *Glaubenslehre* is adequate ground for questioning every assumption that Schleiermacher intended, in any "pure" sense, to open the way to a nonnormative phenomenological methodology.

A second reason for attributing a principle of authority to Schleiermacher traces to the point of origin that he ascribes to piety. He presupposes a definite and definitive a priori, underlying the disposition, or *Gemütszustand,* that the Christian shares with every religious man. This "frame of mind" is said to be rooted in a prereflective immediacy, "the immediate presence of whole undivided being"; [9] and this assertion proves, in fact, to be the methodological axis of his entire system.

Justice should more often be accorded Schleiermacher at this point of prius. It is true that his hand was on the door that was opened to "pantheistic" assumptions in nineteenth-century theology, whether it was there intentionally or inadvertently. It also is true that there are levels of ambiguity that make the case a difficult one to settle within his own system with any assurance. But at the least it should be remembered that he includes a concerted effort to differentiate this "presence," or this fundamental "awareness of God," from all "awareness of the world." He observes that awareness of the world, as such, is not a single, undivided experience of absolute dependence, because it includes a feeling of freedom. He then warns that "the feeling of absolute dependence is not to be interpreted as an awareness coexistent with the world, but only as an awareness coexistent with God as the absolute undivided unity." If it is true that "there is in our relation to God no immediate feeling of freedom," and true that "the feeling of dependence in relation to him cannot be such that a feeling of freedom can come as its counterpart," we must permit Schleiermacher this differentiation. [10] But in any event it is presupposed in his system, and the role that he permits this "awareness" or "immediate presence" to play immediately casts a shadow of suspicion across every suggestion that he was operating theologically without an authoritative a priori.

The third reason that may be given for assuming that he utilized a theological authority appears at first glance to be less important, but in an implicit sense it could have been the one factor that determined the unique constitution and flavor of his system beyond all others. He observes at one juncture that " the more religious he is " the more a theologian " brings his individual religion with him to the inquiry." [11] If we apply this candid admission to his own analysis, what it suggests is obvious: that, as Prof. H. H. Farmer has observed, " in defining religion as the sense of absolute dependence he was drawing on something which was quite basic to his own living sense of God." [12] If this is true, must we not say that there was on this lower level an " original " authoritative element, an element not included in the first instance through analysis of the data of self-consciousness? Must it not be credited, rather, to a living experience of the living God? And does this not mean that it was brought as an a priori to the theological task?

We are, of course, here assuming something that we must presume Schleiermacher would have denied: that there is a basic experience of God that may be said to have been " given " from " outside." In faithfulness to the canons of the philosophical idealism of his day, he contended that this kind of external reference, or "transference of the idea of God " outward, is an arbitrary, " devotional " symbolism that has no place in theology proper.[13] This contention does not necessarily invalidate the point, however; and it certainly does not invalidate our freedom to hazard it. It should be remembered, moreover, that Schleiermacher refers to God as the " whence " of the " consciousness of being absolutely dependent," and that this consciousness, and a consciousness of being in a relationship to God, are not only related but identified. " God means for us only that which is the codeterminant in this feeling, to which we refer the fact of our existence in this feeling. Any meaning beyond this conception must originally be evolved from the basic content assigned to it. This is precisely what is principally meant by the formula: to feel oneself absolutely dependent, and to know oneself to be in a relationship with God, are the same thing." [14]

It is notoriously true that what Schleiermacher intended to communicate when he referred to God as the " whence " and " codeterminant " of the feeling of absolute dependence is not clear. It is possible that his guardedness at this point of referent reflects nothing more than the selfsame sense of mystery or "the Holy" that has prompted theologians as diverse as Aquinas and Barth to warn against all attempts to intrude into the "essence" of God. Or, it is possible that it represents an intention to formulate Christian theology under a purely transcendental norm. The case has remained open, and no doubt will remain open; but, whatever he may have intended, the inference that we have drawn would seem to be a defensible one.

When we turn to the matter of functional criteria, fortunately it is much less ambiguous and much more explicit. It is clear that without inhibition Schleiermacher repudiated the post-Reformation principle, the Bible employed in a *sola Scriptura* sense, and shifted the discussion to entirely new ground. This is symbolized by the relocation of the question of the authority of Scripture, in his system, from the front to the back, or from the section on prolegomena to the propositions that explicate the doctrine of the church.[15] It is important for our purposes to recapture a panoramic view of this new territory within which he wished to rehabilitate the *discrimen,* as it was the site that the nineteenth-century theologians who addressed themselves to our problem attempted to occupy.

Schleiermacher's functional theological authority, in broad outline, encompasses seven specified elements, placed upon one another in a pyramidlike fashion. We find built into the foundation the "original" assumption to which we have alluded, an insistence that feeling, qualified as "immediate self-consciousness," and not "knowing" or "doing," is the constitutive element of all genuine religion.[16] He describes human existence as a dialectical passage between a "remaining in the self" and a "stepping out of the self,"[17] and knowing and feeling are said to be the forms of consciousness of the former. But because cognition, as we ordinarily conceive it, involves the dichotomy of the subject who knows, and the object that is known, it can in fact have reality "only by a stepping out of the self"; and thus, exactly speaking, activity or doing is involved in knowing. This means that feeling alone is completely a "remaining in the self," or that feeling alone can be pure receptivity.[18]

It appears certain that it is first of all at this level, and in this sense, that Schleiermacher's pivotal concept "feeling" should be interpreted and judged. There are recurring references to "religious emotions" and "religious affections" in his system, but when he is read carefully he appears to be clear that feeling is not to be confused with these. It obviously has a noetic dimension, and is intended to denote neither an emotion nor a psychological mood or state. It refers rather to an intuitive immediacy; or, as Prof. Paul Tillich has termed it, to an "immediate awareness" behind the subject-object or idea-thing cleavage.[19]

It is highly instructive that in another context Tillich calls this "awareness" a "mystical a priori," intending the word "mystical" to connote its unmediated character, and that he associates it with his own "abstract translation" of the great commandment as "ultimate concern."[20] It is perhaps due mainly to a misreading of Schleiermacher that the close kinship that exists between these two theological systems has not been widely recognized; and the decisive junction is to be found at this point. Each builds upon the initial assumption of an "inside knowledge," an immediate, prereflective knowledge of an immanent ground of unity that is both logically and ontologically prior to the separation involved in all human cognition and existence. Schleiermacher's notion of feeling probably is no more susceptible to a psychological interpretation and explanation than is Tillich's "unconditional concern." And if this analysis is accurate, it means that at this point of prius the real line of continuity traces from Schleiermacher directly to Tillich, with the nineteenth-century theologians whom we shall consider actually representing aberrations, unintentional misinterpretations, or intentional departures from Schleiermacher. This is the kind of inference that can be drawn only with the highest degree of tentativeness, however, and we shall have occasion to return to it frequently.

The other part of the foundation of the *discrimen* appears when this feeling is further analyzed by Schleiermacher into two constituent elements, one self-originated and the other nonself-originated.[21] It is obvious on the face of the matter that the latter presupposes a cause other than, or "beyond" the self, a "whence." It is said that if our relationship to this Other is examined, we find or "feel" it to be one of *total* receptivity or *absolute* dependence.[22] This "consciousness of absolute dependence" is then designated "the self-identical essence of piety." "The feeling of absolute dependence is in and of itself a coexistence of God in the self-consciousness."[23]

The three criteria that are erected upon this foundation comprise the substratum that supports the distinctively Christian elements of the authoritative *discrimen*. Schleiermacher insists, first, that this feeling drives of necessity to communion, or that it is of its very nature to create a "church."[24] "This participation is always given with faith, of itself."[25] The fact should never be overlooked or under-evaluated, in interpreting Schleiermacher's system, that the basis of his doctrine of the church is found within, and is integral to, his doctrine of authority. It can be said of him, in a sense in which it can be said of no other major Protestant theologian, that he literally begins with the church. And he insists that if a compulsion to fellowship and communion is not present, true piety is not present; which means, in turn, that Christianity cannot be present. In addition to being an initial element, this presupposition of the indispensability of "church" is a continuous and key element of his theology.

He insists, secondly, that genuine religion requires monotheism. A true consciousness that we are absolutely dependent will embrace not only our individual finitude, but a sense of the totality of finitude. This consciousness of the absolute dependence of all is said to exclude immediately all "lesser gods."[26]

It is said, thirdly, that genuine religion will and must issue in a teleological reference and movement, or that motivation and ethical dynamic must be recognized to be integral. If the feeling of absolute dependence turns into itself, and serves only itself, we must conclude that a lower form of aesthetic religion has captured the soul.[27] This point, which will occupy us later, has frequently been neglected, if not denied, within the contemporary theological scene. Schleiermacher struggles throughout his system to remain faithful to it, reiterating that the kind of faith that undergirds Christianity inevitably will find its passive state prompting spontaneous action, or that genuine piety always will know that "some particular thing has to be done."[28]

Upon these three assumptions, which in turn rest upon the two foundational elements, Schleiermacher erects the two unique or "exclusively Christian " elements of his theological authority. The two levels of the substructure support these elements; but the five criteria which we have enumerated cannot function, either individually or taken together, as the Christian *discrimen*. It is only when the " exclusive essence " [29] of Christianity has been ascertained that we can determine whether, and in how far, a particular affirmation or doctrine is compatible or incompatible with the Christian faith. These two upper, " exclusively Christian " elements are: the indissoluble connection of Christian faith with " Jesus of Nazareth "; and the centrality that Christianity, in all its various forms, accords and must accord to " redemption." [30]

It is an unquestioned axiom, for Schleiermacher, that every communal form of religion has a " fixed historical point," which not only marks its origin, but also is the source of the cohesiveness or external unity that is necessary to its survival.[31] It is in this sense of historical reference and continuity that " Jesus of Nazareth " is said to be an essential element of the Christian theological authority: " all Christians trace the communion to which they belong back to Christ." [32] Where we do not find this historical connection and reference, although we may conclude correctly that some form of high religion exists, we cannot concede the existence of Christianity. It is a primary datum of theology for Schleiermacher that Christianity nowhere has emerged, and nowhere can emerge, " beyond all historical coherence with the impulse which proceeded from Christ." [33]

We should notice, for future reference, that there is no suggestion here of a direct " connection," or " I-Thou encounter," that is not mediated through the historical community or the " church." The element of immediacy is located on the first level of the doctrine of authority, which is shared with all forms of " true piety," not on the upper, " exclusively Christian " level. This may also be expressed by saying that for Schleiermacher, strictly speaking, the question of immediacy is a question asked and answered within the area of philosophy of religion, not of theology proper. This forces us to say that the " exclusively Christian impulse " was " direct " or " immediate " [34] only for those who occupied the " fixed historical point " of Christianity. It is indirect, though the continuing Christian com-

munity, the "body of Christ," for all "disciples at second hand." [35]
This is the theological counterpart of the Hegelian assumptions that
prompted the prophetic reaction of Kierkegaard. It also is why
there can be no real element of surprise when we discover Schleiermacher remarking that "it is impossible to see what connection the
resurrection and ascension of Christ have to his redemptive efficacy." [36] It is in a historical sense, and not in any sense of "encounter," that it may and must be said: "If one does not refer the
power of the God-consciousness which he finds in himself to Jesus,
his consciousness is not Christian." [37]

The presence or absence of true Christian doctrine may also be
determined by utilizing the fact that "only in Christianity has redemption became the center of religion." [38] The antithesis of redemption, in its most extreme form, is said to be "Godforsakenness"
or "God-forgetfulness"; [39] and thus the quintessence of this redemption, which is universally shared by Christians, is said to subsist in
"God-consciousness." The first of the propositions that circumscribe
the meaning of the cross, or the work of Christ, is: "The Redeemer
takes believers into the power of his God-consciousness, and this is
his redemptive activity." [40] It must therefore be said, as one of the
exclusively Christian elements of the *discrimen,* that "propositions
which express a reference to Christ are truly Christian propositions
only in so far as they acknowledge no criterion for the relation to
the Redeemer other than the question of the respect in which the
constancy of the God-consciousness is established." [41]

It should be remembered that Schleiermacher in no way implies
that God-consciousness is not present in other communions or in
other forms of piety. This would deny an accepted proposition of
philosophy of religion. He asserts, on the contrary, that pure God-
forgetfulness is never more than approximated in human existence,
so that God-consciousness in some degree is "an integral constancy
of human nature." [42] Thus there is in his doctrine of authority no
claim that redemption is uniquely Christian. The point, rather, is
that "in Christianity the mutual connection of the incapacity and
the redemption is not simply a detached, additional religious element, but all other religious emotions are related to it." [43] In all
other communions redemption is "a derivative element." [44] But in

Christianity it is the *Mittelpunkt,* the center point, like the hub to which each spoke of the wheel is and must be attached. It is in this sense that it becomes a criterion. It coexists with all Christian religious emotions " in such manner that they become distinctively and uniquely Christian "; [45] and therefore it may be said that where redemption does not coexist, as the " middle point," religious emotions and affections are not Christian.

It seems almost redundant to point out that there is no sense in which either the institutional church or the Biblical literature has an essential role in this *discrimen;* so that, in so far as we accept canons of origin, it is neither " Catholic " nor " Protestant." " Communion " is an integral presupposition of the substratum, and of the criteria of religion as such. But it does not appear in the superstratum, and the organized church, or the church as an institution, is assigned no role to play in determining what is or is not distinctively Christian doctrine.

Participation of the Scriptures, as a unique authoritative element, is explicitly repudiated.[46] They are recognized as essential sources of theology, and in this sense are chronologically unique among several *principia* that have derivative authority.[47] But they are permitted no vestige of their former normative role. The negative line of reasoning that Schleiermacher follows at this point is worth noting, as it became a part of popular Protestant theology in the nineteenth and early twentieth centuries.

The Old Testament is almost entirely dismissed, with the observation that if an assertion or doctrine appears in the Old Testament alone, and not in the New, it obviously cannot be held to be " genuinely Christian." Whereas if it does appear in the New Testament, there is no essential need for the Old Testament. " Consequently, it appears that the Old Testament is only a superfluous authority for dogmatics." [48] It also is indicative that confessional statements are elevated above the Bible, for authoritative purposes, because they enshrine a more recent and more direct attestation of the piety of particular communions.[49] Summarily, as products of faith, and in no sense the fountain or the foundation of faith, neither the church nor the Bible is given a place in the *discrimen.*

It is obvious that with Schleiermacher the question has been completely reoriented. The nineteenth-century theologians who struggled with the problem accepted this reorientation and attempted to carry through its implications. The designation of "piety" as the substance of theology in the main took the form of an assumption that "experience" is the material with which the theologian labors; and one or the other of the two "exclusively Christian" criteria became the identification mark on recurrent attempts to resolve the question. When we stand within the context of Schleiermacher's thought and look backward and forward, we realize immediately that, whether he was or was not misread in the nineteenth century, the shift that he symbolizes was of revolutionary proportions. The Biblical material has ceased to be in any sense the formative authoritative element. Theology not only is no longer assumed to be a deductive system that draws upon divinely imparted oracles, but is the fully human construction that results as the theologian labors with purely transcendental materials. The content of revelation is not dogma or doctrine, or the raw material of dogma or doctrine, but "immediate awareness"; and in its substance theology is man's expression of, and commentary on, this consciousness or awareness of God. Theologically speaking, we have passed through a revolution and entered a new world.

2. Auguste Sabatier

It was within the climate of this new world that the great French disciple of Schleiermacher, Auguste Sabatier, drafted his *magnum opus, Religions of Authority and the Religion of the Spirit,* which undoubtedly was the nineteenth century's most notable work devoted directly to Protestantism's problem of authority. It could be said of Sabatier, as has been said of another theologian, that witnessing his struggle with this question is like watching a ship sailing to sea in the teeth of a gale. It was here that the fundamental issues that were raised by the nineteenth-century revolt were first systematically sketched in provocative and unavoidable form. The work is important also because it was the first serious attempt, beyond late orthodoxy, to come to terms with the presuppositions and implications of the Reformation *discrimen.* The conclusions reached are distinctively nineteenth-century conclusions; but they were not offered without a serious effort to demonstrate that they embody the genius and intent of Luther and Calvin. Sabatier's analysis of the Reformers is, in fact, one of the best extant examples of the inevitable filtering process that Reformation thought undergoes as it is interpreted in another age — a lesson not unneeded in our day.

Sabatier orients himself within the context of the second of Schleiermacher's " exclusively Christian " criteria. In his fascinating Socratic dialogue with Adelphi, he brings against himself the charge of opening the door to " unlimited subjectivity." His reply is: " At last the great word is out, the scarecrow with which men think to reply to everything and ward off all dangers. We must avoid subjectivism, and for that reason we will not have a subjective criterion. But can there be any other? " [50] His uncompromising answer to this rhetorical question is, that there can be no other; and this is the consistent thesis undergirding his attempt to resolve the dilemma.

The seeds of this conclusion were securely embedded in the ground upon which Sabatier stood as he began his survey of the problem. He was motivated by two driving desires. He was determined to cut Christianity free from the twin doctrines that he was certain had sapped its life and spirit in the past — the Roman belief in the authoritative church, and the Protestant belief in the authoritative Bible. He was also quite concerned to establish religion as a respectable science among the other sciences, as a branch of sociology. He conceded that religion has its own subject matter, but insisted in true nineteenth-century fashion that it must utilize the empirical, logico-descriptive method that was being universally accepted in his time, and was beginning to prove fruitful in the fields of history and psychology as well as in the natural sciences.

Prompted by this dual motivation, and accepting without question the assumption of the priority of spirit over matter which had been established by German idealism, his initial assertion is that there are two distinctly different kinds of religion, which he calls " religions of authority " and " the religion of the Spirit." He contends that these gave birth to, and nurtured, two incompatible types of theology, " the theology of authority " and " the theology of experience." [51] Between these and the " religions " in which they root, a total and irreconcilable dichotomy is posited. The purpose obviously is to set

Christianity, which is assumed to be supremely " the religion of the Spirit," entirely apart from every type of external authority. And this purpose is completely overt: " That which I absolutely repudiate is authority. The time has come, it seems to me, for those who have broken with authority in their inner life to break definitely with it in their theology." [52]

Sabatier offers this absolute dichotomy of the inward and the outward, or of the internal and the external, as an interpretation of Schleiermacher's methodology and doctrine of authority. Roman Catholicism and Protestant Scholasticism are branded the twin evils of Christendom's past. He observes that the Roman Church, after a slow but steady displacement of the base of authority across several centuries, finally became an unabashed religion of authority when Jesuitism triumphed, and the doctrine of the infallibility of the pope ceased to be debated after the council of 1870. This is regarded as a decisive and final break with original Christianity.

Protestant Scholasticism is said to have made a similar transition when it adopted the doctrine of the formal and material principles of authority. Of this bifurcation, he remarks, " the early Reformers knew nothing." [53] They " proceeded, not by way of external authority, but by way of inward experience, . . . bringing religion back to inward faith, and theology to Christian experience." [54] " With Luther and Calvin the Christian conscience was definitely recognized as autonomous." [55] The overarching conclusion of Sabatier's excursion into Reformation and post-Reformation doctrine is that the root of the tragedy of Protestant theology is to be found in the destruction of this autonomy in Reformed and Lutheran orthodoxy.

This destruction is credited to the dichotomy in the post-Reformation doctrine of authority, which invited the illusion of an inerrant Bible and resulted in the establishment of the Scriptures on the throne pronounced vacant in the Reformation disestablishment of the pope. The view of the Bible as *doctrina divina,* a " supernatural manual of pure religion " whose author was God, Sabatier regarded as a paganism of one genus with the aberration of Roman Catholicism.[56] He says, moreover, that were he forced to choose between the doctrines of authority of Rome, and of late Protestant orthodoxy, he would without hesitation choose the former, which is " of much more grandeur." The principle of orthodoxy is styled, with obvious feeling, "a tissue of abstractions peaceably chained together by a logical link in the closets of doctors or within the precincts of the Schools; a system which has never succeeded in establishing itself seriously either in the churches or in lay society, an artificial and contradictory work, lacking at once basis and conclusion, destroyed by the very Reformation principle whence men have sought to deduce it." [57]

It was because Schleiermacher achieved a decisive break with the past at the level of methodology and authority that Sabatier (literally) lauds him as a new messiah, with whose advent "Protestantism entered upon a new phase." [58] Theologically speaking, Schleiermacher symbolized "the turning point of the age," he says; he "opened a door to the future which no one would thenceforth have power to shut." [59] This unrestrained eulogy focuses upon Schleiermacher's designation of piety, or religious consciousness, as the sole and proper object of theology. Sabatier then proceeds to interpret Schleiermacher psychologically, in an unreserved way. He reveals no hesitation whatever in referring to "religious consciousness" as "emotional experience," which man must "feel." "Emotion, in fact, is the very life of religion, because it alone can show that the human soul has recognized the divine guest which it carries in itself." [60] Tillich is undoubtedly correct in crediting this misinterpretation of Schleiermacher, or this assignment of religion to the nonrational corner of subjective emotions, in part at least to the deep desire to escape the conflicts between religious tradition and modern thought; and it also functioned, when carried to its logical extreme, to free the intellectual and the moral spheres from the claim of faith. This in essence was its danger.

This emotional experience, which constitutes the total material with which theology labors, is available to theology by two approaches, Sabatier said: indirectly through a historical approach, and directly through a psychological approach. At one point he states flatly that the theologian has access to "no sources of information beyond psychology and history," [61] a thesis to which he had devoted an earlier philosophical and methodological work. [62] Also, to complete the psychological interpretation of Schleiermacher's analysis, history is defined as " psychology going back to the past." [63] He bows briefly to "the dumb resistance which historic reality offers," [64] but his subsequent use of "history" for authoritative purposes is thoroughly positivistic. This, in actuality, is the mark of identification that he places upon the " new phase " in theology. The theologian, feeding upon the "two nursing mothers" of theology, history and psychology,[65] will and must confine himself in the new theological age to the critical approach of historico-psychological induction.

Under this methodology, it is apparent that the question of the theological criterion of " religious experience " immediately becomes the crucial issue. Sabatier's answer is as singular as was that of late orthodoxy, although he transfers it to the second side of the Reformation *discrimen*. Christianity is defined as " the religious relation realized in pure spirituality," whose single source is " the inward witness of the Holy Spirit." [66] Thus the " experience " prompted by the *internum testimonium Spiritus Sancti* becomes the sole authority over Christian theology. The Bible and the church are said to be historical and experiential " consequences and effects "; and, inasmuch as neither may be regarded as a *principium* or a " first cause," neither can play a role in the theological *discrimen*. Therefore, with an unambiguous separation of the question from every external element, experience, in the sense of the emotional feeling that can be credited to the Holy Spirit, is established as the singular criterion of theology. And the theologian, laboring with historical and psychological phenomena, becomes in a literal sense a religious historian and psychologist. Summarily expressed, " The accurate delimitation of the object of theology brings in its train the substitution of the method of observation and experiment for the old method of authority." [67] " Religious facts, indeed, belong to the domain of consciousness; they can be grasped, verified, and described only by the observation of the religious psychologist or by the historic exegesis of documents in which the religious consciousness of the past has left its imprint." [68] Hence the conclusion necessarily is: " As the object of theology is to explain the life of piety, it ought to be the ideal reflection of piety, and consequently it should find in life itself the organizing principle of doctrine. From the point of view of experience this principle can be nothing other than the Christian consciousness." [69] "Theology therefore has two sources — psychology and history, and their union must constitute its entire method of observation, direct and indirect." [70]

It is much to his credit that Sabatier did not shy away, or retreat into nebulous ambiguities, when confronted with the necessity of explicating this "Christian experience" which he installs as the single-level criterion or "organizing principle" of doctrine. The description, although brief, is quite important, and more so for what it omits than for what it includes. Following Schleiermacher,[71] he posits a dialectic of "separation" and "reconciliation," or of sin and salvation interpreted as healing. "Both sentiments persist and should persist in the Christian consciousness, ever reacting upon one another," he says; and "the reciprocal passage from one to the other is the constant activity, the very life, of the Christian consciousness." [72]

To this is added the developmental assumption of Hegel's metaphysical idealism. This dialectical "passage from one to the other" is said to propel an upward movement, a "transformation" or "religious evolution," which parallels our physiological evolution. In each "stage" or "phase" man retains "marks" of anterior stages; [73] but because Jesus of Nazareth has become "a living consciousness in the bosom of humanity," and we know through him "a new sentiment, love," the "metaphysical distance and the moral chasm" opened by sin are "filled." Hence, love "brings together and unites that which was divided." "This is why Jesus of Nazareth was not only the Messiah and Savior of his people, but also of all peoples and all men. The religious evolution which took place in him took place in the very bosom and for the profit of all humanity." [74]

We should not overlook the fact that this concise, lucid description of "Christian experience," offered to us as the singular criterion of theology, is itself the most illuminating critique available of the nineteenth-century psychological interpretation of Schleiermacher's reorientation. Viewing it from the vantage point of another century, we recognize immediately that it is in no sense what it purports to be, a timeless sketch of Christian experience, but that it is a report of a characteristically nineteenth-century expression of religious experience. The structural presupposition of a religious evolution is blatantly characteristic. In the area of analysis, the problem is discussed wholly in terms of "sin," defined simply as "separation," with the problem of guilt not mentioned. Correspondingly, the "filial consciousness" of Jesus of Nazareth is represented as the Christian's single need, with the cross not mentioned. The single passage that might possibly be interpreted as an allusion to the atoning work of Christ states that "the metaphysical chasm is filled by the revelation of the infinite love by which God unites himself to man." [75] And these obvious examples of the distinctively nineteenth-century flavor could be multiplied with innumerable less obvious ones.

It really is rather amazing, in retrospect, that Sabatier reveals so little uneasiness that this "autonomy of the Christian conscience" that he advocated would lead to a confusing, destructive theological relativism. He foresaw the possibility; but he dismissed it, somewhat lightly, with an expression of confident trust that it was not a real possibility, because "the state of the soul is essentially the same in individual Christians at all times." [76] He does not even appear to have been disconcerted by the fact that he was forced to repudiate flatly, not only the "Christian experience" described by Protestant Scholasticism, but even Schleiermacher's explication. Schleiermacher's description is "erroneous," he conceded, and credited the error to the fact that he was describing only a "vague sentiment." [77] Nor is there any evidence of a fear that this autonomy of experience would lead to exaggerated or false individualism. He simply remarks, quite simply, in the spirit of nineteenth-century romanticism, that because the fruit of the Spirit is love, the soul necessarily "gives itself to the whole creation and enters into communion with it." [78] The truth is that, notwithstanding the contours of grandeur in this provocative, systematic analysis of the problem, Sabatier would have us resolve it by absolutizing a time-bound, datable description of emotional experience. The suggestion was not new, of course — as it is not obsolete; but, in advocating it, Sabatier was representing a new orientation of Protestant theology at the level of authority. He symbolizes a major nineteenth-century movement that was still struggling to remain faithful to its Reformation heritage, yet determined to come to terms with Kant, Hegel, and Schleiermacher.

3. James Martineau and the Jesus-of-History Movement

If we look farther to the left, we find some who, while attempting to take Schleiermacher seriously, ceased to worry about faithfulness to the Reformation. The high-water mark of the nineteenth-century revolt was represented by James Martineau, who devoted almost twenty years of hard labor to the most ponderous tome that the century produced on the question. Although neither was familiar with his thought, we can almost visualize Sören Kierkegaard and the early Karl Barth lurking in the background, poised to spring upon Martineau's conclusions. Kantian and Hegelian presuppositions pervade every paragraph, and with no trace of critical caution or uneasiness in their use. Nor do we find any evidence of a basic understanding of sixteenth-century thought. The conversation is almost exclusively with seventeenth- and eighteenth-century Protestantism, and is carried on utterly without sympathy or appreciation. He remarks, quite passionately: " The whole conception of an ' orthodoxy' indispensable to the security of man's divine relations — a conception which has had a regulative influence through all ecclesiastical history — is an ethical monstrosity." And the single reference to Luther simply disparages those who would " put back the clock to the night of Luther's birth." [79] Here the umbilical cord has been cleanly severed.

The controlling assumption of this lengthy study of the problem is that God and man are " inseparable partners " in the divine economy, so that religious experience is " like a single drama of two authors." [80] This forbids in principle, and at the outset, any possibility that an institution such as the church, or a book such as the Bible, should be considered to be in any sense a seat of divine authority. To regard either as a special area in which God has been at work would be to sever and isolate artificially one half of the co-operative project of God and man. The approach that is dictated, rather, by a recognition of this " partnership " is a distinction of two complementary kinds of religion, natural and revealed. These are said to emanate from the two " quests " that comprise the form of religion — the quest of man for God, and of God for man. Natural religion is " that in which man finds God," while revealed religion is " that in which God finds man." [81] By following the path of natural religion, we move "out of the finite into the infinite," "reduce the distance," and leave "fewer steps between ourselves and God." [82] This "wayfarer's track" is not said to be sufficient, of itself, to lead us to the necessary criterion of authority; but Martineau insists that it both can and does lead us toward the source of authority. And it directs us to the proper "seat" within man, where God appears in human experience to establish the only sure authority for life and theology.

The fragmentariness and insufficiency of natural religion results from the fact that it produces only "mediate" knowledge. God is not "presented" in nature, but only "represented"; and Martineau presupposes, as a child of his time, that the fundamental condition that we may and must attach to an authoritative revelation is that God shall be known "immediately" in it. His initial, unquestioned axiom is: "The one condition which the desired revelation must fulfill is plainly this: it must be *immediate*." [83] We see at once not only the indirect influence of the philosophical climate, but the direct influence of Schleiermacher's reorientation; and Martineau clings tenaciously to this presupposition. This drives him beyond natural religion to what he calls "revealed religion," within which God "enters our mind to be immediately known."

Man receives, through this gift of immediacy, the self-disclosure of God; and because it is immediate, *self*-disclosure, the noetic content that is given to the mind must be described as a self-evident "intuitive apprehension." Thus revealed religion requires an epistemological "reduction of revelation to intuition"; and this reduction forces us to "limit revelation to the sphere of intuitive apprehension, i.e., of moral and spiritual truth." [84] This contention symbolizes the final break with post-Reformation presuppositions that took place in the nineteenth century. It was a break that required an explicit denial that revelation offers, in any sense, the substance of doctrines or of information about God. What is revealed is "God himself." And presumably this revelation is objectively real and concrete, although it is totally without conceptual content. William Temple's more recent, renowned, and reiterated principle, which is not materially inconsistent with the presuppositions of much contemporary Protestant theology, embodies this contention: "What is offered to man's apprehension in any specific revelation is not truth concerning God, but the living God himself." [85]

The consistency with which Martineau, and the trend in nineteenth-century theology which he represents, clung to this functionally negative epistemological presupposition is indicated by his sharp distinction of "revealed" and "apocalyptic" religion. He insists that the true prophet of revealed religion may be identified, among the many false apocalyptic prophets, if it is remembered that the former points only to what is or may be universally known. "Pretenders and self-deceivers are fond of knowing what no one can know; they have been let into some special turn of the heavenly economy which shall startle the wonder of mankind." The mark of truth that we find upon Jesus of Nazareth, as the greatest of the "true prophets," is that he "again and again thrust aside apocalyptic questions." [86] It was not in bringing something new, but in pointing the way to what is universally and at all times present and available, that Jesus enacted his essential Messianic role. "The sublimest things which he told the people he assumed that they in their secret hearts must know; he gave them a higher truth than they would hear from the scribes in Moses' seat; but nothing that they might not realize in their closet, when alone with the heart-Searcher. In this feature, I believe, was the root and essence of his power." [87]

This leads us directly to the conclusion that theological authority is one-dimensional and must be sought on the single level of universal human experience; and Martineau locates it in part in the "conscience" and in part in the "reason" of man. Conscience is identified as the ability and function of "natural estimate" which every person finds within himself. "As the instinctive impulses turn up within us, one after another, and two or more come into the presence of each other, they report to us their relative worth; and we intuitively know the better from the worse." "We are never left in doubt which of two simultaneous impulses has the nobler claim upon us. This natural estimate is what we mean by conscience." [88]

The Kantian assertion that undergirds this definition is that man has within himself, as part of "the moral structure of the human mind," the recognition of a binding authority that he knows to be a given. He feels that this authority is transcendently, and not merely transcendentally, grounded; and its very existence posits a two-party relationship, for there must be one party to command, and another to obey. The will of man constitutes one of these two parties; and Martineau contends that the key to a correct answer to the question of authority resides in the proper identification of " the other party." Accurately identified, it is said to be the presence of God, residing in man as what we have been taught to call " the Holy Spirit." This is the " inner secret of God which lives as a kernel in each Christlike soul." When this identification has been made, the problem of authority has been solved. We may say with full confidence, " The word of conscience is the voice of God." [89]

Martineau adds, however, that this inner authority must be recognized to have its setting in the larger context of human reason; and thus reason has an indispensable role to play in each judgment or decision that man makes. Or, " if the Holy Spirit is to ' lead you into all truth,' it will not be by saving you the trouble of parting right from wrong, but by the ever keener severance of the evil from the good through the strenuous working of a quickened mind." [90] The function assigned to reason is teleological. Conscience, operating intuitively, furnishes the initial discriminatory power; while reason, in turn, passes reflective, utilitarian judgment upon the decisions of conscience and the consequences that flow from them. Hence the *discrimen* proves finally to be double-edged, although it remains one-dimensional: " Reason for the rational, conscience for the right — these are the sole organs for appreciating the last claims upon us, the courts of ultimate appeal, whose verdict it is not only weakness, but treason to resist." [91]

This somewhat fantastic, pre-Freudian construction is related throughout to the life and teaching of Jesus of Nazareth, and in such a way that the thought of Martineau serves beautifully as a lens through which the essentially nonhistorical character of the nineteenth century, historical-Jesus movement can be recognized. The multitude of Protestant Biblical scholars and theologians who found themselves caught up by the excitement of this movement, which built upon the other of Schleiermacher's two " exclusively Christian " criteria, were seeking a new theological authority at the end of the path of historical research. They were doing so, however, under the overarching influence of German idealism, with its subtle persuasion of a priority of spirit over matter, and thus of mind or idea over "history" in the sense of historical reality, happening or event. Consequently, they assumed — even as they regarded history as the way out of the theological impasse — that it is the ultimate function of revelation, in Martineau's words, to "open our eyes to what really is or ought to be, not to what has happened, is happening, or will happen." The apparent subservience of the movement to historicism notwithstanding, its proponents actually could have asserted with Martineau that the voice of true theological authority "recites no history," or that God wants no "archeological Christians" — Christians who would locate the seat of authority for the living present in the dead past.[92] When we apply this persuasion to the meaning of the man Jesus, it leads to the conclusion, which Martineau explicitly draws, that Jesus is completely misunderstood if we imagine that he came to be in any sense an authoritative Lord or Judge. He came, rather, to be our companion along the way, the one to whom we are to look reverently as life's intended example, the ideal of "the supreme type of moral communion between God and man."[93]

This "moral communion" was the express goal of the historical-Jesus movement, as it sought to "return to Jesus." The project was simply conceived: to "discover Jesus," the "real Jesus," utilizing the logico-descriptive method of historical research. The influence of Kant's sharp differentiation of theoretical and practical reason, in his first and his second *Critique,* had issued in a clear division of religious experience, and the affirmations, dogmas, and doctrines to which religion gives rise. The sweeping popularity of this distinction had abruptly shifted the basic offense of orthodox theology from the dogma of verbal inspiration to the area of Christology; and it led eventually to a thoroughly positivistic bifurcation of the Christian "fact," and the Christological interpretation that the church has placed upon this fact. This was expressed in popular writings by the differentiation of "the religion *of* Jesus" and "the religion *about* Jesus"; and, in Martineau's phrase, it was assumed that the traditional doctrine of the Person of Christ "was made for him, and palmed upon him by his followers." [94] Critical scholarship thus addressed itself to the task of sifting and separating this traditional interpretation, the Christological accretion, to the end of recovering the hard core of fact that was hidden beneath it. The intention was to use this hard core, the biographical picture and such teachings as could be definitely authenticated, as "the essence of Christianity" and the clue to Christianity's intended theological authority.

It was this motivation which prompted the launching of the so-called Jesus-of-history movement during the latter part of the nineteenth century; and it met with such widespread acceptance that it spilled over well into the twentieth century. When we recall the complexity that the problem of theological authority had assumed during the four centuries that separated this new departure from the advent of the Reformation, it is not difficult to imagine the thrill that accompanied this consuming back-to-Jesus pilgrimage. The motivation and the astonishingly free flow that the movement enjoyed early in our century are symbolized by a list that Prof. Henry J. Cadbury cited of "biographies" that had appeared in rapid order just prior to the publication of his effort to formulate a corrective: *The Rediscovery of Jesus, The Man Nobody Knows, The Jesus of History, Our Recovery of Jesus, The Renaissance of Jesus, The Historic Jesus,* and *Discovering Jesus.*[95] And the extent of the eventual penetration of the movement is suggested by a pithy summary statement of Prof. D. M. Baillie:

> During the first generation of the present century there was an extraordinary stream of popular books from the press on the subject of that historical figure as a rediscovery: books by theological scholars, by literary men, by journalists, by poets, by novelists; by Roman Catholics, by Protestants, by Jews, by seekers, by skeptics; books about the Galilean, the Nazarene, the Original Jesus, the Lord of All Good Life, the Spiritual Pilgrimage of Jesus, the Man Nobody Knows, Jesus as They Saw Him, the Jesus of History.[96]

It is vital to our understanding of the Protestant principle of authority, as we struggle to restate it within a theological context that includes a widespread, almost violent reaction against the nineteenth century, that we recognize the inherently nonhistorical nature of this movement. It infolded a structural inability to permit theological authority to be located in a historical happening or event, and turned instead to a Socratic-Platonic type of universal truth. It was presupposed that authority resides in an ideal, which the man Jesus taught, and of which the event " Jesus of Nazareth " was the most notable embodiment. This was "the kernel" that was sought within " the husk." It means that, despite its studied use of the word " history," and its faithfulness to the methodology of history as a discipline, this movement was essentially nonhistorical in its theological orientation, because it was compelled to restrict authority to a universal that could only be exemplified by a particular. This was substantially true even of Ritschl, as Brunner and Barth have pointed out.[97] Despite his basic opposition to Schleiermacher's orientation, and his determination to correct the aberrations of the early part of the century by relocating theology upon its historical foundation, it is "the gospel" that is authoritative, not the man who *was* the gospel. And the value judgments evoked by revelation comprise the core of concern, not the new situation created by what happened in Christ.

This focus of concern is the explanation for the fact that the most popular and influential of the flood of " lives " that issued from this movement were " internal," not " external," biographies.[98] The advocates of the movement could not, and did not, seek the locus of theological authority in " what has happened," or in the particular historical occurrence of the life and death of Jesus confessed to be " the Word made flesh." They sought its locus, rather, in the " ideal " truth that this life and death represented and communicated; and this is why Martineau, who subscribed wholeheartedly to both the assumptions and the project of this movement, was thoroughly consistent when he insisted that our relation to the historical Jesus is " simply spiritual." " The nearer we approach to his presence," he remarked, " the more do we leave every outward form and questionable claim behind, and are left alone with the pure elements of spiritual religion." This necessitated the curious statement, regarding the relationship of the Christian to Jesus Christ, that there is " no lordship and servitude, but the sublime sympathy of a joint worship on the several steps of a never-ending ascent " to God.[99] This is a more radical expression of its final conclusions than would have been ventured by many of the proponents of the Jesus-of-history movement, but it is completely consistent with its original presuppositions. And it is rather blatantly obvious that having reached this point we are not only twice removed from the Reformation, but even once removed from Schleiermacher.

CHAPTER IV

Prophetic Reaction

Early in this century P. T. Forsyth remarked that "nothing produces more uncertainty than a constant reference to subjective experience."[1] The revolt against orthodoxy that we have sketched, symbolized by the reorientation achieved by Schleiermacher, and the attempts of Sabatier and Martineau to carry through his project in the area of authority, left Protestant theologians adrift on this uncertain sea of "experience." Cut free from every "external" mooring, and blown by winds from all directions, they were immediately in danger of shipwreck on the rocks of relativism. It was assumed that theological criteria must necessarily be products of "the method of observation and experiment";[2] and when this inductive-empirical approach continued to spawn violently conflicting results, a cloud of confusion descended.

It is one of the real oddities of the history of theology that the remedial reaction against this situation arose concurrently with the developments that produced it. The nineteenth century had not yet given way when Forsyth delivered his prophetic Boston lecture on "The Evangelical Principle of Authority," in which he anticipated in an uncanny manner correctives that were not to crystallize until near the middle of the twentieth century. Fifty years earlier, Kierkegaard had called into question fundamental assumptions that remained virtually unquestioned by most Protestant theologians until well beyond the turn of the century. The peculiar occurrence that Forsyth had only a modest degree of influence in his own time, and that Kierkegaard was almost completely ignored by both his own and several succeeding generations, while each has been a dominant

influence in our time, will remain one of the most telling enigmas of
history. Each said what needed to be said, and said it when it needed
to be said; but it was to remain for another century to hear and
heed.

1. Sören Kierkegaard

It would be futile as well as erroneous to seek a direct contribution to the Protestant discussion of this problem in the writings of
Kierkegaard. There are several reasons why this is true. Quantita-
tively speaking the balance of his major work deals with what he
termed the aesthetic and ethical spheres of human existence, with no
pretense of being theological in the overt and ordinary sense. The
Philosophical Fragments and the *Concluding Unscientific Postscript*
are the principal works that bear upon our question. The former
embodies a studied avoidance of the "historical costume" of its
problem, or of Christianity as such; and in the latter Johannes
Climacus, the pseudonymous author, avows repeatedly that he is not
to be considered a Christian. Kierkegaard even insists that he is not
raising, in any form, the question of the truth of Christianity, but
simply laboring to produce "a literary work in which the whole
thought is the task of becoming a Christian." [3] His interest is focused
almost entirely upon the relationship and appropriation of the Christian, and almost not at all upon the nature of that to which the
Christian relates himself, or upon what he appropriates.

Three additional significant factors flow from his heuristic style
and methodology. His earlier writings cleave carefully to the Socratic,
or maieutic, method, attempting only "indirect communication"
and reiterating that "begetting belongs to God alone"; and, as has
so often been observed, his consistency in achieving this purpose is
astounding. When he finally concluded that the time had arrived
for him to "speak out," or to employ the method of "witness," he
constantly reminded his reader that he was speaking "without
authority." And, finally, his conviction that "every religious author
is *eo ipso* polemical," [4] together with the persistent polemical tang
even in his more strictly philosophical and theological writings, must
be given due weight.

These circumstances make it virtually impossible for us to identify with accuracy dogmatic or doctrinal positions that may or may not have been assumed underneath Kierkegaard's dialectical discussions. This is the initial reason why most of his writing is properly classified as philosophy of religion rather than as theology. In truth he would appear to have been laboring, although perhaps to a large degree unconsciously, under a structural influence from Luther's law-gospel differentiation, and devoting his literary powers to the project of clarifying and bringing to bear upon the "normal" life of man the full impact of "the law." Thus in large part he was discussing human existence apart from the gospel; and, although the theology is there, predominantly it is implicit theology.[5]

In his *Journals,* Kierkegaard calls authority "the most important ethical-religious concept," and remarks that "Christianity's paradoxical difference from every other doctrine, from a scientific point of view, is that it posits: authority."[6] When we unite this high regard for the role of authority in theology with his reiteration that he is himself speaking "without authority," it suggests a cautious and somewhat unorthodox approach to his contribution. In the interest of an accuracy of estimate, we shall move upstream, endeavoring to retrace the direct and indirect evidences of his influence. In this way we can detect the levels of his thought that were eventually to have a prodigious impact upon the Protestant approach to the question of authority.

Along this path we discover two theses that have proved to be both powerful and remedial. Each was essentially corrective, although only one was predominantly negative. The first was his passionate concern to force an open discussion of the place and function of the historical in Christianity. This crusade succeeded eventually in calling into question both the underlying presuppositions of the Jesus-of-history movement, and the assumptions regarding its theological value that were clustering about the critical approach to the Bible. The other thesis demanded a critique of the content of "Christian experience" and a redefinition of the nature of "subjectivity." This eventually had the effect of provoking a restorative reassessment of the "God-consciousness," "feeling," "intuitive apprehension," and "Christian consciousness" to which appeal was being so freely made as the nineteenth was replaced by the twentieth century.

The original problem that Kierkegaard posed, which was inscribed on the title page of the *Fragments* and reiterated in the introduction to the *Postscript,* was as follows: " Is a historical point of departure possible for an eternal consciousness; how can such a point of departure have any other than a mere historical interest; is it possible to base an eternal happiness upon historical knowledge? " [7] This query had been stimulated by Lessing's essay " On the Proof of the Spirit and of Power." Singularly unimpressed by the traditional " evidences " of apologetics, the attempts to prove the truth of Christianity by appeal to miracles and fulfilled prophecies, Lessing had pondered the problem of historical probability. " If I had lived in the time of Christ, then of course the prophecies fulfilled in his person would have made me pay great attention to him," he mused. But " I live in the eighteenth century. The problem is that this proof of the spirit and of power no longer has any spirit or power." Reflection drove him back to the primal point that " no historical truths can be demonstrated "; and he deduced that " if no historical truths can be demonstrated, then nothing can be demonstrated by means of historical truths." This led to his famous assertion: " accidental truths of history can never become the proof of necessary truths of reason." Lessing concluded this inquiry with a plea: " This is the ugly, broad ditch which I cannot get across, however often and however earnestly I have tried to make the leap. If anyone can help me over it, let him do it, I beg him, I adjure him." [8]

It was from this incisive essay that Kierkegaard adopted both his initial problem and his basic category, " the leap." In order to speak to the question, he launched out to demonstrate that the leap of faith is not made, and cannot be made, through the medium of history or historical knowledge. He did so simply by echoing Lessing, observing that all history, including Biblical history, since it is concerned with the past, and labors with material that has the inescapable elusiveness of the order of becoming, is doomed at best to offer us only proximate knowledge. " Nothing is more readily evident than that the greatest attainable certainty to anything historical is merely an approximation." To this he added the existential axiom: " an approximation, when viewed as a basis for an eternal happiness, is wholly inadequate, since the incommensurability makes a result impossible." [9]

Kierkegaard belabored this point in an almost fanatical way. He leveled a torrential stream of polemics at what appeared to him to be a complacent, ridiculous, and completely indefensible element of certainty in the Hegelian system, resulting from the identification of "reason" and "history." Hegel had written: "While reason is exclusively its own basis of existence, and absolute final aim, it is also the energizing power realizing this aim; developing it not only in the phenomena of the natural, but also of the spiritual universe — the history of the world."[10] This identification required that the attack that Kierkegaard launched upon the presumption of Hegel's "reason" or "idea" be also an attack upon historical presumption, and it was this assault which eventually destroyed the pretensions of the movement that was seeking a new theological criterion through a "recovery of Jesus."

Speaking before the background of his contention that "truth is subjectivity," to which we shall return presently, Kierkegaard reminded the would-be Christian that even "a knowledge of all the circumstances, with the reliability of an eyewitness, does not make such an eyewitness a disciple."[11] This must be conceded to be so, he said, because "no direct or immediate transition to Christianity exists."[12] But the fury of his attack would not permit him to rest the matter here, and he annexed the assertion that "the historical in the more concrete sense is a matter of indifference."[13] This led to two of the most astonishing and provocative statements ever made from within the Christian church. "The historical fact that God has existed in human form is the essence of the matter; the rest of the historical detail is not even as important as if we had to do with a human being instead of with God." He added, "If the contemporary generation had left nothing behind them but these words: 'We have believed that in such and such a year God appeared among us in the humble figure of a servant, that he lived and taught in our community, and finally died,' it would be more than enough."[14]

Here it becomes crystal-clear that Kierkegaard felt that its unavoidable tinge of probabilism disqualifies in a final way every purely historical approach to the Christian faith. He even inverted the point, to drive it home, suggesting that a theological concern for the historical actually is misleading — as, in fact, it had been within the philosophical climate of his time. It is, he said in a typical illustra-

tion, like " what befell the traveler who asked if the road on which
he was journeying went to London, and was told by the Englishman
that it did; in spite of which he failed to reach London, because
the Englishman had omitted to mention that he needed to turn
about, since he was proceeding in the opposite direction." [15]

If we accept the logic inherent in these contentions, two results
ensue, one restorative and the other dangerous. It forces, as we have
witnessed it forcing in the twentieth century, a re-examination of the
theological value of a critical approach to the Biblical material. This
reappraisal has served as a needed corrective for what Kierkegaard
styled the " critical philological occupation-complex " that was ab-
sorbing the concern and energy of Biblical scholars in his time, and
continued to do so until quite recently. It was not until his sharp reminder that a " quantitative approximation " should not be confused with, and cannot be substituted for, the " qualitative leap of
faith " had taken effect that the current, fruitful revival of Biblical
theology began to stir. The matter should not be oversimplified; but
it actually is not too much to say that primarily it was Kierkegaard's
death blow, relayed by Karl Barth, that extinguished the historical-
Jesus movement and freed Biblical scholarship from the stifling historicism inherent in its nineteenth-century preoccupation.

Were Kierkegaard's critique to be taken at its face value, however,
it would bring into question not only historicism, and a purely historical approach to the Scriptures, but all serious concern with Biblical content beyond its use simply as " a witness to the Moment of
the Paradox." Kierkegaard never tired of remarking that when we
attempt to approach the Christian faith along the path of historical
research, we are led astray on irrelevant bypaths and find ourselves
lost in the wilderness of the parentheses. There is obvious truth in
this warning, and it remains a valid and needed one wherever the
temptation is present to regard Scripture as an end rather than as a
means. But if it were embraced in the naked state in which Kierkegaard left it, this assertion would pose a threat to the historical nature of Christianity even greater than that sponsored by Marcion.
And, as we shall see, the shadow of this threat has continued to the
moment to hover over Protestant attempts to speak to the question
of authority.

The posture that Kierkegaard assumed as he fenced with the various forms of the threat of historicism suggests his attitude toward every movement of faith that is less than a direct confrontation of " the Paradox." His basic irritation was agitated by the epistemological presupposition, which had become almost universal in his time under the influence of philosophical idealism, that thought qua thought, or " pure thought," leads one to truth. He believed that this absorption with the abstract, of which the Hegelian metaphysic was the master image, was responsible for the fact that " men had forgotten what it means to exist, and what inwardness signifies." [16] It is almost superfluous, although completely necessary, to remind ourselves that we can understand Kierkegaard only in so far as we take with total seriousness his thesis that all thought that ignores the flesh and blood, passionate and compassionate existence of the thinker, is self-deluded and self-deluding. He remarked of the Cartesian dictum, " I think; therefore I am," that it is " a tautology," and insisted ever and again that the *sum,* not the *cogito,* is the Archimedian point.[17] Hence he contended without compromise, against Hegel and all open or inadvertent Hegelians, that " pure thought," far from being metaphysical reality, is not even the medium of contact with reality. Rather, " existence is the eternal prius." [18]

It is within the context of this anti-Hegelian project that Kierkegaard's uninhibited use of the slippery categories " objective " and " subjective " must be understood and evaluated. It is necessary to remember that he was questioning neither the existence of objective reality nor the value of objective thought within its proper sphere. The target of his attack was abstract, nonexistential thought when the effort is made to employ this " pure thought " for Christian theological purposes. Nor did he make any attempt whatever to limit or confine reality to the sphere of the subjective. He was, as a matter of fact, an idealist in several senses; but not in this sense. His single purpose was to posit subjective or existential knowledge as *the* knowledge in the realm of faith. Were this not clear elsewhere, it was made ultraclear in the literature surrounding " the Adler incident." [19]

He does, however, and without qualification, make the subjective, in the form of existential decision, the sole dimension of faith. He reiterates that religion deals with the final — not with possibility, as does logic; so that religious knowledge by its very nature cannot settle for an " approximation process." The knight of faith must turn his back upon every temptation to repose in the approximations of objective or speculative thought, and seize by decision the truth that man can know only by passionate appropriation. At the heart of Kierkegaard's thought lies the axiom: " An objective uncertainty held fast in an appropriation-process of the most passionate inwardness is the truth, the highest truth attainable for an existing individual." [20] And here " the divine authority is the category. Here there is little or nothing at all for a *Privatdocent* or a licentiate or a paragraph-swallower to do — as little as a young girl needs the barber to remove her beard, and as little as a bald man needs the *friseur* to ' accommodate ' his hair, just so little is the assistance of these gentlemen needed. The question is quite simple: Will you obey? or will you not obey? Will you bow in faith before his divine authority? Or will you be offended? Or will you perhaps take no side? " [21]

It was in this sense that Kierkegaard equated subjectivity with truth. His concern was " eternal truth," and the subjectivity intended bears no kinship to simple psychological or purely cognitive subjectivity. The movement of faith is a movement " outward," toward an objective historical event, the incarnation. And this is to say that we have completely misunderstood Kierkegaard if we imagine that he was a " subjectivist " in the popular sense of this term. Ordinarily speaking, the subjectivist is understood as one who, like Schleiermacher, locates the initial datum of theology in human experience, or in the consciousness of the believer. Kierkegaard begins with the believer; but he begins with him as a nonbeliever, as did Luther. And his whole purpose in doing so is to lead him to the insight that there is no immediate relation between man and God, no continuous movement from unfaith to faith, no " direct transition " from unbelief to belief, no path from man to God. Between lies the abyss created by sin and guilt; and it *is* an abyss. Hence the answer, if there is an answer, must come from beyond.

Kierkegaard's conviction was that it is only when man has looked this fact full in the face, and despaired of every other possibility, that he will open himself to the " absurd " claim that the answer has been given in an objective historical occurrence, a carpenter who was "God in servant form." "Existential subjectivity" is the passionate, decision-making subjectivity of the *whole* existing individual who seizes upon this absurd Paradox as his only hope. In doing so he does not move inward. Having moved inward, and despaired inwardly, he moves outward — to embrace the Paradox. These are the essential presuppositions that were ingrained when Kierkegaard reiterated his axial thesis, "truth is subjectivity." And they must be present in our evaluation, and in any use that we might attempt to make of this assertion. It was not the highest peak reached in the spiraling "psychologism" of the nineteenth-century consciousness-theology. It was the original and decisive break with it.

The service that this remedial polemic of Kierkegaard has rendered to twentieth-century Protestant throught is almost inestimable, as we shall see. A brief summary of the sweep of his dialectic, as he applied it correctively and constructively, is a necessary background to an understanding of his contribution, and its catalytic function, in current theology. When he began with Socrates, for the express purpose of forcing a recognition that man's deepest need is not epistemological but soteriological, although he could not know it, he was speaking to a need of our century as well as of his own. He swiftly relegated the psychological-emotional interpretation of Christian faith, which had followed upon Schleiermacher's reorientation, to the level of the pre-Christian, to the first stage on life's way, or to the "pagan" sphere of "the aesthetic." The plight of man, he reiterated, roots in error, not in ignorance; and thus man needs not only truth, but the condition necessary to an acceptance and understanding of truth. No intuitive feeling, no immediate apprehension, no filial consciousness, no sublime sympathy, no Socratic recollection of universal truth, will serve. What is required, and what is known to be required where the analysis is accurate, is "an advance upon Socrates" that can recognize and appropriate atonement and redemption.

This led him to assert bluntly of the "Jesus of Nazareth" of nineteenth-century theology that he was "God himself," "God in time." He posited an absolute distinction between the finite and the infinite, between history and eternity, refusing to permit man

to " fraternize with God " or to view himself as in any sense a " part-
ner " in the divine economy. " God and man are absolutely different." [22] This is the " infinite qualitative distinction " which dom-
inated Barth's early writing, and was the source of the divine " No "
with which he opened the way for a recognition of the true nature
of the divine " Yes." [23] The crux of Christianity was then identified,
by Kierkegaard, as " the Moment of the Absolute Paradox," the historical miracle that occurred when eternity invaded time, when God
appeared " in servant form." [24] He repeated again and again that
this Moment is unavailable via objective or historical knowledge,
that " objective acceptance of Christianity is paganism or thought-
lessness," [25] and that every approach that assumes a " direct transition " to Christianity suffers from the blindness of a shallow and
false diagnosis of the problem. And because the answer lies only
in " God in time " in the " Absolute Paradox," man must " believe
by virtue of the absurd," through a passionate, " qualitative leap."

The leap, taken from Lessing, was Kierkegaard's vivid category
for the dialectical-existential movement into the Christian faith. Embracing the two Biblical categories " repentance " and " faith " in
a single dramatic description, he pictured this movement as one that
demands a human " no " and " yes." [26] It requires a negative " infinite resignation," a decisive denial and renunciation of the world;
and primarily in the sense of a surrender of every shred of the assumption that truth and " eternal blessedness " are to be had in the
spheres of the aesthetic or the ethical. The positive movement is a
passionate, existential seizing upon the Paradox, or the absurd, upon
the Moment in our existence when the eternal God who appeared in
time makes us contemporaneous with this appearance. It is not by
virtue of any continuity of consciousness, or any sort of immediate
or direct relation to God, but in this discontinuous act of appropriation that man seizes " truth." And in that Moment he becomes what
he is intended to be, the existing individual — an individual existing in God-bestowed freedom, responsibility, and decision. To live
this Moment, this dialectical movement, in eternal repetition, is to
be Christian.

No mention has been made of Kierkegaard's view of the authority
of the Bible. It would be an error to conclude from this silence,

which is merely a repetition of Kierkegaard's silence, that he intended to establish faith, or "subjective experience" in any form, as a singular criterion of doctrine. This conclusion would not only ignore his careful statement of his project, and misinterpret the orientation of his thought, but also fly in the face of clear statements to the contrary. He repeatedly asserted, in various ways, that "truth, from the Christian point of view, does not lie in the subject (as Socrates understood it) but in a revelation which must be proclaimed."[27] Because of the implicit nature of his theology, it is virtually impossible to determine exactly the relationship that he presupposed between this "revelation which must be proclaimed" and the Biblical literature. The scraps of evidence that raise the question of Biblical authority in one form or another are of very little theological value, because of their expedient, polemical, and dated nature. They do, however, clearly prohibit any attempt that might conceivably be made to reassert the *sola Scriptura* principle with his blessing — a move that, in some contexts, he seems to have been anticipating. He observes that "there always lurks some such concern in a man, at the same time indolent and anxious, a wish to lay hold of something so really fixed that it can exclude all dialectics; but this desire is an expression of cowardice, and is deceitfulness toward the divine."[28]

When it is related to the question of authority, the Bible, together with the church, is described as an "approximation object." It is a historical entity, in and subject to time, which is intended to serve as God's witness to the truth.[29] But it also can do "immeasurable harm" when it is misused as the basis of "a religion of learning and law." Kierkegaard felt that this was happening in some quarters in his time; and the typical suggestion that he made is perhaps not completely irrelevant in some quarters in our time. "Let us collect all the New Testaments there are in existence, let us carry them out to an open place or up on a mountain, and then, while we all kneel down, let someone address God in this fashion: Take this book back again; we men, such as we are now, are not good at dealing with a thing like this, it only makes us unhappy."[30] Where this situation prevails, Kierkegaard said, and man has become foolish enough to relate himself primarily to God's book rather than to

God, "a reformation which did away with the Bible would be just as valid as Luther's doing away with the pope." [31] Just so.

2. Peter Taylor Forsyth

The process of transposing Kierkegaard's corrective polemics into constructive theological affirmations was to require more than a century. Forsyth was one of the earliest, if not the earliest, English-speaking theologian to reflect his influence. And just as Kierkegaard essayed a decisive repudiation of subjectivism, and did so in the name of " subjectivity "; so Forsyth attempted a final break with the tyranny of experience that had gripped Protestant theology at the turn of the century, and did so in the name of " the evangelical experience." He posited a clear-cut differentiation between the human seat and the divine source of authority, designating the former " experience," and the latter " the experienced "; and then insisted that the primacy of concern must be shifted to the latter.[32] " The great question," he reiterated, " is not really as to the seat of authority, but as to its nature. The one is psychological, and can wait; the other is theological, and cannot." [33] This pressing previous question of the nature of theological authority continued to be his underlying and major concern to the end of his life, as he fought unceasingly to liberate Protestant thought from the innumerable, subtle psychological milieux with which it had become associated during the latter part of the nineteenth century.

When we view Forsyth's writings in their entirety, we recognize immediately that his overarching purpose was to reaffirm and re-establish the formative motifs of the Biblical faith. This is the most striking characteristic communicated by his epigrammatic style; and it is also why the similarity of his thought to the early writings of Barth, and to the provocative conclusions of the motif research of Bishop Anders Nygren, has so often incited comment.

Forsyth sensed prophetically, and at an earlier date, that the shift of the ground of theological authority, and the anthropocentric, methodological reorientation that had occurred during the nineteenth century, had blurred the formative fact of the primacy of grace, or the *agapē* motif of Christianity — the fact that Christian faith begins, and must be seen theologically to begin, with the movement of God to man, not with a movement of man to God. His writings are informed throughout by his deep, orienting conviction — virtually unique in British and American theology in his day — that confusion at this initial juncture was responsible for a serious malalignment of late nineteeth-century theology. Thus he punctuated his concern with frequent, terse reminders that the quest for "illumination" had almost completely displaced revelation; and that sentimentalized "love" had neutralized the attribute of holiness, and obscured the reality of wrath, in the interpretation of the nature of God. He reiterated that preoccupation with the life of Jesus had almost wholly overshadowed the significance of his death; and that impression had usurped the place of regeneration, and personality integration displaced atonement and redemption, in the interpretation of the Christian life. His great passion was to force theologians and ministers who were championing this pallid, so-called "new theology" [34] to measure their thought once again by "the given," by the essential motifs that emerge if we acknowledge the primacy of grace and discover in so doing that "our authority is what takes the initiative with our faith." [35]

It was to this end that Forsyth defined the authority of Christian theology as "the grace of the gospel," although he frequently used such designations as "the redeeming Christ," "the atoning cross," "creative grace," and "historic grace." [36] He then devoted the only major work that has appeared on the subject of authority within this century to a diversified apologia of this definition. The style is that of the preacher, not of the systematic theologian; and the demonstrated power of the essay lies in its heuristic aphorisms, not in its systematic completeness. But a consistency of formative intention is apparent throughout. And in order to secure this formative intention, he dwelt upon two prerequisites that he felt would always be recognized and acknowledged where Christian theology lives, moves, and has its being under its proper authority.

The initial approach is epistemological. He insists that the true authority of Christian theology is known, and can be acknowledged, only from within the movement of faith; or that the *sola gratia* motif of Christianity necessarily posits a *sola fide* stance on the part of the recipient of grace, whether it be the individual or the church, the unlettered Christian or the theological faculty. This point has been expressed more recently in a pungent way by Prof. Richard Niebuhr, in his widely quoted remark that "there is no neutral standpoint and no faithless situation from which approach can be made to that which is inseparable from faith." [37] This was the initial epistemological presupposition of Forsyth's lengthy survey of the problem of authority.

The psychological problem, with its challenge of all types of religion, was assuming its early twentieth-century composition in Forsyth's time, and he reflects a keen consciousness of its potential threat. He repeated frequently, in varying ways, that the necessary circumscription of theological authority by the circumference of faith is not to be interpreted as in any sense a claim for a separate psychology for Christian experience, or a request for a suspension of normal psychological functions, processes, and "laws" within the domain of theology. "This authority," he remarks, "so super-rational in its nature and action, is yet in its method so rational that it emerges only amid psychological conditions. It is not magical." [38] The point is, rather, that the Christian theologian — by definition if he is, in fact, a Christian theologian — must acknowledge, witness to, and think theologically in the light of an ultimate prius that transcends all psychology where God is known: the fact that man knows God only where, and as, God makes himself known. And this is to say that theology, no less than devotion, must recognize and acknowledge that "his knowledge of us is the source of our knowledge of him." It means, consequently, that all knowledge of the source of Christian authority is of necessity, and first of all, a "being known." This is a remarkable, prophetic parallel to Barth's thesis that "only God speaks of God," or that "God is known through God alone." [39]

This strain of thought is, of course, quite familiar to us in the second half of the twentieth century, even if we are as yet far from having fully come to terms with it in the Protestant pulpit. And it seems obvious, in retrospect, that Forsyth was groping for the noetic delineation that was to be so graphically sketched in Prof. Martin Buber's poetic little *Ich und Du,* and was to become an invaluable tool in the reconstruction of Protestant theology that has been taking place in our time. It was Forsyth who first remarked, as the century opened, that God is the "object" of faith, and the "external" source of Christian authority, only as the "Absolute Subject."[40] And with this emphasis he intended to say both that God is known, and can be known, only on the level of the personal; and that the initiative is with God, and must be his. Buber's word is: "The *Thou* meets me through grace — it is not found by seeking."[41] If theology's "object" were an object in the common sense of the word, it would be open to empirical investigation and verification. But theology's "object" is *the* Subject. Thus man's initial movement must necessarily be one of response; and the response must necessarily be one of grateful acceptance and obedience, as God gives not only knowledge of himself, but himself.

This is why Forsyth frequently echoed Luther, insisting that *assensus,* acceptance and assent simply with the intellect or mind, is insufficient either as the whole or as the first movement of faith.[42] Response to a Subject who claims our lives, and demands allegiance as well as belief, requires *fiducia,* an unqualified trust of the total self. Therefore the first movement of the Christian, from which the Christian theologian is not exempt, must be one of response in the sense of reliance, the acceptance of God's movement to man in the grace of the gospel. Because this is an indispensable prerequisite of all Christian life and thought, it must likewise be an initial recognition in the life of Christian theology, and thus an integral element of the theological *discrimen* of Christendom.

The other prerequisite with which Forsyth secured his formative intention was a recognition and acknowledgment of the historic and thoroughly moral nature of the source of Christian authority. It is difficult to discern at this point the degree of influence exerted by the Kantian and Ritschlian atmosphere early in the century,[43] and the extent to which Forsyth's voluntaristic orientation was merely a reflection of his strong Reformation consciousness.[44] He had studied with Ritschl at Göttingen, in 1872; and there is an obvious influence in the general orientation of his thought, especially in his zeal to "moralize dogma." But much of his later writing was a conscious, constructive effort to correct what he regarded as aberrations in the direction that the Ritschlian school had taken following Ritschl's death. Recent analyses of his theology have dwelt very little upon either the Ritschlian or the Kantian influence;[45] yet there is a strong suggestion in *The Principle of Authority* that the claims of Kant's second *Critique* were a dominant element in determining the direction in which he wished the matter to move.

He endorses Kant's ethical orientation: "his route was right"; and he insists consistently that "the Christian religion involves, if not the solitude, at least the primacy of the ethical."[46] This obviously could have been nothing more than verbal applause for the emerging victory of Kant over Hegel; but it may also be the missing ontological link that explains the perplexing, persistent balance to the side of holiness in his doctrine of God. He quotes with unquestioning approval Kant's metaphysical presupposition, the opening line of the *Metaphysic of Morals,* "There is nothing conceivable in the world, or out of it, which can be called good without qualification except a good will."[47] When this is linked to the conviction that God is absolute, it results in the formula: "Absolute Being must be identical with the absolute moral norm."[48] Here the point has ceased to be merely that the ontological is moral; but, rather, the moral is identified with the ontological. Holiness must then become the primal ontological category; and the holiness of God, as "the identification of the moral norm and the ultimate reality of the world," must be the reality to which all other reality is subjected.[49] This is why it is not surprising to find Forsyth contending, with what is virtually a crusading conviction, that "the great spiritual task for Christianity is to replace its holiness in command of its love."[50]

It is unlikely, but it is possible, on the other hand, that Forsyth intended nothing in this context beyond what Luther implied when he referred to himself as a "modernist." What is certain is that his emphasis led him, as Luther's led him, to a new wedding of authority and soteriology. The pulse of Forsyth's most significant contribution in this area is felt in his reminder, in the spirit of the sixteenth century, that "revelation *is* redemption," and that "faith *is* salvation."[51] "It means that the revelation of the holy can only come through redemption by the holy."[52] This led him to insist repeatedly that the source of Christian authority is known only through what he termed " a moral act in a mystic sphere," and thus that all Christian theology must be " moralized." [53]

It is manifestly unfair to Forsyth to assume that he wished, with this stress, either to substitute morality for faith, or merely to carry through Ritschl's opposition to metaphysics. His concern was much more akin to the Reformation project of establishing " the evangelical way of life," and to Kierkegaard's insistence that a theological affirmation that is not existential is not true.[54] Of Forsyth this project required a concentrated opposition to the aberrations of modern pietism on one side, and to the arrogance of rationalism on the other; and his positive stress was upon a reorientation of Protestant theology under an understanding of faith that centered in the atonement that effects redemption. He saw, with Kierkegaard, that this required that the initial theological referent be historical (in the sense of *Geschichte,* not of *Historie* [55]), not psychological: " it must be the Christ of the historic and redeeming cross." [56] Hence, he would countenance no dismissal and no mitigation of either " experience " or " the experienced," when the point had been made that the latter is both chronologically and logically prior. " All of which issues in this — that authority at the last has no meaning except as it is understood by the evangelical experience of regeneration in some form, which is the soul's re-creation, surrender, and obedience once and for all in a new creation and direct communion with the God of the moral universe." [57]

This was the intended fabric of " the evangelical experience " with which Forsyth combated the cult of experience of his day. He frequently expressed the qualitative distinction that he was so concerned to make by insisting that a miracle occurs in true Christian experience. Transposed into an affirmation bearing upon our question, it means that, in one quite real sense, for Christian theology " authority is in the nature of a miracle." [58] While he was somewhat less sensitive to the charge of " irrationalism " than we today are, he does attempt to forestall this accusation by frequently employing such terms as " alogical " and " superrational " in apposition with this assertion.[59] And his point is clear: that " the last reason for believing is nonrational," which is to say that because the authority of Christianity and of Christian theology is inextricably interwoven with the historic and moral nature of the Christian faith, it is the fruit of a " new creation " — a creation wholly miraculous in its origin and thoroughly redemptive in its nature.[60]

We recognize in retrospect that when the matter is viewed from the side of the question of authority, on the deepest level Forsyth and Kierkegaard were conspirators in a common cause — to break with the nineteenth-century, one-dimensional reinterpretation of Christianity's principle of authority which each confronted in a thoroughly consolidated form in the Protestantism of his own day. Forsyth no less than Kierkegaard was speaking to the nineteenth-century situation; and it cannot be denied that in doing so each was utilizing distinctively nineteenth-century presuppositions in his struggle to overcome the conclusions that had been drawn from them. But we should not permit this historically conditioned fact, and the understandable circumstance that Kierkegaard spoke in the name of subjectivity and Forsyth in the name of experience, to divert us from appreciating the remarkable struggle that each underwent to reorient the theological *discrimen*. When we read them before the backdrop that Sabatier and Martineau represent, we recognize immediately that the nineteenth-century " partnership " of God and man has been dissolved by Kierkegaard's "infinite qualitative distinction." The bald assertion that there is " no lordship and servitude " has been replaced by a question thrust upon man from beyond: Will you obey? or will you not obey? The vital, existential side of the Reformation *discrimen,* which nineteenth-century theology deserves full credit for recovering, has been retained; but the " intuitive apprehension " with which it was identified has given way to " a revelation which must be proclaimed."

It is at this point that Forsyth and Kierkegaard were of one mind: they were united in the attempt to renounce the heritage of Schleiermacher. Each decisively turned his back upon the assumption that an " immediate presence " is the theological prius, and insisted without compromise that we must turn to the Mediator prior to any assertion of immediacy. Each assumed that " the *Thou* meets me through grace " and " is not found by seeking," and that " his knowledge of us is the source of our knowledge of him." This is why each ceased to speak of an " inner secret of God " in the soul, and relocated the initial referent of theological authority beyond human experience, in " the experienced," in " historic grace," in " the atoning cross," in " God in servant form." And this is why at bottom each was profoundly prophetic. Speaking within another milieu, but to us as well, they threw into bold relief the theological decision that no contemporary theologian can avoid when he faces the question of authority.

PART THREE

The Contemporary Milieu

CHAPTER V

The Contextual Approach

NO CONTEMPORARY theologian has approached the question of theological authority more openly and frankly than Tillich, and his candor has forced him to defend a position that differs markedly from both traditional answers and other current efforts. The uniqueness of his approach, which is subtle and complex in the extreme, issues primarily from an insistence that experience, functioning as a medium, transforms the sources of theology and produces the norm in such a way that it may be described as " a product of the collective experience of the church." [1] When this assertion is viewed in the light of the indisputable fact that the *Gestalten* of Christian experience differ within each epoch of history, the theologian is forced to speak contextually, and in the plural, of " norms " or "analogous norms " that are relative to the various cultural configurations within which they make their appearance. This then permits him to seek and identify, and adopt, a specific norm for his own theological era without attributing permanence and finality to it. This is the status that Tillich confers upon the " New Being," the particular norm under which his own theology is formulated. [2]

This unique approach roots, as does all else in Tillich's system, in the methodological presupposition that regulates his apologetic project. The method is itself a theological assertion and affirmation, he observes; and this theological-methodological assertion is intrinsically related, in turn, to his view of the nature and role of theology. [3] He begins with the conviction that the Franciscan element is indispensable, or that there must be *haptus* and *gustus,* touching and tasting; which is to say that theological thought is necessarily " based on a participation of the knowing subject in spiritual realities," so that " participation in a religious reality is a presupposition of all theology." And this participation is " concrete," or theology is, by inner necessity, " positive ": " it works on the basis, in the material, and for the purpose of an actual religion." [4]

The assignment of the Christian theologian, as he works with the material of the Christian religion, is bipolar. He is charged with responsibility for " the statement of the truth of the Christian message "; but he is also responsible for " the interpretation of this truth for every new generation." Thus he must labor not only with the Biblical message, or with the " eternal truth " of the Christian faith that is available in and through its symbols, but also with the specific, temporal, human situation that the church confronts in his own generation. " Situation " is a technical concept in Tillich's thought. It designates " the totality of man's creative self-interpretation," not the historical or socio-psychological plight in which man happens to find himself.[5] The " situation " must be sought within the current cultural media, the artistic, political, scientific, philosophical, and ethical forms that embody and typify the interpretation of human existence that is intrinsic to, and is being presupposed within, the historical period. The theologian's peculiar role is that of relating, or correlating, the symbols of the Christian religion with this situation, as he uncovers it through a running analysis of these forms.

1. The Methodological Problem

Tillich is convinced that this bipolar requirement, if it is taken seriously, immediately exposes the inadequacies of three common theological methods, and that it reveals the necessity for a fourth, the method of correlation. It is with his critique of method that he attempts to chart his " third way," or to assume the stance of " ecstatic naturalism," or " self-transcending realism " (*gläubiger Realismus*), a position that will overcome and avoid the errors of both naturalism and supranaturalism.[6] He feels that the " supranaturalistic " method, which attempts to formulate and apply " revealed truths," has fatal Docetic-Monophysitic traits; and therefore, in principle, it makes the correlation with the human situation completely impossible. Its specific weakness is (if we may use one of the concepts that symbolized the celebrated break between Barth and Brunner [7]) that it has no *Anknüpfungspunkt,* no point of contact between God and man, so that the "truths" of which it speaks are "like strange bodies from a strange world." They are, Tillich says, "thrown at those in the situation — thrown like a stone," and man would in reality have to be something other than human in order to receive them. This is the charge that he brings not only against Protestant orthodoxy and American fundamentalism, but also, with certain qualifications, against Barth's "kerygmatic" theology.

The second possibility, the "naturalistic" or "humanistic" method, fails to meet the methodological demands because, either explicitly or inadvertently, it tends to forfeit every possibility of making the necessary correlation by ignoring the dimension of ontological depth, and thus the eternal truth of the message. Thus this method is in actuality attempting to extract the contents of the faith from the human situation, restricting itself to a level where only the questions may be found. Consequently, it fails to grasp and correlate the depth symbols that communicate, and alone can communicate, the ultimate answers. This was, in Tillich's view, the common basis of the methodological weaknesses shared by the various types of nineteenth- and early twentieth-century liberal theology.[8]

The third alternative, the "dualistic" method, posits two levels, a natural substructure and a supranatural superstructure, and then tries to relate these two. The attempt inevitably fails because of a blindness to the fact that, strictly speaking, there is no "natural theology." Tillich feels that theological method must prize and utilize the philosophical element of so-called natural theology, in its development of the problems that are to be correlated with the Christian symbols.[9] But the weakness of methodological dualism is the failure to recognize that the most that may be derived from this substructure, in itself, is an analysis of the contradictions of finitude. This is, of course, Tillich's critique of the method of Thomism, although he also relates it to late Protestant orthodoxy. He is convinced that every two-level approach is intrinsically unsatisfactory, because it errs at the foundation by seeking and anticipating a part of the answer within a locus where only the questions are available.[10]

This analytical prelude leads Tillich to the conclusion that only the method of correlation can succeed where these alternative methods fail, and avoid the manifest illusions and errors of naturalism, supranaturalism, and the Scholastic approach. The method of correlation strives to develop, through the use of materials available within the sphere of human existence as such, the ultimate questions in their contemporary dress, as they are being asked in the *Fragestellung* peculiar to the human situation of the current period of history. It then correlates these with revelation, or with the symbols that constitute the Christian answers to the ultimate questions. It is the method of question and answer, of existential-philosophical question and theological answer, in which the apologetic concern and element are " omnipresent." It is in this correlative sense that Tillich's thought is " existential theology," and the label is misleading if it is used to associate him directly with any particular type or tradition of philosophical existentialism. The problem within this context is not — as it is, for example, in Bultmann — that his thought appears to be subservient in form or substance to a particular form of existentialism. It is, rather, that he is not clear when he attempts to indicate the precise relation of question to answer, and answer to question; and of each to the situation on the one hand, and to revelation on the other.

He is verbally consistent in the frequent reminder that the results of the analytical project determine only the form of the theological answer and not its content or substance.[11] The primary problem is generally sought here by those who are critical of Tillich's method, under a feeling that he has permitted the philosophical-existential orientation of the system to mold unduly, or distort, the symbols and content of the Biblical revelation. The matter is obviously circular, but the initial methodological problem would seem to lie elsewhere. Tillich himself has remarked, outside of the system,[12] that the type of form-content differentiation that he employs within this context is much too neat to be wholly valid and to solve the problem that the interrelation creates. But he has nevertheless not always been so careful as he might have been in realizing that whenever there is an appeal to this distinction, without qualifications, it may merely serve to divert attention from the genuine difficulty and danger in the kind of correlation that he attempts. We shall return to this puzzling matter of the effect of an existential correlation upon the theological substance of the system when we examine the content attributed to the concept, the New Being. What needs to be recognized here is that the first enigma for the problem of method is not in the effect of the questions upon the answers. It appears when we attempt to determine the relationship of the answers to the questions, and the kind and degree of authoritative theological control, if any, that the former have over the latter.

Correlation has been most recently defined by Tillich as "the interdependence of two independent factors," a relationship that attempts to achieve "a unity of dependence and independence." [13] However, early in the introductory section that deals with preliminary problems of prolegomena, he seems to be saying that the questions are purely existential and are developed with the use of philosophy as the theoretic tool. He states quite clearly that "the analysis of existence, including the development of the questions implicit in existence, is a philosophical task, even if it is performed by a theologian." [14] And, although it is qualified, this apparent independence of the analysis is reaffirmed in the supplementary comments on method in the second volume: "it is impossible to derive the answer from the question, *or* the question from the answer." "The question, asked by man, is man himself," he says; and "in asking it, he is alone with himself." [15]

Tillich remarks elsewhere, however, that "symbolically speaking, God answers man's questions, and under the impact of God's answers, man asks them." [16] Here the analysis presupposes, and is dependent upon, revelation. It is obvious that we cannot have it both ways. If we raise the issue of theological authority, it would appear that a choice has to be made — and, as we shall see, it would also appear that Tillich does make such a choice. Either the critical selection of the particular questions that are to be correlated, and the nature and form that they assume, are *not* determined and in some way controlled by revelation and theology proper; or they *are* in some such way so determined and controlled. The problem, bluntly stated, is that if they are not in fact so controlled, then we must wonder whether Tillich's system is posing the proper questions and is dealing with them in their correct or Christian form. If, on the contrary, the selection and the formulation of the questions are in fact determined by revelation and theology, then the correlation project inherits two thorny problems. One is the inescapable suspicion that philosophy has been made subservient to revelation and theology, rather than correlated with it in the sense claimed. It seems necessary to say that, to the degree that it has become subservient, it has ceased to be philosophy and has become crypto-theology. The other is the possibility that the questions are at bottom those of theology and the theologian, and not necessarily those being asked by the "natural man" or the man who is religiously neutral, or those being asked within the human situation as such. In this event, the method could remain one of correlation, but it obviously would be a correlation of a different kind.

A close reading would seem to offer three possible resolutions of this dilemma. The first possibility is that the entire matter has never actually, or completely, progressed beyond the stage of ambiguity in Tillich's own mind (and perhaps it is not unimportant to notice that he does not entirely shy away from the charge of inconsistency at this point when it is leveled at him by his critics[17]). If this should be the true status of the matter, it would seem rather obvious that our response should be neither to disqualify mentally Tillich's system, nor to forsake his correlation of question and answer as a possible theological and apologetic method — and possibly a peculiarly effective way of communicating the Christian faith in our time. It should be, rather, in the nature of an attempt to push the issue through, and state it sharply, so that its actual and final consequences can be determined.

There is a second possibility toward which Tillich would appear to be leaning in his most recent comments on method. Here independence is claimed for the analysis only in the sense that the questions are not derived directly from the theological answers. It is said to be true in the deepest sense that man's question is "man himself," so that as he formulates it "he asks 'out of the depth,' and this depth is he himself."[18] But this is then qualified by the observation that the "theological circle," a concept developed earlier,[19] is not really a circle. It has now become an ellipse with two central points, one representing the question and the other the answer.[20] What this presumably means is that, although the materials from which the analysis is derived come from the human situation as such, without reference to revelation and theology, it must be remembered that it is the theologian who deals with these materials and states the questions. And, as he selects and formulates them, he is participating existentially in both the human situation and the constellation of a religious commitment, or a concrete ultimate concern. In this sense it can be said that the questions are both independent of, and dependent on, the answers or symbols; because as the theologian seeks and frames them, he does so both as a man and as a theologian.

The basic problem here is that, in order for the questions to remain independent in any actual or genuine sense, it must be insisted that the theologian choose and formulate them solely as a participant in man's finitude and anxiety. That is, he must approach the analytical side of his task " as though he had never received the revelatory answer." [21] This is, to say the least, a strange demand. It is difficult to believe that Tillich is entirely serious in suggesting that a Christian theologian, who has been grasped by the revelatory and redemptive power of Jesus Christ, could and should function in one half of his theological labors as though the Christ had not come and he had not been grasped. If this is what he intends, the sharp, piercing charges of illusion that he brings against the recurring attempts to formulate an empirical or " scientific " theology are equally applicable to his own thought at this particular point.[22]

The third possibility is only suggested, and not systematically developed by Tillich; but it would seem to be consistent with the structure and total content of his system and with his unique turn of mind. The interdependence and independence of the question and the answer may be affirmed dialectically in much the same way as he affirms the essential and existential natures of man.[23] The interdependence, or unity and mutual relation of the form and the content of each, could then be assumed on the basis of the participation of all men in the power of being, and in the " mystical a priori " that logically precedes the self-world and subject-object split in human knowledge. The independence of the question could be asserted on the basis of man's estrangement in existence, his state of sin; and the independence of the answer could be maintained on the basis of revelation. Both dependence and independence could then be affirmed if the affirmation is understood dialectically and not in a structural sense.

This kind of dialectical, correlative relationship might be said to be symbolized by the status of human finitude to which Tillich frequently points: that man, in asking the question of infinity, reveals both his essential union with the infinite and his existential estrangement from it. He could not ask about the infinite if he were not in some sense united to it; and yet, the very fact that he asks reveals his separation from it. In the same way, it could be said dialectically that man's existential questions both are, and are not, determined by his relationship to God. They are so determined inasmuch as they must be, and are, asked on the basis of his essential nature. They are not so determined inasmuch as they are asked within the situation of estrangement and thus on the basis of his existential or sinful nature. Therefore question and answer, in the question-answer correlation, are in this dialectical way both interdependent and independent. And the longer one lives with Tillich's system, the more plausible and certain it appears that this is the basic answer to the methodological puzzle that it posits.

2. The Point of Prius

If this is the real nature of the correlative relationship that is assumed and utilized, it points once more to the continuity of Tillich's thought with the orientation of Schleiermacher, which we noted earlier.[24] Even when we leave aside the question of the content attributed to it, it seems obvious that there is no essential difference, for purposes of orientation, between an identification of the point of prius as " the immediate presence of whole, undivided being " and its identification as " the experience of being over against nonbeing," described as " an immediate experience of something ultimate in value and being of which one can become intuitively aware." [25] Each is a " mystical a priori "; and, epistemologically speaking, each is behind the experience and the application of any distinctively Christian element of authority. The theologian " adds to the ' mystical a priori' the criterion of the Christian message," Tillich says; and here the orientation point, and the basis of the mutual dependence within the correlation, is one logically prior to the Christian revelation. He has frequently attempted to relate this presupposition Christologically, by utilizing his *logos* concept, with his assertion that culture " anticipates " the Christ, and with his doctrine of " the latent church," which is to be developed in the fifth and final section of the system. But none of these really solves the initial methodological problem. There is here no authoritative element that demands that the selection and development of the questions be in some sense Christologically oriented and determined; and therefore, to put it baldly, there is no assurance or guarantee that the questions with which Christian theology deals are Christian questions — and even less that they are *the* Christian questions.

Tillich's system, as he develops it, obviously is not entirely open to the suspicion that this observation suggests, especially perhaps in part three, where the correlation is directly with " the picture of Jesus as the Christ." We shall see, however, that this would seem to be mainly because of the " transformation " that Paul's " new *creation* " undergoes as it is filtered through the medium of experience and becomes normative as " new *being*." [26] The shift in emphasis that is permitted when " creation " becomes " being " in this concept allows him to assume, and to assert, a continuity of the existential (and ontological) question and the Christian-theological answer, which tends to obscure any actual discontinuity that may be present — and to which any method of correlation becomes vulnerable when an attempt is made to adapt it to Christian theology. If we were permitted to reformulate the questions in the light of an explicitly theological and Christological *discrimen,* the problem would emerge immediately and in bold relief.

A single example will suffice to suggest the difficulty, and we will select one that emerges most clearly in this third section of the system. Tillich is forced, when he shares Schleiermacher's point of prius and orientation, to regard the question of being, and the problem of the threat of nihilism or of not-being, as theology's first, fundamental, and formative question. "It is the finitude of being which drives us to the question of God," he says; and this assumption remains formally definitive for all that follows.[27] This, in turn, makes it necessary for him to orient his definition of sin around the admittedly Hegelian (and non-Biblical) concept of estrangement, and to explicate sin in terms of *Sonderung, separation.*[28] The other aspects of sin are then related to, and interpreted within the context of, estrangement and separation; because when finitude, or the threat of not-being, is regarded as the definitive question, estrangement from being or the ground of being must be recognized as the initial problem and the controlling motif in the understanding of sin.

This entire line of development is completely consistent where Christology and soteriology are correlated with a question that has been chosen and formulated with initial and primary reference to the situation and the contradictions of human finitude. It also should be noticed that this reference is entirely consistent with the previous ontological analysis and doctrine of God, where "power" tends to be the controlling category, and where the positive content of revelation is circumscribed by the single, nonsymbolic statement that God is being-itself and the power of being. It likewise is consonant with the assertion that "a kind of split" must be assumed as a prior element in the interpretation of the Fall.[29] In brief, sin is necessarily understood in terms of estrangement and separation when, in Prof. Reinhold Niebuhr's words, "the ontological outweighs the historical," when the "mystical a priori" is the epistemological prius, and when there is therefore no regulative authoritative element that bows to the historical, covenant-incarnational presuppositions that control the Biblical view of the matter.

But what if we are constrained to take our initial stand under a theological *discrimen* that forces us to regard the historical, covenant-Christ presuppositions of the Bible as essentially, and from the first, authoritative? What if the covenant God, who is known in his dealing with Israel and in the crucified and resurrected Jesus Christ of the New Testament — and not in a "mystical a priori" that roots in "the experience of being over against nonbeing" — is the prius? Are we not then forced, with the Bible, to regard man's problem first of all, in every age, as at bottom one of positive, self-willed rebellion and consequent guilt, a rebellion and guilt for which he is responsible? The problem is, to be sure, experienced in varying constellations and in manifold ways within differing cultural configurations. It must be understood dialectically, as both " act " and " fact," with the empirical element of " fate " given its crucial and full weight. And it embraces separation and estrangement, by which man's situation not only may, but must, be analyzed and described. But, as Niebuhr has remarked, it is not without significance that there is no " transcendent Fall " in the Bible; and in the Biblical concept " the emphasis clearly lies upon freedom and responsibility," whereas in Tillich's thought "the emphasis falls upon the fatefulness of sin rather than upon our responsibility." [30]

It is obviously ridiculous to quarrel with Tillich simply because he does not use Biblical categories and expressions; and, where this is the point, he is fully justified in complaining. But the question here is the far more subtle and crucial one of ordering, emphasis, and motif; and this question cannot be avoided. Tillich himself concedes this when he emphasizes that the Fall, the transition from essence to existence, can be only " halfway demythologized," because it is " a story to be told and not a derived dialectical step." [31] And it would seem to be clear that the Biblical frame of reference, where it is authoritative for theology in any controlling sense, forces us to orient the motif of the initial problem, which then circumscribes all derivative problems, in a moral rebellion against the holy God who has revealed his will in the Old and New Covenants, and in Jesus Christ.

It is only when this orienting context ceases to be regulative that the positive character of sin as willful rebellion tends to be neutralized, and the element of responsibility mitigated, within a definition of sin that has an essentially negative motif. At one point Tillich acknowledges that the Bible, in treating the concept of the Fall, has " subordinated the mythical elements to the ethical point of view." But his concern, even here, is to show that " the cosmic presuppositions and implications are not removed." [32] Elsewhere, he has posed for himself the query: " Are sin and grace, if taken into an ontological frame of reference, still sin and grace? " [33] This is precisely the question. And it would appear to be quite clear that we must answer that, even though all the required definitive elements may be preserved within a systematic definition, where there is a shift in order and emphasis that alters the motif, sin ceases to be sin in the Biblical and Christian sense. Then, *can* grace be grace?

It is too seldom recognized that a decision on this difficult interpretive question that Tillich's thought poses simply is not possible apart from a critique of the methodological orientation of his system. The question here is not really whether Tillich's doctrine of sin has a Manichaean streak running through it. Nor is it whether any position that disagrees with him is Pelagian, semi-Pelagian or neo-Pelagian. The introduction of any such labels merely throws the conversation into emotive confusion and obscures the issue. The elements of freedom and destiny are equally embraced, and given the same amount of space, by Tillich; and Pelagianism and Manichaeism are carefully spurned and shunted in a nicely balanced way. The real problem is the semihidden and far more complex one of *a shift in the question.* This immediately has the quiet effect of reversing the Biblical order of concern (so that the problem of " sin and death " in the Bible unobtrusively appears as the problem of death and sin), and it eventually causes a decisive alteration in the entire emphasis. Then *hubris* (spiritual pride or self-elevation), and unbelief or unfaith, are related to estrangement, rather than estrangement's being related to *hubris* and unbelief — and if we may say so, half facetiously (but only *half* facetiously, inasmuch as the Fall is only " halfway demythologized "), it is much as though Adam and Eve had found themselves outside the Garden, and been prompted by this estranged situation to eat the forbidden fruit.

This is why Tillich can say, without a controlling qualification, that "sin is a universal fact before it becomes an individual act." [34] It is why he can reiterate in a naked way that sin is a " state," and remark that the word " ' sin ' should never be used in the plural." [35] Here the crucial qualification of Kierkegaard, that " sin posits itself," has been weakened if not lost.[36] And the emphasis may be traced directly to a shift in the question, *sans façon,* which places the threat of nihilism ahead of the problem of rebellion and guilt as the formative issue, and subsequently forces a reshaping of the controlling motif. We can even venture to say that fundamentally this is why the note of forgiveness is so weakly sounded in Tillich's system, and why atonement receives so little space and emphasis. It is why the incarnation can be defined almost exclusively in a negative way, in terms of the negation of finitude. And it is why salvation is interpreted almost entirely in the sense of *salvus,* healing, and almost not at all in terms of redemption.

Our scrutiny of Reformation presuppositions would seem to confirm the basic conjecture involved here. There is a sense in which, as Tillich frequently points out, Calvin presupposes a correlation, or connection (*conjunctio*), of the knowledge of God and self-knowledge, from the very first line of the *Institutes.* Following Augustine, he remarks that these two are inseparable, and that they are "bound together" in such a way that it is difficult to discern which precedes the other. From one point of view, it is quite true that we will not, and cannot, seek God until we have become dissatisfied with ourselves, and have recognized the precariousness of our self-complacency. Seen from this side, self-knowledge, or a consciousness of our contingency and finitude, is a "stimulus" in our quest for God. Calvin quickly adds, however, that "man cannot attain pure knowledge of himself unless he has previously looked upon the face of God — and then descended from there to examine himself." His doctrine of man forced him to assume that the human condition is such that it even prevents man from understanding his own situation and asking the proper questions, unless he does so in the light of God's self-manifestation in Jesus Christ: "for our natural pride is such that we always see ourselves righteous, untainted, wise, and holy, unless we are convicted with manifest proofs of our unrighteousness, foulness, stupidity, and moral impurity. We are never convicted in this way, however, if we look within ourselves, and not also at the Lord, who is the only criterion by which this can be measured." [37]

A similar presupposition is inherent in the law-gospel structure of Luther's thought. He assumed that only God's law can force and enable man to recognize "his sin, blindness, wretchedness, impiety, his ignorance, hatred, and contempt of God," and bring him to an acknowledgment of his need of the gospel.[38] And since the law is a part of the Word of God, we must conclude that man can neither know the correct existential questions, nor find the intended Christian answers, except as he stands under the Word. In fact, the same observation might be made on the basis of Paul's "correlation" in the letter to the Romans, of chapters 1 through 7 as the question, and 8 through 16 as the answer. This crucial methodological assumption, that man can recognize his real plight and his true need only *coram Deo,* was intrinsic to the Reformation. And it might be added that the subsequent history of theology, especially in its nineteenth-century forms, has abundantly demonstrated its importance. The fact that it becomes quite ambiguous in Tillich's methodology, even to the point that we are forced to ask if it has been forsaken, has almost unlimited implications for his principle of authority and for his total system.

3. THE FORMAL CRITERIA

It is on the methodological level that the question of authority is first treated explicitly by Tillich. It is answered on this level with two formal criteria that are intended to delimit theology as such, or trace the circumference of the theological circle, and thus differentiate theology from science, philosophy, and philosophy of religion. These two "methodological guardians at the boundary line of theology" are formulated as follows: (1) The object of theology is what concerns us ultimately. Only those propositions are theological which deal with their object in so far as it can become a matter of ultimate concern for us. (2) Our ultimate concern is that which determines our being or not-being. Only those statements are theological which deal with their object in so far as it can become a matter of being or not-being for us.[39]

Ultimate concern is offered as an "abstract translation" of the great commandment of Mark 12:29. Tillich employs the translation in both a positive and a negative way, in defining philosophy and theology, and "to prevent mutual interference between theology and other forms of knowledge."[40] The second criterion qualifies the first, leaving it "open" for any particular content, symbol, or doctrine that speaks to the basic question, "to be or not to be." The criteria thus answer early and quickly the question of the relation-

ship of theology to the special sciences, including the " science " of
Biblical criticism. These nontheological disciplines are said to deal
exclusively with objects of preliminary concern. Thus theology,
which deals exclusively with matters of ultimate concern, has, and
can have, no direct relationship to them. It is completely " uncon-
cerned about scientific procedures and results," except as they may
incase a philosophical or theological element.[41]

The question of the relationship to philosophy is much more complex. Tillich works with an (admittedly) arbitrary definition of
philosophy. It is one that virtually identifies philosophy with ontology, defining it as " that cognitive approach to reality in which
reality as such is the object." [42] The philosopher is assigned the task
of investigating reality as a whole (not to be interpreted as " the
whole of reality "), by which Tillich means the " structure of being "
that makes reality a whole, and the concepts and categories presupposed in the " cognitive encounter " with reality. The philosopher
proceeds on the basis of " common rationality " and the universal
logos; and he is by definition, in so far as he is merely a philosopher
and not also a cryptotheologian, operating with " detached objectivity " rather than with involvement and ultimate concern. He is
even permitted, as a philosopher, to inquire into religion. If he does
so successfully, or if he succeeds in maintaining his objectivity and
detachment, and his concepts are consistently " general and abstract " rather than " specific and concrete," he remains a philosopher, operating within the prescribed limits of philosophy of
religion.[43]

The theologian's task, on the other hand, is " the existential, and,
at the same time, methodical interpretation of an ultimate concern."
" Methodical " means that the theologian must " relate the concern
rationally to the whole of experience." The requirement that the
interpretation be existential means that if at any point the content
of the theological circle is viewed and handled in a purely theoretical
or detached way, without involvement, the viewer ceases to be a
theologian and becomes a philosopher of religion.[44] The latter point
is Kierkegaard's: " The basic attitude of the theologian is commitment to the content he expounds. Detachment would be a denial of
the very nature of this content." [45] Hence theology is inherently rela-

tional: "in no theological statement can the relation *to us* be omitted." [46] Even "the God above God," or the "radical abstraction," being, is a relational concept, expressing "the *experience* of being over against nonbeing." [47] Explicit commitment to an ultimate concern, with passion, fear, and love, is — overall, and at every point along the way — essential for, and intrinsic to, theology.

The difficult problems created by these delimitations enter the picture and the unique association of philosophy and theology that is the hallmark of Tillich's system first becomes enigmatic and questionable, with the observation that there not only is an inescapable sense in which theology is philosophical, but also a sense in which philosophy is inevitably theological. Tillich remarks that there is a philosophical element in all theology, even in that of the most scrupulously literalistic Biblical fundamentalism — at the least in the language or semantic tools employed. It is present in a deeper way in that "theology, when dealing with our ultimate concern, presupposes in every sentence the structure of being, its categories, laws, and concepts." [48] Similarly, "there is an element in every philosophy (not only in every philosopher) which is 'existential,' i.e., which has the character of an ultimate decision about the meaning of reality." [49] He reiterates that "the philosopher cannot avoid existential decisions," and that "the theologian cannot avoid ontological concepts." [50] Thus theology is unavoidably philosophical, and philosophy is inescapably theological.

When we draw the logical consequences from these assumptions, two seem inescapable. One is that every philosopher inevitably fails to be what he intends to be, a philosopher, and to some degree is open to the charge of being an unintentional or cryptotheologian. Tillich contends that "philosophers always have tried to reach existential significance, to give a prophetic message, to found a sect, to start a religious-political movement, or to become mystics." [51] The philosopher "does not intend to be a theologian," he says; but he "cannot jump over the concreteness of his existence and his implicit theology." He purposes to be nonexistential, but is unintentionally existential. "Like every human being, he exists in the power of an ultimate concern, whether or not he is fully conscious of it, whether or not he admits it to himself and others"; and thus his philosophy inevitably reveals " existentially conditioned elements." In this sense every philosopher has " theological existence "; and this means that, strictly speaking, " every creative philosopher is a hidden theologian " who utilizes " hidden religious sources." [52]

There are points at which Tillich even goes so far as to insist, when it is expressed positively, that it is " a theological element " that " gives the impulse to philosophy." This permits him to assume and assert that the philosophy or philosophical school that cuts itself off from or neglects the theological element is " noncreative," having only " the shell, not the substance, of philosophy." [53] He remarks, when he expresses this conviction negatively, that except as he is implicitly theological the philosopher in reality stands on " the place which is no place." This means, for example, that he can speak with some degree of success to the problem of the antinomies of reason only as he becomes surreptitiously theological, or only as his philosophy is theonomous and utilizes " ecstatic reason." [54] This is the methodological presupposition in Tillich's definition of theology that recently prompted a leading philosopher to characterize his thought as " bear-hug theology " — a theology that finally embraces even the atheistic philosopher who carefully and explicitly disavows the theological project, and has neither the intention nor the wish to speak theologically.

The other logical consequence of the delimitation is that the boundary between philosophy and theology unavoidably becomes a matter of dispute, and the suspicion recurs on both sides that the relationship that Tillich has actually established is more coalescent than correlative. Correlation demands juxtaposition, interrelation, and interaction. But does it require " interpenetration " and " mutual immanence? " [55] If theology can or must be pursued on the basis of the assumption that philosophy inherently infolds a theological element, and theology has an intrinsic philosophical element, it is, to say the least, very difficult to avoid the impression that the two have in reality, in some way, been united. And if we must presuppose, as Tillich does, that culture is the " form " of religion, and religion the " substance " of culture in the sense of " depth dimension," how could a coalescence be avoided?

He also maintains that the possession of language, or the use of universals, is the *differentia specifica* that divides man and the non-human, and that here philosophy and theology coincide in the universal *logos*. In distinguishing ontological and technical reason, and then the subjective and objective sides of ontological reason, he would appear to be exempting ontological reason on its subjective side, the structure of the mind, from the Fall.[56] He is reported to have said, in a conference on philosophy and theology at Bossey, that " a destroyed, damaged (*zerstört*) structure of reason does not exist," so that reason is " fallen only in the sense of technical reason or reasoning." " What exists is *Verblendung* (infatuation)." [57] This apparently means that the essential structure of the mind, which is the common basis of philosophy and theology, is unaffected by the " state " of estrangement; and philosophy and theology may or must be said to cohere in this sense.

Tillich's explicit statements require that this question remain open. Within the system he insists that a synthesis of philosophy and theology is neither intended nor possible. But in his inaugural address at Union Theological Seminary he clearly seemed to be asserting the opposite.[58] In the reply addressed to his critics, in the analysis and interpretation of his theology written after the first two sections of the system had appeared, he included the observation that such a synthesis, in the sense of union, may and must be affirmed eschatologically. This permits the observation that there is a " present unity " in the sense, and to the degree, that we may affirm realized or partially fulfilled eschatology, or fragmentary theonomy. He states a preference, however, for the expressions " fragmentary unity " and " definitory distance "; and within this context he once more denies that his system establishes a synthesis, insisting that it recognizes a " qualitative difference " between philosophy and theology. Yet in the same paragraph he refers again to the " mutual immanence " of religion and culture.[59] The introduction to the third section of the system confesses that all earlier formulations were " inadequate in clarity, elaboration, and emphasis." But the fresh attempt that is then made to clarify the ambiguity seems quite inadequate to resolve the long-standing suspicion of an unavoidable contradiction at this point — and the question lingers.[60]

It is, of course, obvious that Tillich does not intend to be opaque, inconsistent, or self-contradictory here. It is very difficult to see, however, how ambiguity can be avoided without an affirmation of some intention of synthesis, in view of the inner necessity created by his prius, that ontology and theology should have an orienting point of identity. It would perhaps be better if he were not so conscious of Barth's strictures on this matter, so that the periodic oscillations on the question would not be necessary. It is clear that he intends to stand on the conviction that " the ontological question of being creates not a conflict but *a necessary basis* for any theoretical dealing with the Biblical concept of a personal God." And he is convinced that there is a " structural identity " and an " ultimate unity " of religion and ontology.[61] How, then, can some sort of coalescence or synthesis possibly be avoided, and, under these convictions, why should it be avoided? In *Biblical Religion and the Search for Ultimate Reality,* he very carefully refrains from using the word " synthesis " in the final pages, where he is relating ontology and Biblical religion. But in the earlier pages, where he is framing the question in a radical, negative way, the word is repeatedly employed.

The question must be left open. But we are tempted to agree here with Prof. Hendrik Kraemer (which can be done without sharing either his slight touch of hysteria, or the reactionary alternative that he proposes, the assumption that Biblical thought is " wholly unphilosophical ") that at this orienting point Tillich will continue to vacillate unless or until he openly concedes that a synthesis of philosophy and theology is what he desires and intends. It would appear that he must simply because he must, or because the orienting presupposition of his system condemns him to " imprisonment in opaqueness " when he attempts to sponsor any determinative divergence of philosophy and theology.[62] Nor can the observation be repressed that it would be refreshing if he would revert to his earlier habit of simply speaking as though we may assume that such a synthesis is intended and presupposed.

One further critical comment is needed on this level. In so far as Tillich is merely asserting with his formal criteria that the orientation of theology must dominantly be to *praxis,* even though *theoria* is essential, presumably no Protestant would care to differ with him.

Nor can there be a basic disagreement with his stated intention to
delineate "theological existence" to assure that we recognize the
essential difference between philosophy and theology in perspective
and cognitive attitude — the valuable point that he was most concerned to establish in his earlier writings.[63] But in so far as ultimate
concern is offered as a transposition of "faith," as it clearly is in *The
Dynamics of Faith,* the Protestant surely must quarrel to remain
Protestant.[64] It would seem to be quite clear, even when nothing else
is clear, that what the New Testament means by *pistis* cannot possibly be grasped and understood where there is an undifferentiated
referent.

This demonstrates a basic reason why an authoritative *discrimen*
is inescapable, from the beginning, and at every point along the
way, in Christian theology. "Faith" must be defined in view of its
object; and within Christianity this object must be Jesus Christ, and
not a neutral, undifferentiated "ground." Tillich, in effect, would
appear to be conceding this at certain points. He acknowledges, for
example, that, although the criteria do not indicate the content of
the ultimate concern, yet form and content can only be distinguished
and not separated. And he remarks that the formal criteria are in
reality "derived from the whole of the Christian message." [65] But
if these assertions are to be taken with any degree of seriousness, they
necessarily, and from the first word, set Christian theology apart
from the theology-in-general that Tillich purports to have in view
in the formulation of these formal, negative, "protective" criteria.
And they likewise set Christian faith apart from any "faith" that
has an obscure, ambiguous, or undesignated referent.

Tillich comments, within another context, that "the form, even
in its greatest refinement, is empty if it does not express a spiritual
substance." [66] This leaves two issues unsettled, or two questions unanswered, in any acceptance of the formal criteria. What is the
"spiritual substance" assumed or implied here? And, does the "abstract translation" require that the referent be the covenant God of
Israel, and Father of Jesus Christ, to whom the great commandment
clearly has reference in its New Testament context? [67] The criteria,
as they are stated, may be "open" to the presupposition of a Christological critical element. It is in no way clear, however, that they as-

sume or require this referent, as they are stated and utilized. They illustrate, in fact, an orientation of Tillich's thought that has permitted him, increasingly in his later writings, to employ such concepts as faith, hope, love, revelation, conversion, and salvation without reference to the act of God in history in Jesus Christ. In so doing, they also illustrate the necessity for an explicitly Christian *discrimen;* but within Tillich's system this issue can be pushed no farther without serious consideration of his norm.

4. THE CONTEXTUAL NORM

Tillich's conception of the nature of a theological norm is unique within the scope of contemporary theology. He is convinced that this question was paramount from the moment of the birth of Christianity, and that it was answered from the beginning in the dual material-formal sense, although he acknowledges that this answer was not systematized until much later, and that it apparently was not until the nineteenth century that these particular categories were applied to it.[68] The material principle, or the material norm, is said to have first expressed itself in the early baptismal formula, from which the creeds evolved. The formal principle led to the hierarchy of authorities, which was created in part for the functional purpose of guarding the material norm against heretical distortions.

The significance attached to these historical judgments is that, when the matter is viewed in this way, the Reformation may be regarded as a protest against the subordination of the material to the formal principle, when the ecclesiastical authorities became so powerful in the medieval church that the need for a material norm virtually disappeared. This permits us to see that the cutting edge of Luther's creative contribution emerged following a recovery of the material norm, and that it was in the power of this norm that he was able to break through the traditional formal norm, the hierarchical system of Rome. The basic significance of the Council of Trent can then be traced to the fact that it made the material principle superfluous, in a final way, and extinguished the hope that the Bible might recover a controlling authoritative status, by the identification of tradition with papal decisions. Tillich also assumes that the original Reformers were not directly responsible for the re-

definition of the two principles in Protestantism, and their equation
with justification by faith and the Bible, or with predestination and
the Bible; but that this was the issue of a hardening or absolutizing
process in the slow growth of orthodoxy.[69]

It is this incisive, sweeping perspective on the matter which permits Tillich to assert that the norm of Christian theology has shifted
in form and emphasis through the centuries, so that, rather than
find an absolute theological norm, we find analogous norms developing and appearing in the various periods of church history. Their
growth is said to be a historical process, and one that, "in spite of
many conscious decisions, is on the whole unconscious."[70] They
emerge from the encounter of the church with the Christian message. But it is clear that the process that produces them is held to be in
large part formally determined by the "situation" or by the shift
in the *Gestalten* that the depth problems of human existence assume
in the dynamic flux and flow of history. This assumption becomes
clear when the norms that have appeared are identified. The most
obvious and important are said to be: "the incarnation of immortal
life and eternal truth" in the early Greek church, where liberation
from death and error was the depth problem; "the sacramental
sacrifice of the God-man" in the early Roman church, which was
primarily seeking salvation from guilt; "the picture of the 'synop-
tic' Jesus" in nineteenth-century Protestantism, where a personal
and social ideal was felt to be the deepest need; and "the prophetic
message of the Kingdom of God" for Protestantism in the first half
of the twentieth century, where a theonomous answer to the universal chaos of the time was being sought.[71]

It is important to recognize that Tillich conceives the development
and appearance of these contextual norms to be a depth experience
of the church, and not an arbitrary act of theology or of theologians.
The norm "is not produced intentionally," he comments; and "its
appearance is not the work of theological reflection but of the Spiritual life of the church."[72] This is his view of the norm of his own
theology, the New Being. Presumably he would accept the necessary
judgment that if this norm is not the expression of the deepest Christian experience of the Western church in this era, his system is
ill-conceived and mal-oriented. We should remember also that this

contextual conception of theological normativeness is not offered merely as a historical observation. Tillich maintains that it is both what has happened, and what should and must happen. However, the conclusion that this immediately suggests, that the Christian church is in principle entrapped in a puzzling, if not vicious, theological relativism, must be qualified. It is accurate to say that Tillich's doctrine of authority permits theological truth to be accommodated to the peculiar cultural configurations of changing historical periods. In making this observation, however, a distinction is necessary between formal and material accommodation. When he designates them *analogous* norms, it is intended that the accommodation shall be recognized to be one of form and emphasis only, so that the norms "do not exclude each other in content." [73]

The full implication that this contextual approach has for the question of authority comes into view only when we have identified the functional roles that Tillich assigns to experience, and to the Bible, in this creative historical process which produces a norm. If we compare an early draft of the unpublished theological *Propositions,* which he has used for many years as the basis of his lectures, with his later writings and the completed sections of the system, we discover that there has been an oscillation in the designation of the role of experience. Originally it was included among the positive sources or material with which systematic theology labors. But in an unpublished paper, dated 1947, entitled "The Bible and Systematic Theology," this earlier assertion was withdrawn, and experience is here called the "medium" rather than a source of theology. A published paper that appeared the same year reiterates this shift of viewpoint, observes that the word "experience" needs to be "saved," and then indicates quite clearly the issue that Tillich feels is implicated in this decision.[74]

His purpose manifestly is to regard human experience as a dependent medium of theology and not an independent or a positive source. But it is clear that he wishes at the same time to accept it as a functional source in the sense that it *transforms* all theological sources. It is here, perhaps more than anywhere else within the entire scope of the matter of theological authority, that Tillich's kinship to the *Lebensphilosophie* can be most clearly seen. He frequently reiterates that ontological reason not only "grasps" but also "shapes" reality. He is convinced that the concept "experience" has been, and will continue to be, misunderstood whenever there is a failure to recognize that "in every act of reasonable reception an act of shaping is involved." [75] This is the creative rediscovery credited to Nietzsche and Marx, which corrected "the poverty of philosophy" and reunited insight and action. It identifies a decisive juncture in Tillich's principle of theological authority. It is just at this point that he must define his contextual approach in relation to the Reformers, and in contrast to Protestant orthodoxy, Schleiermacher, contemporary fundamentalism, all types of empirical and experiential theology, and the movement called neo-orthodoxy. He obviously intends to occupy a position that differs to some degree from all of these. He does so primarily with this assertion: that experience, or the formative element of immediacy, functions as a transforming medium.

There is in Tillich's theology an open acknowledgment of the fact that, if we are to stand in the Reformation stream, we must realize that the content of theology is not to be found by "looking at one's self," but must be sought by "looking beyond one's self." [76] His most penetrating critique of Schleiermacher focuses upon this point. The (unintentional) weakness of Schleiermacher's method was an ambiguity that permitted the medium to be treated as a source of theology. It was this ambiguity which led to a confusion of religious consciousness and experience, opening the way for a confounding of revelation with the experience of revelation. This obliterated the crucial distinction between the medium and the source and content; and it is why Schleiermacher's theology led the nineteenth century, in its attempt to derive theological substance from religious consciousness, into an extreme subjectivism and psychologism. In Tillich's view, this fatal error is shared by all types of experiential theology, and it explains why they must presuppose some post-Christian experience or addition to Christian revelation. Orthodoxy and fundamentalism, on the other hand, with an understandable concern to affirm the finality of the Christian revelation, are prone to precisely the opposite error. They are blind to, or refuse to acknowledge, the intermediate and mediating role of experience. Thus they attempt the impossible and illusory task of sponsoring a mere repetition of the sources and content. Neo-orthodoxy is said to share in this illusion when it denies that there is any sense in which experience is a source of Christian theology.[77]

The correlative, synthesizing position that Tillich wishes to occupy, between these alternatives on the left and the right, makes it necessary for him to assert that experience both is, and is not, a source of theology. In referring to it as a medium, he is attempting to settle the claim of all " enthusiasts." This requires that in every use of the word " revelation," beyond the final revelation in Jesus as the Christ, the qualifying adjective " dependent " be added. It is presupposed that the original constellation of (objective) " miracle " and (subjective) " ecstasy," which constituted the final Christian revelation, cannot recur. Thus every Christian revelation beyond this is necessarily a dependent revelation, because its reception has to be correlated with both the objective and the subjective side of the original constellation.[78] In this sense, Tillich holds, it is quite crucial to acknowledge that experience is not a source of theology. It cannot produce, or provide, anything that could displace, add to, supplement, or replace the original revelatory constellation.

It is said to be equally important, however, to acknowledge that experience is a theological source in the sense of transformation. The element of immediacy imbedded in the point of prius of his system requires the recognition that experience, functioning as a mediator, " determines the interpretation of what it receives." Once more he adds the curious qualification that this process must be primarily an unconscious one and must be unintentional. This is an effort to exclude all intentional subjectivity. But in this carefully defined sense, " the mediating experience " is said to be an indispensable source. It contributes neither a mere repetition, nor new positive material, but a transformation of all of the given sources of theology.[79]

This analysis of the mediating and transforming role of experience immediately precedes, but it is not applied directly to, the question of the origin of the contextual theological norm. This tends to obscure one of the most formative presuppositions underlying Tillich's system. The Bible is described as one of the sources of theology, and it is in this way that it is related to the method of correlation, to the content, and to the norm of the system. It receives its authoritative status as one of the two sources of the contextual norm, as it is when the Christian message found in the Bible is encountered by the church, within its concrete historical situation, that the norm emerges. But the exegetical and interpretive identification of this message is not a movement chronologically prior to the emergence of the norm. The Bible is assumed to be a complex and diversified document, which itself requires a norm in order to be understood, interpreted, and put to theological use.[80] Thus Biblical content must be filtered through the medium, and must participate in the process of unintentional transformation, before the norm (which then becomes the norm of the Bible) may emerge.

This is why Tillich reiterates that the norm of systematic theology is not discovered or determined by Biblical exegesis and is not available to Biblical theology as such. The norm is "Biblical," but only in the sense that it emerges from the encounter of the message of the Bible with the receptive possibilities of the church in a particular historical period. The content of the norm is not Biblical content per se, but the contextual substance of the "encounter," and the unintentional process of transformation is necessary in order for this substance to be available. This presupposition is sometimes obscured by the remark that the Biblical message is the content of the norm. This is true; but it obviously is true only in an "analogous" sense. And it is not true when the qualifying assumption that experience as the medium transforms all the sources of theology, including the Biblical material as one source, is not present. This is why it can be said, and must be said, that "the norm grows within the medium of experience"; and it also is why the Pauline "new creation" can be "transformed" to New Being as the norm of Tillich's system.

It is rarely noticed that the explicit justification that Tillich offers for this normative transformation is that New Being is "more adequate" than the Pauline concept because it has "a metaphysical and logical character" and "mystical implications" that are not overt in "new creation," and because it explicitly introduces the classic philosophical notion of being into Christology.[81] He must and does insist, however, that this is the norm that is demanded by, and that has emerged from, the situation within which the church exists in our time. " It is not an exaggeration to say that today man experiences his present situation in terms of disruption, conflict, self-destruction, meaninglessness, and despair in all realms of life," he argues. " This experience is expressed in the arts and in literature, conceptualized in existential philosophy, actualized in political cleavages of all kinds, and analyzed in the psychology of the unconscious." [82] The contention necessitated by this analysis is that when the Biblical message encounters the church, within this contemporary situation of estrangement, New Being is *the* theological norm, or the contextual norm that inevitably emerges in the correlative way that has been described.

New Being is defined by transposing the negative analysis into positive theological substance as " a reality in which the self-estrangement of our existence is overcome." [83] This " reality " is identified with the final revelation in Jesus as the Christ. When it is necessary to explicate its content, the orienting presuppositions of two areas of the system are involved, the doctrine of revelation in the first section, and the Christology of the third section. The initial, major assertion utilized is that revelation is unavoidably conditioned by the objective medium in and through which it makes its appearance. The finite nature of this conditioning medium is then said to demand the axiomatic principle: " a revelation is final if it has the power of negating itself without losing itself." This axiom is, in turn, applied to the revelatory, historical figure, and the definitive Christological conclusion is: " He who is the bearer of the final revelation must surrender his finitude — not only his life but also his finite power and knowledge and perfection. In doing so, he affirms that he is the bearer of final revelation (the ' Son of God ' in classic terms). He becomes completely transparent to the mystery he reveals." This negative, self-sacrificing " transparency " of the incarnation, to the ground and power of being, thus becomes the all-embracing meaning of the Christ event. His " uninterrupted unity with the ground of his being and the continuous sacrifice of himself as Jesus to himself as the Christ," is made the basis of both his revelatory and his redemptive significance.[84]

This principle is the foundation not only of all Christological statements, but also of all statements regarding the principle of authority, in Tillich's system. This is why there is no sense whatsoever in which " Jesus," the historical manifestation, may be said to be theologically authoritative. This would violate " the Protestant principle " that nothing finite and relative can be elevated to the status of an absolute, and made an object of ultimate concern. It thus would contradict the formal criteria, which require that every finite object be no more than a matter of preliminary concern. Any theological statement that in any way implies faith in Jesus, rather than in the " ground " to which he was transparent, is said to be " demonic."

The radical reorientation that this involves obviously stems from the epistemological point of prius, which we have discussed, and the ontological frame of reference that knits the system together. And it is permitted by the " transformation " that injects definitive, normative " mystical implications " of nonhistorical immediacy in the name of the apostle Paul. But it also issues in large part from Tillich's determination to define theology out of the reach of Biblical studies by cutting the question of authority entirely free from the results, either positive or negative, of historical research and Biblical criticism.

He tells us that he posed for himself quite early the two-edged query, What fate would the Christian faith suffer if skepticism as to the existence of the man Jesus should prevail, or if criticism should so alter the picture of this historical figure that it became entirely incompatible with the Christ of the Gospels and of Christian tradition? He felt that this threat, which was quite real when Tillich framed the question in 1911, called for a serious attempt " to answer the question, how the Christian doctrine might be understood if the nonexistence of the historical Jesus should become historically probable." [85] And, for whatever reasons, at its deepest level this is precisely what the principle of authority developed in Tillich's system endeavors to accomplish.

In his initial approach to this problem, he reflects a strong influence from Kierkegaard's reply to Lessing, and he utilizes a significant distinction that is to be fully developed in the fifth part of the system. He differentiates the subjective and the objective in history, dividing objective fact and the subjective reception and interpretation of objective fact. Fact or " event " is regarded as the necessary material of history, but not in itself history until it has been received and interpreted. Just as revelation cannot accurately be called revelation except as it is received, so events have no meaning until they are experienced, and no historical significance except as they are interpreted. This is not intended to be a bifurcation, but only a necessary correlative distinction. Tillich insists, however, that when it is accepted in this way it both can and must be applied to the Christian event, Jesus of Nazareth who was received as the Christ.

Its application is then said to require the methodological conclusion that the concern of Christian theology is not Jesus Christ, but the " believing interpretation," or " the picture of Jesus as the Christ." " Jesus as the Christ is both a historical fact and a subject of believing reception," Tillich remarks; and " the *concrete* side of final revelation appears in the picture of Jesus as the Christ," or in the believing reception and interpretation.[86] Neither the facticity of the fact, nor the content of the interpretive reception, can be ignored or dismissed. But the distinction does permit a *functional* elimination of the content of the fact as an element in the principle of authority — and, at the same time, it permits the introduction of ontological and mystical elements that admittedly are not an explicit part of the content of the Biblical witness to the fact.

None of this is a matter of conjecture in Tillich's system. Many critiques of his theology veer toward irrelevancy, not because they are inaccurate or untrue, but because they struggle laboriously to convict him of questionable assumptions and conclusions to which he openly subscribes; and this is the only genuine risk involved in a criticism at this point. He consistently assumes that Christianity is " based on the witness to the messianic character of Jesus by people who were not interested at all in a biography of the Messiah." He has been thoroughly faithful in eliminating every use of the positive content of the " fact," beyond its formal affirmation, and appealing only to " the picture of Christ as it is rooted in ecclesiastical belief." [87] This is the decisive epistemological principle of the *analogia imaginis*. Under this principle, the only Biblical event that Tillich utilizes theologically for other than occasional illustrative purposes is the Caesarea Philippi confession, the classic "believing interpretation." As the Biblical symbol of the response or reception of the revelation, this is the single historical rock upon which the system is built. We realize how thoroughgoing this shift is — from the historical manifestation, and the historical orientation of the Biblical material, to the "picture" of the incarnation — when we find him openly attributing "unconditional and universal validity" to the picture, and even, both in the system and in sermons, locating the transforming, redeeming, and saving power of the Christian faith in "the *picture* of Jesus as the Savior." [88]

This question has been treated in critical detail elsewhere; [89] but a brief, positive comment on Tillich's project is necessary here, because the crux of his principle of authority recedes ultimately into the heart of this very difficult problem which was bequeathed by Lessing and Kierkegaard. His entire approach rests upon this methodological differentiation of fact and interpretation, which prohibits an organic bifurcation, but permits a working, functional dichotomy. This cannot be permitted to pass without question. Is there not a definite and inescapable, although admittedly a limited, sense in which every historical statement, and thus every theological-historical affirmation, is intrinsically dependent upon the self-interpreting nature of the fact that is interpreted? And is this not true of the incarnation, which is more than historical but also historical? If this is true, its truth inescapably becomes involved as a datum that plays a definitive role as we make the basic decision that determines the formative place of the Bible in the *discrimen* of Christian theology.

If we disregard this undeniable methodological fact, we falsify history; and this is just as true of its neglect within the Christian faith and Christian theology as it is elsewhere, when we permit Christianity to remain what it is, a historical religion. To cite an ultrasimple example, Jesus was a man. In various periods, especially in America in recent years, artists have tended to depict him with feminine features. This falsifies history by contradicting the self-interpreting nature, and the self-interpretation, of the fact. Anyone who is even vaguely familiar with American Protestantism is conscious of the part that this particular falsifying tendency has played in recent years, in the substitution of various types of sentimentality for Christian faith.

Moreover, we cannot ignore the uninterpreted fact that Jesus was a Palestinian man. Throughout the centuries the license granted with artistic freedom has been employed to depict him as Chinese, Negro, or Indian (yellow, black, or red). As a symbolic expression of the conviction of the universality of the Christian revelation, this is beyond criticism. But as history, it is not historical; and, taken as history, it obviously falsifies history. Aside from the question of the relative importance or unimportance of the color of the " flesh," when " the Word became flesh " it did become flesh; and this means — if it means anything — flesh of a particular biological constitution and pigment. To ignore this willfully is to contradict and destroy an element of the interpretation that is intrinsic to, and that arises from, the fact of the Christian faith; and, as we know too well in the twentieth century, the quiet but deadly consequence always is that Christianity is lifted out of its Hebraic incasement. As trivial as it may appear at first glance, it is precisely this kind of neglect and falsification of the self-interpreting character of the history upon which the Christian faith rests which tends to sever it from its historical rootage. It unavoidably mitigates or destroys the crucial feeling for the particularity of the Christian revelation that knows it to have been bound to a certain space at a certain time.

It would appear that there actually is no instance, however seemingly trivial, where a similar effect is not implied to some degree by the methodological assumption under question. A more basic example is found at the cross. That Jesus died is a part of the Christian fact. May the elaboration of this to the statement " he suffered and died " be regarded as the imposition of an interpretation upon the fact? Or is it necessary to hold to this elaboration as first of all a self-interpretation, or a part of the self-interpreting nature of the fact? Whenever the former method has been followed, some form of Docetism has resulted. Even without the benefit of modern enlightenment on the psychosomatic nature of suffering, it is obvious that objective " flesh " is involved here, and that any attempt to skirt or mitigate this, or to deny its importance, is a subtle distortion and denial of the full implication of the Biblical claim that the Word became flesh.

It is in large part this self-interpreting nature of historical fact which demands what Prof. Herbert Butterfield has called " the vivid apprehension of material things " that is intrinsic to the Christian faith. How can we possibly escape, or methodologically reverse, the traditional recognition of the Christian church in all centuries that no more positive and absolute a relationship of God to human history can be conceived than that implied in the incarnation? And how can we escape the witness of the history of doctrine that whenever we cease to regard it in this way the very foundation of the Christian faith is threatened? Tillich is quite right, and his reminder is extremely valuable, when he warns us against any tendency to move back to a new historicism, or to a new Jesus cult. But this is in no sense necessarily implicated in a determination to take seriously the essential nature of Biblical Christianity as self-interpreting revelation rooted and grounded in history. If we do so, it would appear that we are led inescapably to the binding conclusion that the fact and the interpretation of the Christian faith are organically and inextricably joined: not only formally, but essentially; and not only originally, but continually. In the deepest and most literal sense, the fact not only gave rise to the interpretation, but it gives rise to the interpretation. It is this recognition alone which can keep the Jesus Christ of Christian faith from evaporating into a transparent symbol of an undifferentiated ground.

What is needed here is a fresh occasion of the recurring reaction of the church through the centuries against any trend that seems to abstract " the Word " from " the Word made flesh." Embarrassing as it may seem at times, and as difficult as it may make the apologetic task of theology, this is essential if we are not to do violence to the given nature of the Christian faith. In one sense this is what was involved in the classic affirmation that the humanity of Jesus, as well as his deity, was resurrected. The philosopher who restricts himself to the frame of reference of classic ontology may find his hair standing on end at the suggestion that we must affirm that the human nature and personality of the man Jesus were not obliterated by death, but were resurrected, consummated, and survive.

Yet, this is the witness of the Scriptures; and this is just what the church has said. Furthermore, it would appear that it is what the church must say if its faith is to remain faith in Jesus Christ, and not an *analogia imaginis* kind of faith in a "picture," or an empathetic faith in the faith of Peter in the Christ.

There are obvious theological dangers here, and we can enter this area only in the spirit with which Paul approached the discussion of I Cor., ch. 15. But it is difficult to circumvent the evidence that there is more danger where the area is not entered. What is crucial is that a false abstraction or dichotomy be avoided from either side, and that we affirm, as Prof. D. M. Baillie expressed it, that our experience in knowing Jesus Christ beyond the crucifixion, and in the church today, is "not less, but greater" than that of those who confronted him merely as flesh within history.[90] Tillich acknowledges in his reply to his critics that "there is a real danger felt by those who are uneasy about the system; namely, that its form becomes self-sufficient and determines the content."[91] This is the question that is necessary at this point, that locates the heart of the principle of authority under which his theology is written. It should not be regarded as in any sense a depreciation, or a lack of appreciation, of the manifest dimensions of theological profundity and grandeur that Tillich's system represents to suggest that this crucial, determinative question has not as yet been given a satisfactory answer.

It still should be remembered, however, that the decisive question is the prior one. What is maintained here, at the center of the principle of authority, is materially consistent with the "mystical a priori," the "immediate experience of something ultimate" that is the point of prius. Tillich's Christology, as well as his doctrine of revelation and his doctrine of God, is thoroughly consonant with the delineation of the formative question as one that roots in and is evoked by "the experience of being over against nonbeing." The issues that result from this initial decision for the primacy of immediacy are genuine issues, but in the most basic sense they are necessarily subsidiary. The previous issue is the formative and crucial one, and it marks the juncture at which the theological decision must be made in our time.

CHAPTER VI

The Scientific and Normative Approaches

THE most unique attempt to answer the question of authority within the purview of contemporary theology is sponsored by the Lundensian theologians. Nygren and Aulén have been the most influential representatives of the school, with the former contributing the philosophical and methodological basis of the answer, and testing it in the area of the history of doctrine, and the latter applying the method to systematic theology. The regulating presupposition is that theology is a " science," and they observe in apposition that if a science becomes normative, it thereby ceases to be scientific. This assumption forces a reverse, or negating, reply to the question of theological authority; and it leads to an effort, which would appear to have no parallel in the history of Christian thought, to fashion a completely nonnormative theology.

Kant and Schleiermacher were the dominant influences underlying the origin of the Swedish *motivforskning,* the motif research through which they approach systematic theology. It originated with an unreserved acceptance of Kant's transcendentalism, and a subsequent attempt to move beyond him on his own ground. Kant had contended that human reason poses questions to itself that it cannot decline, but that it cannot answer on the basis of experience alone. It thus is driven by these quandaries beyond the transcendental to the transcendent, or to " principles that transcend the region of experience " and that on examination reveal " endless confusion and contradiction." Foremost among these unavoidable questions which are posed by reason is that of " a Supreme Being." Kant insisted that for theoretic or " speculative reason " such a Being must remain merely an ideal, " the objective reality of which can neither be proved nor disproved by pure reason." [1] He then transplanted the question in the realm of practical reason and " moral theology "; [2] and, in his renowned attempt to " remove knowledge to make room for belief," he pronounced " speculative metaphysics," or theology as it had hitherto been widely conceived, " a bastard form of knowledge." " Without looking upon myself as a remarkably combative person," he commented, " I shall not decline the challenge to detect the fallacy and destroy the pretensions of every attempt of speculative theology." [3]

Kant's critique resulted not only in a new conception of philosophy, but in new definitions of the problems, and the areas of concern, of both philosophy and philosophy of religion. The problem of objective reality, which had tended to dominate the philosophic scene since the days of the pre-Socratics, was replaced by the problem of objective validity, and the question of value displaced the question of origin. Kant then proceeded, by logical analysis, to establish his a priori categories. The categories are intuitive or pure perceptions,[4] which are not based, and do not rest, on empirical perception, but which are at the basis of, and are included in, all perceptions. The intention, in designating them a priori, was not to claim a chronological or psychological priority for the categories, but to demonstrate that they are necessary and universal. The claim is that they are logically prior, and that necessity and universality are their exclusive attributes.

It is at this point that Nygren attempts an advance upon Kant, and reflects the influence of Schleiermacher's conviction that religion is a self-authenticating and independent type of transcendental experience, which can be validated on a level deeper than that of the moral. Accepting the conclusions and implications of Kant's critique, he proceeds to establish religion as an a priori experience by demonstrating that it enshrines an additional necessary and universal category that validates it, the category of " eternity." His point is that when something is termed " valid," it is, and must be assumed to be, valid apart from temporal or spatial reference, or without regard to time or place. Where this " eternal " presupposition is not present, he contends, validity cannot be presumed; and thus eternity is a necessary and universal form of every claim of validity. " *Every* judgment — even the nonreligious — must refer back to the category of eternity in order to be valid." [5]

This is joined with the assertion that eternity is the basic and distinctive transcendental category of religion, inasmuch as " it is the very claim of religion to lift human life above the givenness of the sensuous, finite sphere." [6] The recognition of this fact is said to establish religion as a unique and independent form of transcendentally valid experience, because it possesses its own universal and necessary, or a priori, category. It is clear that the category is intended to be purely formal, with no content that may or must function normatively. But Nygren insists that it serves to validate religion as a proper object of scientific study.

Quite apart from the matter of the equivocal meaning that this assertion assigns to the word " eternity," and the difficulty that has previously been discussed in conjunction with Tillich's method of correlation — that here Christianity must permit its definitive question to be thrust upon it from without — there are some additional questions that project themselves at the beginning, provoked by the Platonic tinge of this presupposition. Granted that it is necessary, for purposes of codification, to regard Christianity as one type of " religion," is it really possible so to validate it with a formal, theoretical category if the Reformers were correct in their assertion that Christian faith is intrinsically redemptive or soteriological? And, apart from the question of other religions, does not an enucleation of Christianity actually lead us, not to a distinctive category or " idea," but to a concrete (and temporal and spatial) historical event? Moreover, one cannot but wonder if this validation is true even to its own Kantian orientation. It would appear that Kant's method prohibits the presupposition of any such " form " of knowledge, devoid of content and valid beyond time and space. It can be observed that if Nygren arrived at his formal category by inference from an experientially known content, the form must be acknowledged to be subject to the fluctuations inherent in all human experience. Or if, on the other hand, it has merely been posited — by, so to speak, an epistemological leap of faith — the basis of its claim of necessity and universality must remain in question. In either event the validation that is asserted on the basis of the category lapses into difficulties, as did Plato's "forms." And what is the third alternative?

1. THE LUNDENSIAN PROJECT

Theology enters the field of inquiry, for the Lund theologians, at the conclusion of this Kantian excursion into philosophy of religion; and it is undertaken on the basis of the philosophical validation that Nygren has attempted. It is presupposed that the theological enterprise has been freed in advance of all concern with the question of objective reality, so that the remaining tasks are a definition of its nature and its methodology, and a subsequent implementation of the method. Aulén's lucid work, *The Faith of the Christian Church,* is to the moment the classic example of a system that professes to have been created wholly within the boundaries of the "scientific" methodology that ensues. The assertion is that theology must be defined, and distinguished from other disciplines, neither in terms of its epistemology, nor of an exclusive or distinctive norm, but entirely in view of its unique object. "Systematic theology has a special object — as does every science. The object of systematic theology is the Christian faith as a living reality."[7] The word "object" indicates a composite of "historically given, organic convictions which are localized in time and place, available in written sources and available for examination by ordinary historical methods."[8] It is this which sets theology apart from the other sciences; and this "object" is the only "given" for the theologian. The total task of theology is "to explain the significance of this faith, to make clear what essentially belongs to it, and to bring to light, wholly and completely, its own characteristic viewpoints."[9]

This attempt to establish systematic theology as a science is the identification mark of the Swedish school, and the scientific claim is advanced in an unequivocal way. "The function of systematic theology is *purely* scientific," Aulén argues; "it must be emphatically stated that systematic theology is confronted with the same situation as are all other scientific disciplines, namely, that it is concerned with the study of a definite object."[10] No distinction is permitted between theology and the other sciences on grounds of intent, as theology attempts neither to prove reality nor to explain the real. This means, Aulén says, that "all presuppositions which limit the investigation beforehand are then removed. It is not a matter of setting up verifiable goals which cannot be scientifically attained. The study is carried on simply to understand and eluci-date, which is the purpose of all scholarly research. Thus, systematic theology is not influenced by secondary aims which lie outside its purview and warp the scientific nature of the work."[11] Further-more, it is explicitly maintained that the theological task embraces neither a final judgment as to the truth of theology, nor prelim-inary, normative judgments as to the relative truth or falsity of particular theological affirmations and positions. Wingren remarks that "it is clear that any concern about 'the question of truth' in theology is very quickly and radically eliminated from Nygren's view."[12] Theology is "a type of scientific analysis, and that alone is enough to show that there can be no question of any value-judg-ment," Nygren says. "The task of science is to understand, not to appraise. . . . Admittedly we are dealing with 'values,' but our attitude to them is that of an observer who wishes to understand, not of a valuer assessing their worth."[13] Thus theology requests only what each scientific field must request, that it be permitted to conform itself to its own object, and examine and elucidate it with the logico-descriptive tools of science.

The implementation of the method requires both an inductive and a deductive movement. The Christian theologian begins with the acceptance of "the Christian faith" as his given, proper object. He then proceeds inductively, with purely critical and descriptive tools, to investigate and enucleate the "ideas" that compose this faith. His goal is an objective, unbiased "unveiling" of "the very heart of the matter," to the end of exposing the meaning that lies concealed beneath the particular configuration that the "idea" has assumed within a given cultural milieu. This is the process and the stage in the theological project which is referred to as "motif re-search." Motif research can be described as a dispassionate, descrip-tive quest, pursued inductively, which is intended to lead beneath the surface, "penetrate through the shifting forms," and expose the controlling *grundmotiv*.[14] Where this quest is successful, it is said to permit the theologian to recognize and describe how the total complex, which we call " the Christian faith," groups itself about, and communicates its inner meaning in terms of, a distinctive center. The Lund school is convinced that this is the only approach " which desires nothing else than to understand faith from within," and " which intends nothing else than to allow the ideas and viewpoints of faith itself to appear in their rightful place." [15]

This initial process is then followed by a deductive movement, which produces the materials of systematic theology. The inner elucidation, which is achieved through motif research, is utilized to " brush aside all nonessential and foreign elements, to remove all unnecessary accretions." As he makes this second movement, the theologian does not appeal to any preconceived or external norm or criterion, but only to " the inner logic of faith itself," or to the *grundmotiv* that has been exposed by the prior logico-descriptive exercise. The motivating and guiding conviction is that whatever survives this deductive and diastasic process can be regarded as " the genuinely Christian," and is thus the intended material of systematic theology.[16] When this residue has been arranged and interrelated systematically, the theological project is complete.

It is obvious that this approach incases a unique answer to the question of theological authority. Acceptance of the Lundensian definition of the task of theology immediately commits the theologian to a flat, formal repudiation of all normativeness, and consequently to a methodological exemption from every theological value-judgment. Aulén formulates this requisite unambiguously: " Theology does not write laws for faith, nor act as lord over faith. The task is neither demonstrative nor normative, but analytical and critical. Its purpose is neither to furnish proofs for faith nor to determine what ' ought to be believed.' " [17] The introduction to his influential little work, *Christus Victor,* repeats this conviction, insisting that the question of value is implicated in no way, or that " the question of origin " is the single concern in this attempt to recover the " classic " doctrine of the atonement.[18]

This repudiation implies two things, the first of which might be called a commitment to radical theological openness. The analogy of this characteristic of the Swedish methodology to Husserl's project is striking.[19] The theologian, as a theologian, is not permitted to favor one religion, or a specific confessional tradition, over others, or to value one higher than the others. The conviction dictated by the method is that religion " has *centra* but no *centrum*," so that each manifestation must be approached and examined with equal seriousness, and purely in the light of its own *grundmotiv*. It is interesting to contrast this with the attitude of Barth, who is forced to state in a similar context, regarding the matter from the point of view of his own understanding of the nature of Christian theology, that "there is, strictly speaking, no dogmatic tolerance." [20] Aulén must insist, on the contrary, and with striking resemblance to the restrictions of pure phenomenology, that theology cannot judge among the religions either as to their truth in terms of objective reality, or as to the truth of their separate theological pronouncements, or even as to their comparative value. [21]

It thus is no surprise when we find the Lund school contending strongly for the ecumenical nature of theology, and supporting the theological efforts of the ecumenical movement. They disqualify at the outset every attempt to establish an intrinsic relation between systematic theology and confessional symbols or standards, insisting that theology " can be confessional only in so far as this is of assistance to the comprehension of that which is genuinely Christian." "Theology is not looking for denominational expressions of Christianity but for genuine Christianity itself," Aulén remarks; " and it does not recognize a denominational expression unless it can document itself as genuinely Christian." [22] It also is quite interesting to find him protesting that Luther is only one among the various possible sources of theology, and that the recurrence of Luther's name and thought throughout *The Faith of the Christian Church* is due solely to the demonstrable fact that he " penetrated deeper into the meaning of the Christian faith." [23]

The dismissal of normativeness implies, also, a formal wariness toward all hidden criteria, and toward the constant pressure of the temptation to exercise subjective or personal, selective judgments. The theologian must content himself with the methodological decision that places the limit of theology at the end of the inductive-deductive process that determines what is, and what is not, consistent with the distinctive motif of the religion under investigation.

The logical inference that this limitation immediately suggests, that the Lund project entails or encourages theological relativism, is probably an unjustifiable and unfair one. It is possible that a certain relativity of result is inevitable in the very nature of the project, especially where it is pursued without revision by the second and subsequent generations. But it is quite clear that relativism is the diametrical opposite of what is intended. Theoretically — or, perhaps, idealistically — the *grundmotiv* of Christianity, which is said to be available to any impartial observer, is identical for all Christian theology and every Christian theologian. Thus the subjective preferences and whims of individual theologians and theological schools, and the continual recasting of the configuration of Christian faith by the movement of history and the flux and flow of Christian experience, are formally neutralized. Whether such a neutralization is actually possible, given the nature of human nature, is another question; and it is completely clear that the Swedish movement regards its method as the best, if not only sure, corrective of the theological relativism that prevailed during the latter part of the nineteenth and the early decades of the twentieth century.[24]

It is quite in order, however, to pose the previous question as to whether the kind of dispassionate objectivity that this theological method demands is, in reality, a human possibility. The question is particularly provocative when there is a consciousness of the recent confessions by representatives of other disciplines, or other "sciences," that value-judgments seem inescapable. It is now widely conceded that the possibility of objectivity in scientific pursuits decreases in inverse proportion to the abstractness of the object under investigation. Few successful attempts to solve the problems of theoretical physics are decisively affected by the subjective bias of the physicists. But may the same be said of the fields of history, sociology, and human relations? And is not the theologian forced to deal with the least abstract, or with the most existential, facets of human life and experience? Tillich has candidly remarked that in every theological system "there is a point where individual experience, traditional valuation, and personal commitment must decide the issue." He annexes the observation that although this point may not always be discernible to the theologian, it is easily identified from the outside.[25] This would appear to be unavoidably true; and perhaps one indication of its truth is the consistency with which Aulén's methodological "neutrality" or "objectivity" leads him to peculiarly Lutheran affirmations and conclusions. Another is the observation that Wingren feels must be made about the results of Nygren's research in quest of the "*agapē* motif," that when it emerges it is "really purer in Luther than in the New Testament." [26]

The suspicion that these observations suggest should not be permitted to detract from the proved, and almost inestimable, preliminary and leavening value of Swedish motif research to contemporary theology, a value that can be expected to increase rather than decrease in the next decade. It does, however, suggest a necessary misgiving, lest this attempt to reorient the matter has, in truth, only succeeded in avoiding, rather than in answering, the crucial question of theological authority; and that it has done so by permitting a trace of illusion to disfigure its methodology. This misgiving proves to be neither an idle nor an insignificant one when we notice that it cuts to the very heart of our conviction about the nature and the mission of Christian theology, and its relationship to the life of the church and the individual Christian. If we could follow Aristotle, or simply define theology etymologically as a recounting of the myths about the gods, no question would be necessary. But Protestantism has generally persisted, for reasons that safeguard the very nature of the Christian faith, in siding with Duns Scotus against Aquinas, regarding theology basically not as a *scientia speculata* but as a *scientia practica*. This means that although theological problems both can and should be analyzed and clarified *supra nos,* and their answers both formally and materially affected by the history of ideas, yet theology simply cannot be reduced to an exercise in the history of religion. The living present must be permitted an intrinsic share in the theological process, and the theological task must be pursued both by the church and for the church. If this necessarily puts the theologian on guard against even the most subtle reductionistic transposition of theology into history of doctrine, it would appear that where the Lund school has succeeded in being faithful to the limits of its original method, the incisive results of its research must be accepted and utilized as *praeparatio,* and not regarded as theology proper.

2. THE NORMATIVE THEOLOGY OF NELS F. S. FERRÉ

This in effect appears to be how the Swedish-born American theologian, Prof. Nels F. S. Ferré, has attempted to relate himself to the Lundensian school, and make serious use of its contributions. Ferré's system is posited on the presupposition that the central conclusion of Nygren's research is accurate. He then balances everything on the assumption that *agapē* is the distinctive motif of Christianity.[27] Ferré has differed with the Lundensians from the outset, however, at two fundamental points, both methodological. He contends that *agapē* is not only the distinctive, but also the inclusive and explanatory motif of the Christian faith, and is therefore normative. We shall return to the question of his reasons for making this decisive break. What must be noticed from the beginning is that this requires a full repudiation of the posture of neutrality that is inherent in the scientific claim of the Swedish theology, and forces the adoption of an entirely different methodological stance.[28]

The other major difference results from the unlimited scope, and the final authority, that Ferré grants to *agapē* as the norm. The Lund method was directed only to the discovery and exposition of motif, and to its comparison and contrast with other conflicting and supplementary motifs. Ferré insists that when it has been recognized that the *agapē* motif is normative, the theologian falls under an unavoidable obligation to acknowledge that "everything is ultimately subject to God's love," and thus to apply the norm both critically and formatively to every area of theology and ethics.[29] He must sift all extraneous elements and accretions that are in any way in conflict, or are inconsistent, with *agapē*. He then must reformulate the whole of the Christian faith, together with its philosophical involvements, and its theological, experiential, and ethical implications, under the point of view provided by this adoption of *agapē* as its singular norm. This is the nature, and the thesis, of Ferré's theological project. The guiding and ruling conviction is explicit and unilateral throughout his system: that "this claim that God as *agapē*, or unlimited, objective, self-giving love, is central for both faith and life constitutes the fulfilling and revolutionary uniqueness of Christian faith, which should dominate its very last and least doctrine." [30]

Ferré enters the theological circle by posing the explanatory question of philosophy of religion, insisting that " although explanation in thought is not central," it is nevertheless " native to the human mind," and therefore is necessary to religion.[31] He quickly disqualifies both reductionistic and nonreductionistic naturalism as live alternatives in the quest for an explanatory point of view. The former is repudiated because it rests on a principle of continuity, and mechanistic assumptions, that are unwarranted, because it is unjustifiably anthropocentric, and because in the end it seems to deny more than it explains. The latter is said to be unsatisfactory because, although it achieves an impressive degree of success in answering man's " how? " it cannot answer his " why? " and thus it does not contribute the " whole-explanation " necessary to the " whole-response " which is crucial if life is to find its intended meaning.[32] The explanatory perspective that he sponsors is one that canvasses the natural and historical process, and acknowledges " the most high as the most real." Everything is then examined under, and explained in terms of, " the most significant novel emergence in history." Ferré calls this highest novel emergence the " selective ideal-actual," and insists that it will offer both the best key to an explanation of past process, and the best indication of " the position toward which process is going." [33] It is in this sense that it is said to be ideal as well as actual, and to speak to man's question, "why? "

This brief tussle with explanatory alternatives, and injection of Christianity's historical element into the philosophic conversation, suggests the earliest movement away from the Lundensian orientation that is discernible in Ferré's writings. We discover a marked shift of basic concern. It is a shift from the question of validity to the problem of adequacy, or from the kind of occupation with the matter of a principle of philosophical certification that is represented by the early writings of Nygren, to the more Kierkegaardian pursuit of " saving adequacy." Ferré recognized and conceded even in his earliest writings that it seems inevitable that, " from the point of view of life, adequacy must be obtained at the expense of validity." This is said to be true because " knowledge is most demonstrable and most objectively communicable at the extreme abstraction of either form or fact." It means, he observed, that " as science develops its body of knowledge, its specific validity decreases while its general applicability to the actual world increases." The same is said to be true of religion. "The more interpretation moves from the two opposite extremes of fact or form into the midst of fullness of life, the more difficult interpretation becomes, and the less validity it has, but the more it obtains applicability and adequacy." [34] Thus, while he can forsake neither, the theologian no less than the scientist must choose which he will serve with the primacy of his concern — the cause of validity, or that of adequacy. The decision of the Swedish movement at this juncture is hardly as clear, but Ferré's increasing intention has quite obviously been to make adequacy, and not validity, the initial concern of his theology.

This intention is specifically identifiable in the fact that after a brief effort to rehabilitate Nygren's approach — by a substitution of the category "fellowship" for the category "eternity" [35] — we can trace in Ferré's writings a waning of the dialogue with the more predominantly philosophical problems that theology confronts. It is replaced by the steady rise of a more existential and soteriological preoccupation.[36] One telling symbol of this shift which bears upon our problem has been his increasing awareness of the centrality, and the enigmatic nature, of the matter of motivation. An increasing consciousness that "the problem of motivation is one of the deepest of our age" prompted the recognition that this is a question which can only artificially be severed and excluded from the discussion of authority. This has led to the emergence in Ferré's theology, in a new context and with a new cast, of the Reformation strain that we saw to have been renewed by Forsyth — the insistence that a proper Christian theological authority must have a soteriological dimension. Ferré attempts to meet this demand with the reiterated assertion that "in *agapē* motivation and authority are inseparable." "When the most high is believed through whole-response to be the most real," he says, "we have an adequate authority and motivation. When life is lived for anything less, our problems become many and vexing. For our own day, we need desperately, humanly speaking, such authority and motivation." [37] This existential-motivational concern appears to be one of the controlling reasons for Ferré's uncompromising insistence that, even theologically speaking, "everything is ultimately subject to God's love."

When we pose the pivotal questions, why Christian theology must be normative, and why *agapē* must be acknowledged as the singular norm of the Christian faith, we find that it is necessary to canvass the whole of Ferré's writings in search of the answer, or answers. He is careful to speak to these questions negatively, or to indicate what is not advanced as a justification of these claims. We find, surprisingly enough, that there is no contention whatsoever that this status of absolute priority may or must be attributed to *agapē* on precedential or traditional grounds, as though this were " the way of the fathers," or of the main stream of Christian tradition, or of the most trustworthy theologians of the past. Ferré acknowledges quite openly that if this is the path to true Christian theology, there are few who have found it. He expressly states that " when it is claimed that the New Testament idea of love is the determinative principle of Christianity, this principle is in no sense equated with either the ideological or the sociological history of Christianity." [38]

There is, likewise, no attempt made to afford the normative elevation of *agapē* a simple or a final Biblical justification. Ferré insists, and in this he would seem to be in accord with the dominant, current trend of Biblical theology, that there is a demonstrative sense in which *agapē* (in the recurrence of *chesed,* and in the centrality of " covenant love ") may be said to be at the heart of the Old Testament configuration. He also assumes that love is the controlling and distinctive motif of the New Testament. We can even conjecture quite safely that he would contend that this centrality of love, in the sense of *agapē,* constitutes the proper principle of a doctrine of the unity of the Scriptures. It is clear, nevertheless, that he sponsors no claim that the idea of love is a pure or singular norm in the Bible, or even in the New Testament. He freely concedes, per contra, that much of the Old Testament does not justify this principle of authority, and even that " many ideas in the New Testament are either contrary to or not fully up to the level of this idea." [39]

When we pose the question of the ground for this decision for the normativeness of *agapē* from the positive side, an answer is much more difficult to discover and explicate. This is true principally because of the complexity and interweaving of the factors that are implicated. When they are unraveled, it would appear that, summarily speaking, there are four basic reasons that may be identified. High priority is accorded to the inductive conclusion, which presumably Ferré would say can be reached only across an experimental path of trial and error, that *agapē* is crucial to the Christian faith to the conclusive degree that "it constitutes its very essence, in the light of which the several Christian doctrines can best be understood." [40] This degree of cruciality and conclusiveness is then said to constitute love "the key" to all else, and therefore necessarily the norm of Christian theology. [41] Ferré reveals an uneasy consciousness of the predominantly theoretical and explanatory (or nonexistential and nonsoteriological) cast of this claim, however. Thus his reliance upon it is always qualified in such a way that it is never permitted to stand alone. [42]

A second strand of justification that appears attempts to anchor the norm in the historical. The man Jesus is said to be accurately understood, and properly understandable, only as he is seen to have brought the truth, and to have been the incarnation, of *agapē*. "It seems an undeniable fact of history," he remarks, "that through Jesus there came into full historical awareness the idea of Christian love." [43] But there are two difficulties that block the way to an unqualified attempt to justify normativeness on this ground. Ferré is conscious of the dilemma of historical probability, or of the problem posed and formulated by Lessing and Kierkegaard. We therefore find him reflecting the realization that any final or unquestionable "proof" that the life and death of Jesus incarnated the love of God is beyond the reach of theology or the theologian. He also acknowledges certain philosophical difficulties that are said to be bequeathed by the nature of *agapē* itself, and comments that "it is a matter of real importance to understand clearly the fact that God's *agapē* comes to us absolute *in content only,* not in historical expression nor in perfect personal form." This qualification he feels to be necessary because "history is characterized by change, by decision, by a measure of real freedom." Because this is incontrovertibly true, and its truth cannot — and should not — be ignored by theology, "any authority for history must be open; it must be embodied absolutely in content only, but never in form. We must be free to give our own creative forms to our own historic decisions." This is said to necessitate the conclusion that " while the source and reality of authority is absolute, the form in history must always be relative." [44] This is why, while contending that the historical as such contributes both necessarily and substantially to the methodological conviction of the authority of love, Ferré acknowledges that a decision for the normativeness of *agapē* cannot rest upon the historical element alone.

The third strand that may be identified involves a qualified appeal to the Bible as a canon and to the visible or historical church. Ferré does not suggest that the church, even as it existed and was represented by the original apostles, incarnated or maintained the standard of *agapē*. He does insist, however, that it is demonstrable fact that the realization that " God is love " has controlled the most authentic periods of church history, and produced the highest levels of Christian experience and accomplishment in the church. He also argues in the same vein — even as he is acknowledging that there are levels of meaning and truth in the Scriptures, and that some of these are below the level of the norm of Christianity — that *agapē* undeniably constitutes itself " the core " of the Biblical material.[45] This leads deductively to two conclusions: one, that the Bible can be correctly interpreted only when it is read in the light of *agapē;* and, the other, that the deepest currents in the stream of church history can be identified only as we recognize that they had as their common source " the agapaic motivation." These observations are assumed to be of indispensable but insufficient importance. Or they are regarded as acceptable but not as autonomous and self-sufficient reasons for attributing theological normativeness to *agapē*.

The fourth summary strand of justification is somewhat more elusive. The prevailing temper of Ferré's writings suggests, however, that it could be regarded as of primary importance and given the most weight in his methodological decision. It embraces the entire complex that is indicated by the recurring, complementary categories, " the Holy Spirit " and " personal experience " — referents to which, somewhat to the embarrassment of the main stream of contemporary theology, and of most contemporary theologians, and to the delight of a large lay following, Ferré appeals in a quite unabashed way. He suggests that for those who have received the Holy Spirit, and who live and think under the guidance of the presence of the Spirit, *agapē* becomes a " self-authenticating " or " self-verifying " theological norm.[46] " Not until we share Christ's compassion for men," he says, " not until we want to take up our crosses to follow him, not until we enter into his concerns, does he become alive in us and to us. The key is not any intellectual formula. The key is not turned except by the Holy Spirit." [47]

Whether we approach Ferré's theological system logically or chronologically, we immediately encounter this experiential cast and this assertion that it " turns the key." We also are reminded of it whenever reference is made either to a valid or to an adequate principle of authority. It is this more than any other single factor that reveals how far he has moved from the presuppositions of the Lundensian methodology. " The truth that saves must come out of some actual whole-response," he says. " It must be existential. It must be something to which we must bow because it grips us with the intensity of a mystic intuition, subduing us." [48] Oddly enough, the weight that Ferré gives to this side of the matter stands out most clearly when he relates it to the question of the authority of the Bible. His constant emphasis upon theological " creativity " and " the creative " prompts him to warn frequently, in references to Scripture, that " we must be careful not to limit the Spirit." It is interesting to contrast his intended meaning in this context with Calvin's contention that the Spirit not only " attests " the Word, but the Word must also be used to " test " the Spirit. Ferré remarks that " wherever the Holy Spirit is, there is the Spirit of truth who shall lead us increasingly into all truth." He adds, indicating clearly that he feels that an openness not permitted by Calvin's *discrimen* is necessary: " God wants to write new and even better Scriptures, both in life and in books. The Holy Spirit is no ancestor worshiper. *God* never closed the canon of Scripture." [49] Therefore, " we need the fuller edition of the Bible in life." [50]

It has to be said here too, however, that this strand of verification is not permitted to stand alone. Ferré manifestly holds it as a constituent element; and he apparently regards it as the most important element, or as the key to all else. His reliance upon it is frequently qualified, however. Perhaps it would be both fair and accurate to say that, although it is *suggested* that the self-authentification and self-verification that come with a personal experience of the God of love are in themselves sufficient justification for making *agapē* theologically normative, this is *not* asserted. Rather, this experiential strand is associated with the others that have been enumerated, and always appears in juxtaposition to them.

The difficulties that are encountered in attempting to answer this crucial, pivotal question in Ferré's theology indicate a level that has remained ambiguous, despite his concentrated effort to dispel the cloud of confusion that has settled upon this whole matter of theological authority in twentieth-century Protestant theology. The functional use that he attempts to make of *agapē* as a critical principle, or as a theological authority, is necessarily material as well as formal. This immediately subjects his doctrine of authority to a prior question — the question about the decision, and the authority for the decision, that determines the precise content attributed to this New Testament category. Nygren has attempted to forestall any assertion that the conclusions of his study stand or fall with this decision, by insisting in advance that in his use of the category *agapē* he has reference only to a "formative motif," or to a "general attitude," and that this involves him in no ontological assertions or authoritative claims.[51] Ferré, on the other hand, in the act of making *agapē* normative, erects his entire theological system on the singular, ontological assertion that "God *is* love"; and he then proceeds to utilize this "love" not only formatively, but also functionally and regulatively. In so doing he necessarily, and methodologically, obligates himself to defend a particular and precise definition of the content of the category *agapē*.

This immediately involves Ferré with difficulties that Nygren has managed to avoid, at whatever cost, by his methodological decision. He cannot avoid, for example, the difficulty that even his principle of authority, not to speak of the particular positions assumed in his system, is contingent upon correct answers to such questions as that of the relationship of love and holiness in our knowledge and experience of God; that of the relation of justice to love, and love to justice, in the nature of God; and that of the relation of *agapē* to *erōs* in the spheres of both creation and redemption. That the answers to these prior questions about the content of *agapē,* and the determinative nuances that must be attributed to it as a category, are hardly self-evident, is clearly indicated by the intensive criticism to which Nygren's statements on the matter have been subjected during the quarter of a century since *Agape and Eros* first appeared. And Ferré has been one of the participants in this criticism.[52]

It is this attempt to use " love " as a single-level, regulative, and functional theological authority, as well as to permit it to be the formative motif, which creates the ambiguity, and the touch of opaqueness, in Ferré's position. It makes it necessary for him to insist, inherently if not explicitly, that a singular category with specific inclusive and exclusive content must be the unilateral criterion of all Christian theology. While this probably does not justify the criticism that is sometimes made, that he attributes ontological status and absoluteness to a " principle " or " idea," and thus sponsors a hidden, twentieth-century type of theological Hegelianism, it does entail a problem that appears unsolved — or, at the least, a question that remains unanswered.

Even if we leave aside any inquiry about the accuracy or inaccuracy of the particular definition of " love " that Ferré utilizes, the fact remains that the question of the precise content of the category *agapē* has remained open — and, undoubtedly, will remain open. The question that must be asked is, In the very nature of the case, how can — or could — this question be closed without appeal to a specific theological *discrimen?* When Ferré makes not simply *agapē,* but a particular definition of *agapē,* theologically regulative, he thereby obligates himself to an explanation and explication of both the composition and the exact authoritative status of the *discrimen* that permits this decisive move. We may regret, or even deplore, this circular nature of the matter. But we cannot deny it; and we should not oversimplify it.

CHAPTER VII

The Confessional Approach

THE frequent ultravibrant words that Karl Barth has spoken on the matter have tended to mislead many in this country who find his theology uncongenial, as well as some of his less attentive adherents of the second and third generations, into the assumption that he regards the question of authority as one that Protestants can ask and answer on a single level. This misconception has been due much less to what Barth has said than to the way in which he has said what he has said. Many years ago Prof. H. R. Mackintosh attempted to alert English-speaking readers of Barth to his oratorical style of writing, and to the fondness that he has for an absolute type of statement that almost always has its complement but sometimes not for many pages.[1] Numerous remarks that he has made on the subject of authority have been of this nature, and through the years they have prompted many to leap to the conclusion that Barth regards the question of the authoritative status of the Bible as the single issue implicated in the Protestant problem of authority. It is difficult to conceive of a conclusion that could be more inaccurate, whether we have in view his earlier or his more recent writings.

In view of the controlling tendency at present to speak of two Barths, an earlier and a later Barth, it should perhaps be said at the outset that his position on this particular matter has not changed materially since the appearance of his epoch-making commentary on Paul's letter to the Romans. Then, as now, he insisted that theology is inherently normative, and that the dogmatic norm is the Word of God revealed in Jesus Christ; and he was meticulously careful, as he is today, to forestall any tendency to equate the Word of God with the Bible. It is sometimes overlooked that the principal object of Barth's polemics, as he fought to re-establish a Reformation type of "theological exegesis" in the decades following the First World War, was not nineteenth-century subjectivism. It was what he keenly felt to be a false objectivism in the critical approach of twentieth-century Biblical studies. He became convinced at an early date that "there is no subjectivity quite as dangerous as that which is based on the presumption of a false objectivity," and that the enthusiasm that had been created by the proved values of the historical-critical method had led Biblical scholars into just this kind of trap, into a subtle, repressive type of historicism that tended to obscure the church's vision of its theological task and norm.[2] It is in fact difficult to suppress the feeling that even today, or perhaps especially today, Barth would completely agree with Kierkegaard that where we are too preoccupied with the words to hear the Word, it would be better to gather all Bibles, carry them to the top of a hill, and burn them as a tribute to the long-suffering of God and a sin offering for the stupidity of man. There has been an unbroken continuity in Barth's warning that it is fatal to the mission of the Christian church to rest secure with either a crass or a sophisticated type of Biblicistic *Historismus* that obscures "the beyond," the "eternal Spirit" who lies behind and who would speak in and through the pages of this book, unremittingly demanding "a criticism of the letter by the Spirit."[3]

This was the conviction that motivated Barth's early, methodical quest for "the Word beneath the words," the Word of God which is "exposed in the words" of Scripture. It is quite easy to understand why, in this quest, he was attacked on both flanks. He was assaulted from the right because he steadfastly refused to equate the Word of God, or revelation, with the words of the Bible, and consistently maintained that the words of Scripture are not, as such, the final authority of theology. And he was attacked from the left because he was determined to force Protestant theology to relocate the Bible in the center of the circle circumscribing its principle of theological authority and thus vigorously assaulted every answer that did not include a fresh, serious confrontation with "the strange new world within the Bible." Barth's approach to this question, and his treatment of its manifold ramifications, have changed often, and sometimes drastically, during the intervening decades. They have not changed materially, however; and his way of framing the issue has in substance remained the same: How may we reaffirm and reestablish the Reformation principle of the theological authority of the Bible, and at the same time preserve the freedom of the sovereign grace of God which was threatened by the formulation of the principle of authority in old Protestant orthodoxy? [4]

1. The Confessional Nature of Theology

Barth defines systematic theology (or dogmatics) as the church's reflective criticism of its preaching or proclamation, " the self-test to which the Christian church puts herself in respect to the content of her peculiar language about God." [5] Four preliminary, orienting observations which bear directly upon the question of authority are necessary regarding this conception of the nature of theology. The first is that here all theology is church theology in the most stringent sense. Theological labor is carried out under a commission granted to the church, and it must be pursued within and for the benefit of the church. This implies that there is no neutral standpoint from which it may be approached, and no outside voice to which it must listen. Barth quotes Zwingli with approval, insisting that the theologian must remember that the church " heareth not the voice of a stranger " unless perchance it is in some clearly discernible way an echo of the voice of Jesus Christ.[6] The Christian preacher, and the theologian in so far as he is also a proclaimer of the Word of God, should be sensitive to the voices of the world, or to the cultural situation to which the Word is to be spoken. But he should not expect that these voices will offer a theological word that can be materially determinative for, or will in any way supplement, the church's theology. This word, which is always the word about Jesus Christ, can be spoken only from within the church, which means within that concrete body of believers which knows Jesus Christ as its essense.[7] Barth has remarked in one of the most recent volumes of his *Dogmatik* that this has been his " thesis," the theme of his entire project, from the beginning: that " the being of Jesus Christ is the being of the church," and that this must determine both questions and answers, both problems and solutions, or, in brief, theology in its entirety.[8]

This is why Barth insists that theology can be only relatively and indirectly a " science " if this word is understood in the sense in which the Lundensians appropriate it. It is within the context of his remarks on this question that we recognize that his view of the nature of theology places it at such a distance from the contentions of Nygren and Aulén that, methodologically speaking, the two approaches have almost nothing in common. Barth concedes that theology may be described as *wissenschaftliche,* as a " scientific " discipline, if we mean by this that it strives to speak relevantly, and not simply arbitrarily, as a human effort after truth. It also is obviously true that when it is viewed from the side of the world, it certainly occupies a place beside other human disciplines or sciences. Not only so, but he acknowledges that the results of other sciences may well assume importance for theology indirectly after they have been submitted to a theological interpretation in the light of Jesus Christ or under the criterion of the essence of the church.

It is much more crucial to Barth, however, to recognize that theology is not a science in the sense that it can, or should, conform to principles that are foreign to it as confessional service of Jesus Christ. This is the point that he has been most concerned to make in the conversation that has surrounded this question. Christian theology, because it rests upon and moves out from God's self-revelation in Jesus Christ, cannot under any circumstances whatsoever " submit to measurement by the canons valid for other sciences." This means, for Barth, that when we are speaking in terms of fundamentals, " it has nothing to learn in their school as regards method." He views theology as in every sense and both materially and methodologically an independent discipline. This is why he must say, completely contrary to the " scientific " aspirations of the Lund school, that whenever an effort is made to capture a place for theology in the system of the sciences, or when an offer is made to assign it such a rank, it must politely reply that " this is too lofty — and too mean — an honor." [9]

We should notice, secondly, that this understanding of the nature of theology implies that it is a task assigned to the church as a whole, and not to select individuals within the church. Barth insists in the strongest possible manner that where the church understands its theological vocation, there is, strictly speaking, no "laity." The obligation of critical reflection upon its halting, stammering, equivocal, ambiguous language about God is one laid upon the entire church, "without the exception of a single one of its members." Every Christian must be sensitive to the "severe temptation" (*schwere Anfechtbarkeit*) to which we are exposed in daring to speak about God at all. And to be critically sensitive in this area of human endeavor and experience is in the most elemental sense to be a theologian. Barth insists that the theological task must be understood and interpreted in this comprehensive way, and that the corporate body which we call the church must respond as one body to this essential call to theological confession and obedience. He adds also that it is only as the church is obedient in this specific sense that it may truly be said to have acknowledged that in its inmost nature it is human as well as divine, as Jesus Christ was human and divine.[10]

The third necessary observation is that under this definition of theology the position that the theologian occupies, and that any Christian occupies as he participates in the dogmatic task of the church, must be clearly marked and remembered. He stands in the *Mitte,* the middle zone that is located between Scripture and proclamation, between *explicatio* and *applicatio,* between the Bible and the church, or between what we commonly call Biblical theology and practical theology. Barth sometimes refers to this as the razor's edge. It is the precarious, sharp line of demarcation that identifies the transition from exegesis to proclamation, and from hearing to teaching, and upon which dogmatics or systematic theology is balanced. Every Christian, including the theologian, is a part of the *ecclesia audiens,* the hearing church. And every particular dogmatician will also participate in the exegetical and practical tasks of the church, as a member of the church. But it remains important that he should be conscious of the position that he occupies as a theologian. Barth's major concern as he emphasizes the need for such a consciousness is that we see that there is no sense whatsoever in which the theologian is above the preacher, and no sense in which the preacher is above the theologian. They stand side by side; and, what is more important, the two inseparable obligations and functions that they represent, of kerygmatic proclamation and theological reflection, should exist side by side in the life of every congregation and of every Christian, lay or ordained.

This emphasis is not permitted to blur the fact that theology and proclamation both may and must be distinguished, especially in regard to the constraint or necessity under which they come into being. The constraint of proclamation issues from "the divine mandate" to the church. Thus preaching is motivated (or should be motivated) by a necessity that is essentially divine. The constraint of theology derives, however, from the secondary fact that all proclamation is to a degree opaque, as a human venture. This means that the necessity in which theology roots is unmistakably human in its origin. Theology exists only because preaching is fallible human work. This difference of constraint requires a clear distinction, and a functional differentiation, of proclamation and theology — and it may even justify the presence of "professors" or "professional theologians" within the church. The distinction should in no sense be interpreted as a division, however, for theology and proclamation cannot be separated within the historical existence of the church. The preacher and the theologian are inextricably bound up with one another in such a way that each becomes impotent without the other. Or, even better, proclamation and theology are so interdependent that the kerygmatic witness of each individual Christian tends to become impotent precisely to the degree that these two roles are not inseparably united in his person as he serves the church.[11] It would be difficult to cite a point that needs more desperately to be made at the moment in the American scene, where "lay participation" has become a consuming fad but is hardly understood and interpreted on this level.

The fourth orienting observation required by Barth's definition is that the "stuff" or raw material with which systematic theology labors is the message that the church proclaims from its pulpit. He regards theology as in the most direct way the servant of preaching, and in this absolutely concrete sense *ministerium verbi divini,* service of the divine Word. "The normal and central fact to which dogmatics relates itself is quite plainly the Sunday preaching of the church, of yesterday and tomorrow, and it will continue to be so." [12] " Even concrete dogma is nothing but kerygma tested by the church." [13] This is why we can say, with a certainty very nearly akin to that of a mathematical equation, " bad theology — bad preaching: good theology — good preaching." [14]

Theology takes its rise from the intrinsic " unrest " that is an inescapable part of the existence of the church within history, because of its human, all-too-human side. This restlessness is born of the deepest concern of the church, the concern that man's words about God shall in fact become and be the Word of God. Thus it is so fundamental a part of Christian life that it prohibits the church from in any way acquiescing in the ambiguity of its language about God, and drives it day by day to theological reflection and labor. It is this concern which designates the subject matter to which theology must turn its attention, namely, " the totality of what it hears from the church, the actual, contemporary church, as its human speech about God." [15]

This is the first and most obvious reason why a theological system can never be " final," and why the task of theology is never finished (and why every theological system, although it may exceed twelve thousand pages and six million words, remains in the last analysis " a marginal note"). The statements that Barth has made about the legitimacy of " scholasticism " notwithstanding, he simply cannot be likened to an architect constructing a cathedral, who has his materials delivered beforehand and can survey them and visualize his finished creation from the outset. If we may adapt a much more mundane simile from Heraclitus, he is like a man fishing in a stream, who stands on the same spot apparently casting in the same stream, but who knows that because of the very dynamics of the matter one cannot fish in the same stream twice. The theologian stands in the stream of the living church, with new raw material being committed to him every day. And his call to obedience requires that every day he say something (old and) new in his reflection on this new material in the light of the theological norm. It is somewhat puzzling that both critics and camp followers of Barth seem hesitant to take him at his word here, and recognize and acknowledge that he is completely serious in holding reflection on proclamation as, both theoretically and practically, the exclusive and inclusive limit of the dogmatic project. His definition of systematic theology requires that the theologian look in one direction only for his raw material. The all-embracing obligation of his vocation as a theologian is "to test the church's speech about God in order to discern whether as the word of man it is capable of serving the Word of God."[16]

It is because theological reflection is fallible human labor, and thus an enterprise within which success is possible only as the church stands under justifying grace as it reflects theologically, that Barth describes theology as an *Ereignis* and a *Glaubensakt,* an "event" and an "act of faith." It is with his application of the formal category "event" to the nature of theology that he systematically cuts his principle of authority free at the outset from that of late orthodoxy as well as from Roman Catholicism (and also, were he concerned to do so, from American fundamentalism). This renders theologically impossible any conception of the nature of theology where it is assumed or asserted to be a reception, summary, and recitation of given propositional content or "truths of revelation." Barth's all-embracing, regulatory presupposition is that "God is known through God alone," so that "revelation has its truth in the free decision of God."[17] His most characteristic way of voicing this definitive, actualistic conviction is with the potent little expression *je und je,* "now and then," or "from time to time," which recurs again and again in his *Dogmatik.*[18] Revelation, and theological truth, in so far as it is true, rest upon God's free grace, which issues from God's free decision and is given "from time to time"; and this, and nothing less than this, is the ultimate basis of the problematic nature of theology. Man "has" the Word of God, or the norm and the substance of theology, "only in virtue of the freedom and sovereignty of the Word." Thus the conviction must be embraced, without qualification or compromise, that "dogmatics is what it is either by the sovereign act of God or not at all."[19]

Another familiar way that Barth employs to give voice to this principle is by repeating that the expression *es gibt,* "there is," whether it is intended in the Roman Catholic or in a Protestant

Biblicist way, is " profane " — and in the deepest sense, even though it be unintentional, a blasphemous denial of the sovereignty and freedom of God. We cannot say for methodological purposes that " there is " revelation, or truth, or " correct doctrine " — or a theological authority! The inescapable necessity for " God's contingent visitation " circumscribes all theological truth, and should mark the outside limits of every theological enterprise. Here the theologian can only confess that he always seems to presume too much; and that, for all of his labors, troubles, and sorrows, he appears always to remain with empty hands. He stands confined within the limits of the *je und je;* and (even if his *superbia* and *hubris* do not permit him to acknowledge the fact in his conception of the theological task) there is no place other than this where he can stand. This is a limitation that cannot be circumvented by any theory of theonomy, any claims of an infallible authority for church or Bible, any doctrine of inspiration, or even by a refinement or redefinition of theological method.

Barth is less clear in drawing the conclusion, but his delimiting assertions force us to say also that precisely the same is true of the principle of theological authority. Normatively and materially we may state, variously within different loci but without qualifications, that God, the Word of God, or Jesus Christ is theologically authoritative in an absolute way. The Word of God is known to us, however, and is accessible as we operate with the functional *discrimen* of theology, only as an " event " and " from time to time." This means that we cannot say that " there is " such a theological authority, as though it were available to us as a norm that we can " handle." We must say, rather, that " when and in so far as a word is spoken by God to the church, then and only then is there any right, and any meaning, in speaking in the church about God; and then and only then is there a criterion." [20]

It follows that theology must also be regarded as a confessional venture, or as an " act of faith." This is the principal reason why it must be confined within the boundaries of the church and viewed as a privilege and function of the church. To be in the church is to be called to serve Jesus Christ and to act in obedient response to this call. As faith is the primary and necessary response, theology is a secondary and derivative response to this call. This requires that theology be "confessional" not only in the more narrow, accidental sense of being bound to the symbols of a particular tradition, but also in the prior, more essential, sense of being a part of the act of faith. The quest of theology is for truth in the form of *reine Lehre*, understood not as "correct" but as "pure doctrine"; and pure doctrine is an "event."[21] It is human language about God which is made transparent to the Word of God by the action of God.[22] This is why not only proclamation, but also theology, must "discern God in faith." And if we remember that faith is not something that man can determine and command at will, but is first of all a gift, we know that the theologian, to be a theologian, must rest solely in God's promise of revelation to the church and the given power of faith to grasp this promise "from time to time." His hope — even his hope for theological success as a theologian — is "from on high."[23]

2. PHILOSOPHY AND THEOLOGY

It is when the implications of these assertions regarding the nature of theology are applied to practical questions of procedure that the sharp contrast between the confessional approach of Barth and the contextual approach of Tillich first becomes obvious; and — as each has recognized for many years, having separated at this initial juncture and proceeded in different directions — it is extremely difficult to find a point beyond where their paths actually cross. We have seen that Tillich is deeply convinced that theology must speak, and basically concerned that theology shall speak, *ad hominem,* to the "situation" in which man is inextricably enmeshed. He believes that this apologetic obligation is so intrinsic to the nature of theology that it must share in the formative decisions that define its task and method. This is why he contends that theology that is irrelevant to the cultural milieu is untrue. It also is why he insists that the symbols of revelation not only may, but must, be correlated with the existential situation, including the ontological, epistemological, and anthropological presuppositions that are operative in the emergence of the questions that root in man's depth problems.

It has to be said immediately, and unfortunately in the face of

diverse notions to the contrary, that Barth is likewise deeply concerned that theology should communicate with "the varying present," or with the human situation — so much so, in fact, that there
are places even in his *Dogmatik* where this concern is a decisive factor in the procedure that he adopts and in the arrangement of his
material.[24] He believes that it is of the essence of the theological vocation that the promise that is given to the church should be "made
intelligible in contemporary language," and that the theologian who
defaults his share of this obligation, and contents himself with irrelevant repristination, or "mere repetition," has misunderstood
and unintentionally betrayed his calling as a Christian theologian.
Nor should we fail to appreciate the disciplined struggle through
which Barth has gone in an effort to fulfill this obligation in his own
way. If we juxtapose his *Romans* and the latest volumes of his
Church Dogmatics, and compare them in such matters as lucidity,
style, and the tendency to rely upon esoteric terminology, it is difficult to believe that the two could have come from the same pen. It
is unfortunate that so many ministers in the United States, who were
discouraged from reading him by the cumbersome mode of expression that he employed earlier, are unaware of this change.

   The contrast between Tillich and Barth makes its initial appearance when we attempt to identify the primacy of concern that informs each system. It needs to be recognized that Tillich's deepest
concern is to be an evangelist. If this has a strange sound to some
(and it will, and more often than not for diametrically opposite
reasons), we should remember that a sophisticated evangelist is
still an evangelist, and in certain circles the only kind of evangelist
who can have any hope of a hearing. When it is viewed from the
side of motivation, Tillich's thought is strikingly similar to that of
the Schleiermacher of the "Speeches" to cultured despisers of religion, and to that of Bultmann, both of whom should be appreciated
as sophisticated evangelists. He shares with Bultmann an attitude of
integrity and openness that compels him to recognize, and acknowledge methodologically, that "human nature is on the move." Each
assumes that there is an unavoidable sense in which "man is constantly redefining 'man,'" and that it is therefore theologically

fatal as well as futile to act as though the twentieth century were either the sixteenth or the first.

This is why the apologetic element is omnipresent in Tillich's theology, and why he insists that the Biblical message must be " de-literalized." It is why his relationship to the Reformers is essentially one of expediency, and why he virtually lives his theological life in search of a new vocabulary and new means of expression and communication. To be sure, he intends to be and is a theologian of the church. The first line of his system reads: " Theology, as a function of the Christian church, must serve the needs of the church." But he has become increasingly sensitive through the years to the isolation and obsolescence of the church. He is much too honest to try to explain away the failure of the church to break out of its stereotyped patterns of thought, and of the little ecclesiastical circles that it traces with its petty routines, and genuinely confront a world gripped by revolutionary turmoil and suffering from malignant decadence. Thus, while Tillich is standing within the church, he is not facing the altar as he thinks theologically. He faces the world outside the church, his basic concern being that those for whom Christ died shall not fail to hear of him because of unnecessary clinging to tradition, to ineffectual Biblicism, and to outmoded forms of thought. It is this evangelistic turn of mind which prompts him to allow his theology to flow from the compulsion to speak *ad hominem,* and to permit the cultural situation a share in the definition of the theological norm.

Barth's most basic concern, on the other hand, is ecclesiastical, and thus theological in the strict sense; and his formative preoccupation is simply " to say what must be said " in the light of the Biblical witness to Jesus Christ. It is characteristic that he insists that the most pressing problem is not unbelief outside of the church, but the difference of belief within. We may feel, and we should feel, that these two concerns are not exclusive of one another, and certainly neither Tillich nor Barth intends that they should be. The fact is, however, that the decision as to which must be the primary concern has led them down two fundamentally variant theological paths. Barth has become increasingly sensitive to the danger that the influence of Kierkegaard and philosophical existentialism, and the current concern that theology should be existential, could quietly metamorphose it to the degree that it could become anthropocentrically oriented in a new and hidden way — and thus merely be the old theological ghost of the nineteenth century stalking again, albeit disguised in new clothing.[25] He is determined that this shall not happen, and thus is constantly on guard to see that "the experience and attitude of man" does not become a secret theological criterion, even unconsciously.

This is why, as Barth stands within the church, even as a theologian he is facing the chancel, with its lectern (supporting the written Word) and its pulpit (supporting the proclaimed Word). It is also why he has consistently refused to be disconcerted by the clamor outside the sanctuary. We should notice that he reiterates that theology that is in any basic sense nonexistential, or that casts itself in the role of "the wisdom of an onlooker," cannot be Christian theology; and he will not permit the theologian to assume any illusory "scientific" stance of neutrality. When Barth requires that theology be "existential," however, and that the theologian be involved, what he primarily means is that theology is possible only in the fear of God, and only as a *Glaubensakt*. His emphasis is unfailingly upon the fact that "the free grace of the Word and of the Holy Spirit, the act of being called into the church, which the theologian must encounter from time to time from the God who has dealings with man in order to be what he is called to be," are not merely desirable but necessary to the inner nature of theology.[26] It is therefore to be expected that the "situation" with which he is concerned as a theologian is that of the church, and when he permits culture as such to enter the picture, it is merely because of the accidental fact that worshipers and theologians confront the world when they are elsewhere than in the sanctuary. From first to last, he views the dogmatic task as one to be plied within the sanctuary, whatever may be the necessary concerns, obligations, and avocations of the theologian when he is not plying his trade.

We thus are not surprised when we find that Barth locates the "correlation," or "connection," at the point of transition where the preacher proclaims the kerygma to a given congregation, and not, as in Tillich's system, at the point where the norm of theology is determined and the content of the Christian faith is explicated under the norm. For Barth, "theology is what it is intended to be [*Sachlichkeit*] when it makes the exposition of revelation its single task."[27] The necessity for a sensitivity to culture is therefore an obligation laid principally upon the preacher, who must proclaim the Word of God to worshipers who have been conditioned by a particular cultural configuration. The theologian's interest in this obligation is secondary. And his relationship to it, although it is both negative and positive, or both critical and constructive, must be primarily diastasic because of the prior decision as to the nature of the theological task.[28] The theologian's initial and consuming obligation is to cling to the Biblical norm, devoting his efforts to a penetration of the Biblical language. Then, permitting the Word of God that speaks through these particular words to be theologically authoritative, with Luther he must strive to separate "the doctrines of man" from "the Word of God" (*Menschenlehre* from *Gottes Wort*) in church proclamation.

This makes it necessary for Barth to regard the cultural situation as, first of all, a problem for theology; and it is in large part this radically different procedure in regard to the relationship of theology to all "profane" cultural forms which determines his attitude toward the specific problem of the interrelationship of philosophy and theology. He is fully cognizant of the fact that theology is "also a philosophy, or a conglomerate of all kinds of philosophy"; and that it is merely a radical reversal of the foolishness of the Greeks, and just as foolish, to despise or attempt to escape this philosophic involvement.[29] It is inescapable in an elemental sense because "man's language is the concrete problem of dogmatics," and all human language is, in its very humanity, inextricably interwoven with philosophical presuppositions and nuances. But Barth reminds us that it is intended to be inescapable in a far deeper sense, as this is an essential part of "the mystery of the worldliness of the Word of God." The failure to recognize and acknowledge the worldly *Gestalten* in which man receives and knows God's Word is analogous to the Docetic heresy in Christology. It is symptomatic of a paralytic blindness to the "veiling" and the "riddle" (*ainigma*, I Cor. 13:12) that interposes itself in all of man's knowledge of the Word of God.

Barth leans heavily upon Luther at this point. He adapts Luther's doctrine of the *larva* of God, the creaturely "mask," or "veil," behind which even the revealed God remains the hidden God, as a model for his own doctrine of the "double indirectness" of our vision of God.[30] Luther reminds us that within the limitations of this life we cannot expect to know "the naked God," or to know God "face to face," because he is always veiled and shadowed when he appears before us. He then speaks of the ability that is given to man by the Holy Spirit to distinguish the mask, or "the veil of God, from God himself, the person from the word."[31] He insists that both this distinction and the given ability to make the distinction are necessary to faith because of the misleading character that the Fall has given to man's reason, and because of the persistent indirectness of God's self-revelation. "For faith says, 'I believe you when you speak, God.' But what does God say? If you consult the reason, he says things that are impossible, things that are deceitful, things that are foolish, things that are weak, things that are absurd, things that are abominable and heretical and diabolical."[32] This is not to be deplored, however. To desire that it be otherwise would be both to seek for a *theologia gloriae* and to attempt to establish a new, more subtle doctrine of righteousness by theological works. We must simply acknowledge, therefore, that man never knows God directly, that this is both how it is and how it must be. "If there is to be a place for faith, everything that is believed must be hidden."[33]

Barth contends that this is the *conditio sine qua non* of man's knowledge of God. He employs this *conditio* positively, as "an assertion of revelation," as well as to deny that man has any "capacity" that permits him to comprehend or apprehend God. "There is a double indirectness of our vision: the first, that the Word of God encounters us in a form which must be distinguished from its content; and, the second, that this form is a 'riddle,' a veiling of the Word of God."[34] This is said to be the *terminus a quo,* the point from which every theological statement must proceed, "the fundamental and decisive thing which determines not our ignorance, but our knowledge of God."[35] Barth parallels this, in his doctrine of God, with the assertion that man confronts only the "secondary objectivity " of God: " we believe in him in his clothed objectivity, not in his nude objectivity." [36] This presupposition is then present in every assertion or denial that he makes in reference to the theological use of human language, concepts, and categories, including Biblical words, concepts, and categories. It is here that he separates himself in a final way from the doctrine of inspiration, and the principle of authority, of late orthodoxy. The very mystery of revelation and of the Bible as the Word of God is to be found in the fact that God hides himself behind " worldly " forms and words in revealing himself, and in doing so permits them to remain altogether worldly.

It thus is not entirely unexpected, and it is quite significant, when we find Barth paralleling the inextricable philosophic element in theology to the presence of sin in the Christian life. He remarks that as every Christian is *simul peccator et justus,* so all theology is at once philosophical and theological.[87] It is accidentally inevitable, although not essentially inevitable, that all of man's language about God, as human language, shall be ambiguous and equivocal, just as it is inevitable that the sinner shall remain a sinner even as a justified Christian. The attempt to escape philosophy, as though in some grand *sacrificium intellectus* we could transcend the structure of ontological and epistemological assumptions that unavoidably determine our understanding, and achieve " a pure Biblical point of view," then proves to be analogous to the illusion that moral perfection is a practical human possibility. The concern of theology cannot be to escape philosophy: it must be to place it in the service of Jesus Christ.

If this is to be accomplished, the Word of God must be permitted to control all philosophy that is to be utilized for theological purposes. It is perhaps not too gross an oversimplification to say that, while Tillich's thought proceeds from philosophical questions, Barth's thought recedes to philosophical problems. This is in fact the way in which he has stated the noetic principle of his theology. " The kind of thinking that wishes to begin with the question of the knowability of God, and then advance from there to the question of the fulfillment of the knowledge of God, is not grateful but covetous, not obedient but self-affirming. It is not theological thinking." [38]

Theological thinking is recessive thinking (*rückwärts*): it necessarily is a posteriori thought.[39] " It is to move back from the knowledge of God and ask about the presuppositions and conditions on
the basis of which God is known." [40] Barth is convinced that the
" ascending way," the way that moves from the valley of human
perplexity and human questions and problems to the heights of
God's answers and solutions, leads not to God but to false gods and
no-gods. Only the " descending way " is theologically faithful. This
is the way that begins and moves down from the God whom we
know because we are known, and strives however unsuccessfully
to think God's thoughts after him. " We have no grounds for saying
' no ' where God in his revelation has said ' Yes '; but the decisive
factor is whether we only say ' yes ' where God himself has said
' Yes ' in his revelation." [41] This is Barth's prius.

Barth feels that here Calvin has been taken seriously. If " all true
knowledge of God is born of obedience," then only the knowledge
that issues from the response of faith can be true and trustworthy
theological knowledge.[42] This means that the knowledge of God
must be given in the moment and movement of free, obedient response to God's movement to us in Jesus Christ. This is why Barth
will entertain no possibility of an " outside " position from which
theology may proceed. It is also why he will countenance no assumption of an anthropological possibility, a prius in or under human
experience, as a point of departure. And it is why his thought com-
prises the most radically consistent Christocentric system ever created
in the entire history of Christian doctrine. He will not even grant
that man may pose the correct questions, except as they are posed for
him by the Word of God. Man " must permit himself to be lifted
out of himself into this Word and *its* concerns and questions." [43]
This encompassing noetic point which he has been so concerned to
make has been reiterated succinctly and sharply in a paragraph in
the most recent section of his *Dogmatik,* his doctrine of reconciliation:

> If the crucified Jesus Christ lives, and if the church is the
> gathering of those who know this, have taken it seriously, and
> among whom it has rightly become the one axiom of all axi-

oms, they cannot rely upon any other word that God may have spoken, before, after, in juxtaposition to, or outside of this Word — words that he willed to have proclaimed by this Word. The church hears and proclaims this one Jesus Christ as the one Word, the first and the last Word, of the true God. It hears in him the fullness of God's Word of comfort, commandment, and power. It is therefore completely bound to him, and completely free in him. Thus it interprets creation, the course of the world, the nature of man, his grandeur and his misery, in the light which comes from him; and not somehow vice versa. It need hear no voice beside this voice as authoritative, because the evaluation of all other voices is contingent upon whether they are, or are not, an echo of this voice. It is quite true that, as the church seeks this voice, it also has both the permission and the command to hear other voices. And it can do so without hesitation or anxiety, because they may be permitted a share in his authority as an echo of his voice. However, it will always wish to return once again to hear this special, original voice, and place itself in its service. And, because he lives, the church will always be permitted to hear this voice, and effectively commit itself to its service. In this sense we can say with Zwingli (and against all alleged "natural theology"): "The holy Christian church, whose sole head is Jesus Christ, is born of the Word of God; and in this same Word it remains, and hears not the voice of a stranger." [44]

This leads Barth finally to two broad assertions regarding the theological use of philosophy. The first is that the theologian must always be conscious of his philosophical presuppositions, and aware that they inevitably are to some degree inconsistent with those of Scripture. He feels that the danger invited by the utilization of philosophy enters the picture in the moment when any philosophy is employed uncritically, or is regarded as a "fit" or adequate vehicle for the formulation and expression of theology. Therefore it is of first importance that we "not think that any of our schemes of thought is of itself fitted, or even peculiarly fitted" to the theological task.[45] The theologian's controlling obligation is to remember that " the Word of God did not found an academy but a church," and to strive for " imitative thought " as he seeks to fathom the words of the Bible in his quest for the Word of God. In doing so, however, he must always remember that he cannot divest himself of the inbred philosophical assumptions that he has brought to this task. These he must offer in an overt act of obedience, sharply aware of their inadequacy. If he is obedient, even philosophically obedient, he will know that every use of human language, concepts, and categories must remain provisional and tentative, and that he cannot commit himself without reserve to any philosophical school or point of view. But he will also know that he has nothing to fear from any particular philosophy. It is quite interesting that, having made this point, Barth's own use of philosophical elements in various parts of his *Dogmatik* seems surprisingly free and natural. As a matter of fact, he appears much more relaxed and unreserved than does Brunner, who has been consistently critical of Barth's negative premises and attitude in this area. This means, however, that the analytical and critical process, through which every major theological system passes, will be a much more lengthy one in Barth's *Dogmatik,* because he so rarely bothers to identify the species of the philosophical assumptions that are inescapably if not obviously present.

The other broad requisite to which he frequently returns is that philosophy must be kept in an instrumental position and permitted no constitutive role in theology. Barth contends that if philosophy is in any way permitted to frame the theological issues, or to determine the concerns, interests, methodology, or limits of theology, the true God will always be displaced by false gods. All use of philosophical assumptions and schemes must be subjected to the object reflected in the Biblical text. This requires that the Bible be the critical instrument over philosophy, rather than that philosophy be permitted formal or critical authority over the Bible and theology. The fundamental principle to be followed, Barth says, is that of " subordination " (*Unterordnung*).[46] He will not agree that this in any way represents an attempt to return philosophy to its medieval role as the handmaid of theology. We leap to this conclusion, he remarks, only if we attribute much too exalted a status to theology. The question, in reality, is not whether philosophy shall be made a servant of theology, but whether philosophy and theology alike shall be servants of the Word of God offered in Holy Scripture. For Barth there is no methodological question that is more pressing in the contemporary scene than this one.[47]

3. THE AUTHORITY OF HOLY SCRIPTURE

It is evident in what has been said that Barth's view of the nature of theology casts it in an essentially critical role, requiring that it consistently be corrective, or reformation, theology. It is quite clear, however, that he does not intend to imply by this that theology speaks, or can speak, from some higher or superior position, or in the confidence of some more sure and accurate grasp of the norm of theology or of the Word of God. The theologian stands with the church, in the church; and such " insight " as he may be granted is not his own but is given to the church. The seriousness with which he intends this limitation is illustrated by the fact that he refuses to attribute to theology as such, or to theologians, any special, unique function whatever when articles of faith must be defined and heresies must be anathematized. These manifestly are theological acts. But they are acts that can be performed only by the church, acting as the church. Theology, when it is understood in its most comprehensive sense, is the church engaged in the obedient act of reflective self-criticism, clarifying and purging its faith in quest of pure doctrine. Therefore the principle of theological authority must be a church doctrine.

This principle emerges in the theological process when the church recognizes that its critique of proclamation must conform to a concrete criterion, the Holy Scriptures. Thus in Barth's system the problem of theological authority becomes in its final stage the quite practical question of the pragmatic " authority of Holy Writ." There are levels of subtlety and profundity present in this apparently single-minded answer, however; and they can be recognized only as we bear in mind Barth's earlier doctrine of the three forms of the Word of God, and remember that he says explicitly that this threefold distinction is analogous to the doctrine of the Trinity.[48]

Barth states bluntly, and reiterates, that when we are speaking

materially, or with reference to content, we must acknowledge that
the authority of theology is " the Lordship of the triune God in the
incarnate Word through the Holy Spirit." [49] Here the Bible " can
only represent the divine authority." Nothing that follows is permitted to mitigate the cruciality of this basic confession of the
ground of all authority in theology. But we must notice, Barth points
out, that this answer is not created *ex nihilo,* or plucked from the
void. It is inseparable from and logically dependent upon a prior
decision, the decision to accept the witness of the prophets and
apostles in the Holy Scripture, through which we receive this answer. This does not mean the establishment of a chronological
priority for the Bible in principle; for, if we have accepted the
witness of the Scripture, this was an " event " and an " act of faith "
originating in God's free decision and act. Nor does it make the
normative authority of God in any sense subservient to, and contingent upon, our acceptance of the authority of the Scriptures. What
it does mean is that when we speak of theological authority we must
speak on two levels, and that we do not even know what we must
say on the level where we acknowledge the normative authority
of God except as we recognize what must be said about the authority of the written Word.[50]

The relative clarity of Barth's approach to the question of the authority of the Bible, which is found in the second half-volume of
his prolegomenon, is possible because of the foundation that he has
constructed for this discussion in the previous half-volume. He contends that we must recognize that the church encounters the Word
of God in three forms: as it is proclaimed, as it is written, and as it
is revealed by God. This doctrine of the three forms of the Word
of God has been the subject of much discussion and has proved to be
rather enigmatic when approached abstractly. Its function as a
part of Barth's larger doctrine of authority becomes clear, however,
if we view it before the backdrop of his assertions about the relationship of the affirmation of the Trinity to the doctrine of God,
and then notice the crucial, protective distinctions that it permits
when he delineates the authority of the Bible. In order to do this,
we must remember that the relationship of the three forms is said
to be analogous to the three-in-oneness of God, as the triune God.

We must also remember that revelation, the third form, is said to be materially the first form, or to be analogous to *Deus a se et per se,* to " God in and of himself." " Revelation is originally and immediately what the Bible and church proclamation are derivatively and mediately," he says; and " for revelation, Scripture, and proclamation we can substitute the divine ' person '-names, Father, Son, and Holy Spirit." [51]

It is then necessary to remember that, structurally speaking, the very uniqueness of Barth's theology traces to the place of primacy that it grants to the doctrine of the Trinity, and that the effects of this methodological decision permeate every layer of his thought. God is known through God alone, and this God is none but the triune God. Barth is convinced that the most formative error of Protestant orthodoxy, which eventually cast its shadow over the entire theological enterprise of Protestantism, must be traced to its unspoken assumption that a doctrine of God can be developed on a basis other than that given in the act of God in Jesus Christ. This in turn permitted the development and formulation of a doctrine of the nature and attributes of God prior to the formulation of the doctrine of the Trinity, and hence a conception of the aseity of God abstracted from a Trinitarian context. The characteristic, corrective conviction that informs Barth's entire system is that " when we ask questions about the being of God, we cannot in fact leave the sphere of his acts and work." [52] It means that, although we may and must make a theological distinction between *Deus a se* and *Deus pro nobis,* God in himself and God for us, as we must distinguish the First from the Second and Third " Persons " of the Trinity, we can no more speak accurately of the first abstracted from the second than we could of the second abstracted from the first. There is no way whatever in which we may move behind the acts of God to some supposed being beyond his action. " What God is as God, the divine individuality and characteristics, the *essentia* or ' essence ' of God, is something which we shall encounter either where God deals with us as Lord and Savior, or not at all." No part of Barth's *Dogmatik* can be understood unless it is viewed before the background of this all-embracing conviction. It is axiomatic that " there is no possibility of dealing with the being of any other God, or with any other being of God, than that of the Father, the Son, and the Holy Spirit as it is in the revelation of God and in eternity." [53]

This is the formative conviction that lies behind Barth's doctrine of the three forms of the Word of God, the doctrine that constitutes itself the context of his view of the authority of the Bible. It necessitates three protective acknowledgments, which clear the air and give the discussion of Biblical authority a new footing and a renewed seriousness, without permitting the re-entrance of the quasi-rationalistic assumptions that led to the downfall of orthodoxy's " Scripture principle." First of all, it permits the frequent reminder that Scripture is not revelation, but a witness to revelation. When the written Word is made dependent upon the first form of the Word of God, this orients it, together with proclamation, in the locus of becoming and not of being. It also places it in the line of the further contingency of revelation as " act " and " event " grounded in the freedom and love of God. Here the two levels that are necessary to a Protestant doctrine of theological authority, which is not covertly striving to establish itself on a singular level alongside the Roman Catholic doctrine, are recognized and acknowledged.

The Bible *a se,* in and of itself, testifies that revelation has occurred in the past; and it prompts us to expect it in the future. But it does not replace revelation, or displace or detract from the authority of God. Now the unity of the revealed and the written Word of God may be affirmed, even as the fierce temptation to identify or fuse them theologically is being rejected. The Bible *is* the Word of God: it " is the Word of God in so far as God lets it be his Word, in so far as God speaks through it." [54] Barth insists that this is what we must affirm if we are to recognize that, when we say that the Bible is the Word of God, this is a confession of faith; and that it is a confession of faith in God through Jesus Christ, the object of Scripture, and not a confession of faith in Scripture itself. He remarks that this is an " analytical statement," one grounded only " in its repetition, description, and interpretation," and not rooted in some major premise beyond itself. " The Bible must be known as the Word of *God* if it is to be *known* as the Word of God." [55] The weakness of the doctrine of authority formulated by late orthodoxy was not that it took the Scripture principle too seriously, he says. It was rather that it did not take it seriously enough, and thus imagined that it needed external proofs and props. We can say no more than that " Scripture is recognized as the Word of God by the fact that it *is* the Word of God." [56] How else may we really affirm the necessity for the second noetic office of the Holy Spirit, or for the *internum testimonium Spiritus Sancti?*

Moreover, the truth of this affirmation, like that of every other affirmation of faith, is rooted in the free decision of God. It is an " event " and one that occurs " from time to time." [57] This is why the church, with its Bible, should bear no resemblance whatever to a widow left with her deceased husband's legacy. " The Bible *becomes* the Word of God in this event, and it is to its *being* in this *becoming* that the little word ' is ' refers in the statement that the Bible is the Word of God." [58] This prohibits any doctrine of authority that would, either explicitly or implicitly, move Scripture from under the grace of God and commit it into the hands of man. " What we are really dealing with in this equation is the free grace of God and the gracious freedom of God. The statement that the Bible is the Word of God cannot mean that the Bible, together with other attributes, has the attribute of being God's Word. Here we would trample on God's Word, which is God himself, on the freedom and sovereignty of God. God is not an attribute of something else, even if this something else is the Bible. God is the Subject: God is Lord. He is Lord even over the Bible, and in the Bible. Thus the statement that the Bible is the Word of God cannot mean that the Word of God is bound to the Bible, but must mean inversely that the Bible is bound to the Word of God. And this means that in making this statement we look beyond, to a free decision of God — not in uncertainty, but in certainty; and not without basis, but on the basis of the promise which the Bible itself announces, and which we are permitted to receive in and with the church." [59] When this is acknowledged, the danger that the Bible will displace or replace God, and the authority of the Bible the authority of God, is no greater than (or is precisely analogous to) the danger that in confessing the man Christ Jesus to be the Word of God, and the Second Person of the Trinity, we will forget that God is God.

It is for Barth no less crucial to acknowledge, secondly, that theology knows nothing of God's revelation of himself, and therefore cannot even speak of the third form of the Word of God, apart from the Bible or its written form. " There is authority and freedom in the church," he says, " only because Scripture has already told us what we are asking about when we ask about God's revelation." [60] This requires that theology be bound from first to last, and methodologically no less than in content, to the Biblical witness. Once more, thinking analogically we must say that theology that attempts to speak without regard to the witness of Scripture is analogous to theology that attempts to speak of God, the First Person of the Trinity, on the basis of some anthropological possibility or general revelation, without regard to his revelation of himself in Jesus Christ, the Second Person of the Trinity.

This is why Barth can insist in some contexts that where the matter of authority is the concern, the basic question of theology is the question of its obedience to Jesus Christ, and then can say in other contexts that the fundamental question for Protestant theology is per se the question of its obedience to Holy Scripture.[61] When we view them before the backdrop that he has erected, we see that the question of the authority of the Lordship of the truine God revealed in Jesus Christ, and the question as to whether theology shall be " subjected to, measured by, and executed according to the Biblical witness," are in reality the same question asked within different loci. The Bible must be clearly distinguished from revelation, as the man Christ Jesus must be distinguished from God the Father. But it is in and through the second form of the Word of God, the Biblical witness, and for Barth it is only in view of this Biblical witness, that man knows the revelation that is materially the first form of God's Word. Therefore Christian theology, if it would in fact be Christian theology, is bound to the Bible which witnesses to Jesus Christ. This is why, when we are speaking on the functional level, we must say that *the* theological decision is as such the decision for Holy Scripture.

The third acknowledgment that this analogy demands is that the Bible, even as it becomes " from time to time " the Word of God in and for the church, is a thoroughly human document. " Where the

Word of God is an event, revelation and the Bible are in fact one." However, in this event the words of Scripture remain in every respect creaturely *larvae*.[62] "Holy Scripture is like the unity of God and man in Jesus Christ," Barth remarks; and, as with Christ, it is in the humanity of Scripture that we find its divinity, and nowhere else.[63] When it is considered historically, the Bible is "a very human literary document"; and, just as no Docetic compromise can be tolerated in Christology, so no view of the nature, place, and authority of Scripture can be acceptable if it in any way denies or compromises its full humanity. This point is seldom argued by Barth, but it is assumed throughout to be indispensable.

When he turns to the question of the use of the Bible for authoritative purposes, Barth consistently relies upon the two categories *Zeichen* and *Zeugnis*, "sign" and "testimony." The Bible is said to be a "sign" of revelation, or when he is speaking more accurately he refers to it as "a sign of a sign." This is the necessary acknowledgment that the authority of the written Scriptures which we possess is dependent upon the prior existence of the prophets and apostles, whose original testimony was the original sign. It means, Barth says, that revelation "in itself" never comes within our purview: "even on the basis of the Biblical witness, we cannot have revelation except through this witness."[64] This makes apostolicity as crucial for Protestantism as for Roman Catholicism, although locating its meaning in the office or function of the apostle rather than in his person. It also precludes any notion that, on the basis of a doctrine of inspiration, we can dispense with the witnesses once they have testified to the Word and cleave only to the words. Barth insists that as the words of the Bible become "from time to time" the Word of God for the church through the *testimonium Spiritus Sancti*, their voices become living voices. It is in these living voices that we hear "the voice of the one who called them to speak, which is the authority in the church."[65] But again, the canon is our only access to this "sign," to their voices, and to his voice.

The purpose of the written "sign" is to "testify" or witness; and while "a witness is not identical with that to which he witnesses," it is his function "to place before him that to which he witnesses." This defines on the one hand the restriction, and on the other the affirmation, to which we are bound as we employ the Bible as a functional theological authority: the absolute distinction of this fully human book from the Word of God, and its actual and real witness to the Word of God. Barth repeats frequently that " if we wish to understand the Bible as an actual testimony to God's revelation, obviously we must unremittingly have, and must permit to influence us, both views, the restriction and the affirmation: its distinction from the revelation, in so far as it is only a human word about it; and its unity with it, in so far as the revelation is the ground, object, and content of this word." [66] The all-embracing conclusion is that on the most practical level, theological fidelity is fidelity to this testimony in the trust that God will find us faithful to its content, Jesus Christ. This requires that the theologian have at all times a " Biblical attitude," the attitude of one who testifies to the " sign " which has been given to him, and to which he is bound as a Christian theologian.[67] In this sense " Biblicism " (*Biblizität*) is not merely acceptable, but completely necessary to theology. The " Biblical attitude " requires that the theological issues to which we speak, and our way of speaking to them, be uniform with the Biblical prototype or the " frame of mind " (*Geistesverfassung*) of the Biblical writers. It is once more, and from first to last, the demand for " subordination " and " imitative thought."

The Theological Decision

IT IS a matter of first importance that we recognize that the recurrent decision that Protestantism makes on the matter of theological authority is never one made *in vacuo*, but that it always is made at a particular time and place, and within a given historical setting. This is why in the very nature of the case the decision of the church cannot be abstract, but must be concrete. It is a choice that must be made in the face of a given set of theological circumstances with which the church finds itself confronted *hic et nunc;* and this means that the decision always must be made for, and against, specific alternatives that are presented to the church by these circumstances. This does not require that we choose between theologians. A theologian who solicits disciples has in this very act ceased to be a Christian theologian; and a Christian who projects his allegiance upon a theologian has in this act ceased to be a Christian. Nor does it require that we choose between systems of theology. Every theological system is like a shattered mirror: at best it merely reflects the light of truth, and even when it succeeds in accomplishing this, it is only a fragmentary reflection of a part of the truth. But it does mean that the church must decide between the theological alternatives that are presented to it by the historical setting in which it finds itself; and from this choice there is no escape. Even the refusal to choose is in itself a choice, made by default.

We should recognize, moreover, as philosophical existentialism has recently reiterated, that every decision is at once both an affirmation and a negation. When we choose one theological alternative, we inescapably negate another or others. Luther's decision for the

Word of God was also a decision against the tridentate principle of authority of Rome; and the decision of Calvin for the Word-Spirit *discrimen* was at the same time a negation of the claims of the left wing of the Reformation. The development of the *sola Scriptura* principle in orthodoxy was a decision against pietism and philosophical rationalism; and Schleiermacher's choice of "the immediate presence of whole, undivided being" and "God-consciousness" as the point of orientation for theology was in itself a negation of the principle of authority of late orthodoxy. Every affirmation unavoidably involves a negation; and from this also there is no escape, even by default.

When we recognize the inevitability of this fact, it has a dual value. It nurtures an attitude of caution that proves to be an invaluable tool in the critical evaluation of the contributions of previous periods, for it prohibits us from discounting, or writing off in one bold stroke, what was said in some past age under the false impression that it has no value for us simply because it does not formally say what must be said today. This is in fact the primary prerequisite for the fundamental theological discipline, the study of the history of doctrine. But it also has an even greater value, in that it reminds us that we too occupy a quite definite position within history. The church of today finds itself within a given historical setting, as has the church of every period; and this inescapably implies that we are confronted with a concrete complex of theological circumstances to which we must speak both positively and negatively as the theological decision is made in our time. Perhaps it is not too much to say that the theological ambiguity that pervades Protestantism in the mid-twentieth century may be traced directly to our failure to recognize this fact—or to our hesitancy, where we have recognized it, to meet it candidly. The unavoidable outcome has been that the affirmation and the negation that theological fidelity and obedience demand of us have in the main not been forthcoming in the church in our time, and thus the theological decision has largely been made by default.

The conditioning that is brought to the question of authority within the American scene at the present time makes it imperative that we recognize two things. One is that although a decision at the point of prius for the self-disclosure of God in history, and for the Scriptures through which we learn of this revelation and its meaning, is necessarily a decision against the "immediate awareness" or the "intuitive apprehension" upon which Protestant theology was reoriented in the nineteenth and early twentieth centuries, it is not a decision against immediacy as such. Nor does it in any sense necessarily negate the indispensable existential and experiential nature of Christian faith. It has had this effect in various periods in the past, but unnecessarily so; and when this has happened, the theological decision has not been faithful either to the Reformation or to the Bible for which the decision was made.

What is required if this decision is made is the acknowledgment that the immediacy of Christianity is a historically mediated immediacy, or that all experience that may be called Christian is intrinsically inseparable from the Mediator who lived and died within history, and who was raised of God to live eternally in and with his church. The point is the crucial one of which we are reminded by virtually every prayer of the Christian church, that the only immediate knowledge or experience of God of which a Christian speaks is his knowledge and experience "through Jesus Christ our Lord." To take seriously the theological implication of this liturgical practice is to negate every suggestion of nonhistorical immediacy at the point of prius of Christian theology; and this is, viewed from one side, the theological decision that the church cannot avoid in our time, the decision that it will make in obedience or by default.

It is no less important to recognize, secondly, that the decision for the historical revelation and the Scriptures need be in no sense a decision for the *sola Scriptura* principle of orthodoxy. In fact, it cannot be, for the circumstances that called forth the orthodox decision, and that it was framed to meet, are now totally obsolete, even if broad analogies to them can be found in our time. We have no obligation whatsoever to choose today between the principle of authority of orthodoxy, and the experiential criterion of the nineteenth century; and we need not take seriously the recent spate of literature that has attempted to frame and force the issue in this way. It is imperative that this be recognized in American Protestantism if the church is to be liberated from the deadly illusion of false alternatives that has now plagued and crippled it for almost a century.

One of the difficulties created by this illusion in the recent past has been the almost universal assumption that the opposite of the word " absolute " necessarily is the word " relative." But the correct theological antonym for the word " absolute " is " derivative." The theological circumstances of the moment obviously require that a doctrine of authority, to be acceptable in our time, initially and openly subscribe to the First Commandment, acknowledging frankly that because God is Lord, he alone is absolute. This has the necessary effect of placing the whole of creation under the justifying grace of God; and it has the further effect of establishing all theological criteria under the absolute, normative authority of God, with derivative authority. It would appear that history has made it clear that no acknowledgment other than this can destroy the heteronomous pretense that recurringly infiltrates the Protestant principle of theological authority, and subsequently reappears in the theological attitudes and affirmations of Protestants, and that is completely contrary to the very genius of the Reformation.

The absolutistic threat is always with us, and has to be met in every generation; and one of the most valuable lessons that can be learned from church history, in both its Roman Catholic and its Protestant forms, is that this threat will be met and conquered only as we confess that every authority at our disposal is a derivative authority, which exists and must be employed under the sovereign grace and normative authority of God. It is this acknowledgment which opens the way for a theological *discrimen* that permits the Bible to retain, or if need be, to regain, the authoritative status to which it was restored in the Reformation. If the word " norm " is permitted its original connotations, and theology bows in all things to the normative authority of God, we should not hesitate to insist that the Scriptures are not the norm of Christian theology, but are one of the criteria within its theological *discrimen*. This then permits us to wed the Bible to the action of a living God, his acts in history in the past, and his continuing action in the present through the Holy Spirit.

The anomaly of the theological situation in American Protestantism at the moment is that one part of the church tends to negate or default one side of the Reformation *discrimen,* while another part of the church tends to neglect or neutralize the other side. One need not be a prophet to recognize that the authoritative criterion most desperately needed in large areas of the church today is the written Word of God, which not only speaks to, but also stands over against, and brings theological judgment to bear upon, the church. The need is for a recognition and acknowledgment that we stand under an authoritative criterion that possesses the attribute of sheer givenness, a Word of God that the church cannot manipulate, to which it must listen, and that it must obey if it is to be the church of Jesus Christ.

We have seen that it was the clear intention of Luther and Calvin that the Bible should be permitted this critical role in the life of the church — that it should be granted the status of a prosecuting attorney *vis à vis* the church, subjecting it to unceasing, rigorous theological cross-examination; and it is, if it is nothing else, a clear breach of our heritage when we do not acknowledge that the Bible is not in our hands but in God's hands, and that it speaks against us as well as to us. The vitality of Biblical studies in recent years has been almost fantastic; but those familiar with the situation will concede that with marked exceptions this expanding breadth and depth in the understanding of the Scriptures has caused hardly a ripple in the church. Here the theological decision that is called for is a decision for the Word of God in Holy Scripture. Theological obedience requires that we permit the Bible to speak its Word before we speak ours, that we allow it to witness to its own Christ, frame its own issues, and proclaim its own message to these issues as the *regula* of faith and life.

There is likewise a deep need to recognize that if the Bible is to be the authoritative Word of God, it must be kept organically related to the revelatory, reconciling, and redeeming action of God, and this is the need felt in other quarters in the American church. God's act in giving us the Scriptures and his act as he makes the message of Scripture his Word for us today are reciprocal coefficients that must be held in an "inviolable union." Only this can prevent a renewed acceptance of the authority of the Bible from leading to the renewal of a "religion of learning and law," and preserve the vital, dynamic side of the *discrimen* of the Reformation which was recovered in nineteenth-century theology. Perhaps what is required here is a serious reaffirmation of the *filioque* clause. We need in fact to take this conviction even more seriously than it was taken in the Reformation, by acknowledging methodologically as well as formally and materially that the Holy Spirit who is given to the church, the very Spirit who makes it possible for us to accept the authority of the Bible, " proceedeth from the Father *and* the Son." This implies that where the Scriptures in any way become a composite of dead words, or where they are employed for any purpose other than as God's witness to the revelation and redemption that he has wrought in Jesus Christ, they have ceased to be God's Word for us. The Bible can become the Word of God for the church, for theology, or for us as individuals only by the action of the Spirit of God; and this Spirit we know only as we also know and are known of the Son of God, Jesus Christ the Lord. To this must be added the Reformation word, " to know Christ is to know his benefits "; and in this resides our knowledge that the Bible and God's Holy Spirit are given to the church for its nurture and for the healing of its wounds, and our assurance that they can and will serve this purpose in our time.

Notes

Prologue

1. *Die kirchliche Dogmatik* (Zürich: Evangelischer Verlag, 1932 ff.), I, 1, pp. 35–43 (*Church Dogmatics,* I, 1, pp. 38–47). Quotations from *Die kirchliche Dogmatik,* Vols. I, II, and IV used by permission of Evangelischer Verlag.

2. Daniel Day Williams, "Authority and Ministry," *Union Seminary Quarterly Review,* Vol. XIV, No. 1 (November, 1958), p. 17.

3. *The Faith of a Moralist* (London: The Macmillan Company, 1930), Series II, p. 198.

4. Heinrich Heppe, *Reformed Dogmatics* (London: George Allen and Unwin, Ltd., 1950), pp. 12–41.

5. R. M. Grant, *The Letter and the Spirit* (London: S.P.C.K., 1957).

6. *De principiis,* iv. i. 11–13.

7. Beryl Smalley, *The Study of the Bible in the Middle Ages* (Oxford: Clarendon Press, 1941).

8. R. M. Grant, *The Bible in the Church* (The Macmillan Company, 1948), p. 70.

9. F. W. Farrar, *History of Interpretation* (London: The Macmillan Company, 1886), pp. 266–267.

10. G. H. Gilbert, *Interpretation of the Bible* (The Macmillan Company, 1908), p. 195.

Chapter I. *Martin Luther*

1. A. Harnack, *Outline of the History of Dogma* (London: Hodder and Stoughton, 1893), p. 558.

2. A. Harnack, *Lehrbuch der Dogmengeschichte* (Freiburg: Akademische Verlagsbuchhandlung von J. C. B. Mohr, 1890), III, p. 696.

3. Martin Luther, *Vorreden, historische und philologische Schriften* (St. Louis, Mo.: 1880 ff.), XIV, p. 438.

4. The word "subsume" is used here in its original, positive (and not in its current, negative, and polemical) sense: *sub sumo,* to take into by drawing under.

5. *Lehrbuch,* III, pp. 693, 745–746.

6. *K. D.,* I, 1, p. 292 (*C. D.,* I, 1, p. 316).

7. *K. D.,* I, 1, p. 294 (*C. D.,* I, 1, p. 319). Cf. Edgar M. Carlson, *The Reinterpretation of Luther* (The Westminster Press, 1948), pp. 140–150.

8. Reinhold Seeberg, *Textbook of the History of Doctrines* (Baker Book House, 1952), II, p. 297.

9. *Lehrbuch,* III, p. 737.

10. *Prüfstein, Probierstein, Streichstein, Regel, Richtschnur, lapsis lidius.* Martin Luther, *Werke* (Weimar: 1883 ff.), XLVI, p. 780; VII, p. 640; XXXIII, pp. 276, 304; XXX, 1, p. 276.

11. *St. Louis Ed.,* XIV, p. 439.

12. *W. A.,* I, pp. 525–527.

13. *Vocem tuam vocem Christi. W. A.,* I, pp. 528–529.

14. Preserved Smith, *Luther's Correspondence* (Lutheran Publication Society, 1913), I, p. 159.

15. *W. A.,* VI, p. 413.

16. Some interesting and diverse examples, in addition to those discussed, are found in *W. A.:* VI, pp. 512–513; VII, pp. 313–315, 429–431, 662–663, 667; XI, p. 409; XII, p. 217; XVIII, pp. 627–631; XXX, 1, pp. 643–645; XXXI, p. 214; L, p. 639.

17. *W. A.,* I, p. 234.

18. *W. A.,* VI, pp. 560–561.

19. *W. A.,* X, 2, pp. 61 ff.

20. *W. A.,* X, 2, p. 86.

21. *W. A.,* X, 2, p. 92.

22. *W. A.,* VII, p. 614.

23. *W. A.,* VII, p. 675.

24. *W. A.,* VII, p. 640.

25. *W. A.,* VII, p. 663.

26. *W. A.,* VII, p. 639.

27. *W. A.,* VII, p. 641.

28. *W. A.,* VII, p. 632.

29. *Die Schrift allein. W. A.,* VII, p. 641.

30. *W. A.,* VII, pp. 662, 673. Some additional examples of this kind of direct, unambiguous use of the Scriptures as the criterion of doctrine, in quite different contexts, are found in *W. A.:* II, pp. 64, 727 ff., 291–292, 296–297, 301–302, 322, 357 ff., 411 ff.; VII, pp. 311–317, 429–431, 451–453; X, 2, pp. 88–89, 91–92; X, 3, pp. 2–4, 22–23, 33–40; XVIII, pp. 291 ff.; XXXI, pp. 207–209; L, pp. 519–520, 524–526, 543–547, 572–573, 606–607, 615–616.

31. *Zisscheten eintrechtiglich. W. A.,* XXXI, pp. 208–209.

32. *W. A.,* L, p. 572.

33. *W. A.,* VII, p. 639.

34. *W. A.,* VI, p. 301.

35. *W. A.,* VII, pp. 639–640. It was not unusual for Luther to refer to the text of the Bible as the *words* of God, or the words of the Holy Spirit; and, of course, because he was writing *before* the development of the hermeneutics of Protestant orthodoxy, he did so without the reserve prompted by a consciousness of the problems that we today necessarily associate with these expressions. E.g., *W. A.:* VI, pp. 286, 313, 316, 509, 512; VII, pp. 341, 342, 422, 598; XII, pp. 217, 240, 241; XVIII, pp. 704, 707, 712, 748; XXXI, p. 193.

36. *W. A.,* VII, p. 650.

37. *W. A.,* VI, p. 509. Cf. *W. A.,* XVIII, pp. 701–704.

38. *W. A.,* VII, pp. 647 ff.

39. *Zungen oder sprachen Sinn; grammaticum, historicum sensum. W. A.,* VII, p. 652.

40. *W. A.,* X, 1, p. 576. *St. Louis Ed.,* XIV, p. 4.

41. *W. A.,* VII, p. 658.

42. *St. Louis Ed.,* XIV, p. 109.

43. *St. Louis Ed.,* XIV, p. 4.

44. *St. Louis Ed.,* XIV, p. 89.

45. *St. Louis Ed.,* XIV, p. 95.

46. *St. Louis Ed.,* XIV, p. 14.

47. *Legislator. W. A.,* XL, 2, p. 43.

48. *W. A.,* XL, 1, p. 479.

49. *W. A.,* XL, 1, pp. 259, 480.

50. *W. A.,* XL, 1, p. 481.

51. *W. A.,* XL, 1, p. 259.

52. *W. A.,* XL, 1, p. 509.

53. *Inst.,* II. vii. 12 (*C. R.,* II, p. 261).

54. *W. A.,* L, p. 643.

55. *W. A.,* VII, p. 656.

56. *W. A.,* XL, 1, pp. 207, 486.

57. Bernard Ramm, *Protestant Biblical Interpretation: A Textbook of Hermeneutics for Conservative Protestants* (W. A. Wilde Co., 1950), pp. 31 f. n., 53 ff.

58. Rupert E. Davies, *The Problem of Authority in the Continental Reformers* (London: Epworth Press, 1946), pp. 34, 36 (italics mine). Used by permission of the publisher. Cf. Auguste Sabatier, *Religions of Authority and the Religion of the Spirit* (McClure, Phillips and Co., 1904), pp. 155–160.

59. *St. Louis Ed.,* XIV, p. 128.

60. *Ibid.*

61. *St. Louis Ed.,* XIV, p. 91.

62. *St. Louis Ed.,* XIV, pp. 127–129.

63. See, e.g.: *W. A.,* II, pp. 125–126; Preserved Smith, *The Life and Letters of Martin Luther* (Houghton Mifflin Company, 1911), p. 269. Luther's question about Hebrews, James, Jude, and Revelation reached its highest degree of intensity when he separated them from the other New Testament writings in his translation of the New Testament in 1522. See also, as the other side of this coin, his apparently serious suggestion, in *De Servo Arbitrio,* that the *Loci Communes* of Melanchthon should be included in the canon. *W. A.,* XVIII, p. 601.

64. See, e.g.: Karl Barth, *K. D.,* I, 1 and I, 2, *passim.* Emil Brunner, *Revelation and Reason* (The Westminster Press, 1946), *passim; The Christian Doctrine of God* (The Westminster Press, 1950), pp. 107–113; Gustaf Aulén, *The Faith of the Christian Church* (Muhlenberg Press, 1948), pp. 359–370; R. E. Davies, *op. cit.,* pp. 15–61; E. M. Carlson, *op. cit.,* pp. 116–127; Philip S. Watson, *Let God Be God!* (London: Epworth Press, 1947), pp. 149–189; Wil-

helm Pauck, *The Heritage of the Reformation* (Beacon Press, 1950), pp. 31–38; J. K. S. Reid, *The Authority of Scripture* (London: Methuen & Co., Ltd., 1957), pp. 56–72; Gordon Rupp, *The Righteousness of God* (London: Hodder and Stoughton, 1953), pp. 320–322.

65. *W. A.*, X, 1, p. 158.

66. *W. A.*, XI, p. 223.

67. *W. A.*, X, 1, pp. 186, 188.

68. *W. A.*, VIII, p. 491.

69. *W. A.*, II, p. 213.

70. *W. A.*, X, 1, p. 80.

71. It is interesting, and quite informative, that so many of the scholars who posited " two Luthers " as the solution to this problem were completely divided among themselves, with some tending to absolve the "young Luther" or "earlier Luther," and others the "old Luther" or "later Luther," of Biblical literalism and an authoritative Bible. Cf., e.g.: Sabatier, *op. cit.*, pp. 159–160; Ernst Troeltsch, *The Social Teaching of the Christian Churches* (The Macmillan Company, 1931), II, p. 486; Seeberg, *op. cit.*, II, pp. 298–302. Harnack, *Lehrbuch,* III, pp. 733–737; Hartmann Grisar, *Luther* (London: Kegan Paul, Trench, Trübner and Co., 1915), IV, pp. 407–408; George Park Fisher, *History of Christian Doctrine* (Charles Scribner's Sons, 1899), p. 280; A. C. McGiffert, *Martin Luther, the Man and His Work* (Century Company, 1912), p. 332; Julius Köstlin, *The Theology of Luther* (Luther Publishing Society, 1897), II, p. 228.

72. *W. A.*, L, pp. 520, 544.

Chapter II. *John Calvin*

1. *Inst.*, I. vii–ix (*C. R.*, II, pp. 56–72). Quotations from the *Institutes* are taken from the Allen translation, John Calvin, *Institutes of the Christian Religion* (Presbyterian Board of Christian Education, 1936). The references in the *Corpus Reformatorum* (*Calvini Opera*) have been added parenthetically for convenience. Where there is a departure from the Allen translation, the form has been reversed, with the reference in the *C. R.* given first.

2. *Inst.*, I. vii. 5 (*C. R.*, II, p. 60).

3. *Ibid.*

4. Cf.: Edward A. Dowey, Jr., *The Knowledge of God in Calvin's Theology* (Columbia University Press, 1952), pp. 86 ff.; Benjamin B. Warfield, *Calvin and Augustine* (Presbyterian and Reformed Publishing Company, 1956), pp. 48 ff.; T. H. L. Parker, *The Doctrine of the Knowledge of God* (London: Oliver and Boyd, 1952), pp. 41 ff.; Ronald S. Wallace, *Calvin's Doctrine of the Word and Sacrament* (London: Oliver and Boyd, 1953), pp. 96 ff.

5. John Calvin, *Tracts Relating to the Reformation* (Edinburgh: Calvin Translation Society, 1894), p. 37; *Inst.,* I. vi. 1 and IV. viii. 4 (*C. R.,* II, pp. 53, 848).

6. *C. R.,* II, p. 54 (*Inst.,* I. vi. 2).

7. *W. A.,* VII, p. 650.

8. *W. A.,* XVIII, p. 609.

9. *Sensus divinitatis; semen religionis. Inst.,* I. iii. 1 (*C. R.,* II, p. 36).

10. *Inst.,* I. ii–iii (*C. R.,* II, pp. 34–38).

11. *Inst.,* II. i (*C. R.,* II, pp. 175–185).

12. *Inst.,* II. ii–iii (*C. R.,* II, pp. 185–224).

13. Commentary on I Cor. 1:20. John Calvin, *Commentary on the Epistles of Paul to the Corinthians* (Edinburgh: Calvin Translation Society, 1848), I, p. 82 (*C. R.,* XLIX, p. 325).

14. *Inst.,* I. vi. 1 (*C. R.,* II, p. 53).

15. *Doctrinam Dei viventis. Inst.,* Vol. I, p. 23 (*C. R.,* II, p. 12).

16. John Calvin, *The Mystery of Godliness* (Wm. B. Eerdmans Publishing Company, 1950), p. 139.

17. *C. R.,* II, pp. 1059–1060 (*Inst.,* IV. xviii. 12).

18. *Totam coelestis doctrinae summam. Inst.,* III. ii. 13 (*C. R.,* II, p. 408).

19. *Inst.,* I. xv (*C. R.,* II, pp. 134–143).

20. John Calvin, *The Deity of Christ and Other Sermons* (Wm. B. Eerdmans Publishing Company, 1950), pp. 243–244.

21. *Inst.,* IV. viii. 4 (*C. R.,* II, p. 848).

22. *Inst.,* I. vi. 4 (*C. R.,* II, p. 56).

23. *Inst.,* I. ix. 1 (*C. R.,* II, p. 69).

24. *Inst.,* III. xxi. 2 (*C. R.,* II, p. 680).

25. *Inst.,* I. vi. 1 (*C. R.,* II, p. 53).

26. *C. R.,* II, p. 850 (*Inst.,* IV. viii. 8).

27. *Inst.,* I. vii. 5 (*C. R.,* II, p. 60).

28. *Inst.,* I. vii. 5 (*C. R.,* II, p. 60).

29. Commentary on I Peter 1:25. John Calvin, *Commentaries on the Catholic Epistles* (Edinburgh: Calvin Translation Society, 1855), p. 60 (*C. R.,* LV, p. 230).

30. *The Mystery of Godliness,* p. 131.

31. Warfield, *op. cit.,* p. 63.

32. Cf. Dowey, *op. cit.,* pp. 90 ff.

33. *Inst.,* IV. viii. 6 (*C. R.,* II, p. 849).

34. *Inst.,* I. vii. 4 (*C. R.,* II, p. 59).

35. *Inst.,* IV. viii. 6 (*C. R.,* II, p. 849).

36. *Ibid.*

37. *Ibid.*

38. *Ibid.* Cf.: Commentary on Jer. 36:4–8; Commentary on John, ch. 1; Commentary on II Tim. 3:16.

39. *Inst.,* IV. viii. 9 (*C. R.,* II, p. 851).

40. *Inst.,* I. vii. 1–2 (*C. R.,* II, pp. 56–57).

41. Commentary on II Tim. 3:16. John Calvin, *Commentaries on the Epistles to Timothy, Titus, and Philemon* (Edinburgh: Calvin Translation Society, 1856), p. 249 (*C. R.,* LII, p. 383).

42. Commentary on Gal. 4:22. John Calvin, *Commentaries on the Epistles of Paul to the Galatians and Ephesians* (Wm. B. Eerdmans Publishing Company, 1948), p. 135 (*C. R.,* L, pp. 236–237). Cf. *Commentaires de Jehan Calvin sur le Nouveau Testament* (Paris: Ch. Meyrueis et Compagnie, 1855), Tome Troisième, pp. 621–622.

43. *Ibid.* (italics mine).

44. *C. R.,* II, pp. 34–35, 41, 73, 402 (*Inst.,* I. ii. 2, I. v. 1, I. x. 2, and III. ii. 6).

45. Commentary on II Tim. 3:16. Calvin, *Commentaries on the Epistles to Timothy, Titus, and Philemon,* p. 249 (*C. R.,* LII, p. 383).

46. *Inst.,* I. ix. 1 (*C. R.,* II, p. 70).

47. *Inst.,* I. ix. 1 (*C. R.,* II, p. 70).

48. A. Lecerf, *Estudes Calvinistes* (Paris: Delachaux and Niestle, 1949), p. 85.

49. *Religions of Authority,* pp. 155 ff.

50. *Tracts Relating to the Reformation,* p. 37.

51. *Inst.,* I. vii. 5 (*C. R.,* II, p. 60).

52. *Inst.*, III. ii. 36 (*C. R.*, II, p. 428).

53. *Inst.*, II. i (*C. R.*, II, pp. 175–185).

54. *C. R.*, II, p. 403 (*Inst.*, III. ii. 7).

55. *C. R.*, II, p. 428 (*Inst.*, III. ii. 36).

56. *Inst.*, I. vii. 4 (*C. R.*, II, p. 59).

57. Westminster Confession of Faith, Ch. I, Sec. 5.

58. *Estudes Calvinistes*, p. 84.

59. *C. R.*, II, p. 70 (*Inst.*, I. ix. 2). Cf. Luther, *W. A.*, XVIII, p. 653.

60. *C. R.*, II, p. 71 (*Inst.*, I. ix. 3).

61. *C. R.*, II, p. 70 (*Inst.*, I. ix. 2. The English translation of this passage apparently was unduly influenced by the French edition. Cf. *C. R.*, III, p. 112).

62. *Inst.*, I. ix. 2 (*C. R.*, II, p. 70).

63. Heppe, *op. cit.*, p. 12.

64. J. K. S. Reid, *op. cit.*, p. 78.

65. Heppe, *op. cit.*, p. 43.

66. *Fundamentum fidei* or *articuli fundamentales* and *articuli non fundamentales*.

67. Heppe, *op. cit.*, p. 17.

CHAPTER III. *The Nineteenth-Century Revolt*

1. Cf., e.g., Friedrich Schleiermacher, *Der christliche Glaube* (Halle: Verlag von Otto Hendel, 1830), 130.

2. Chapter 6.

3. Cf. Ferdinand Kattenbusch, *Die deutsche evangelische Theologie seit Schleiermacher* (Giessen: Alfred Töpelmann, 1934), II, pp. 20–21.

4. *Die protestantische Theologie im 19. Jahrhundert* (Zürich: Evangelischer Verlag, 1952), p. 380.

5. *C. G.*, 18. 3.

6. *C. G.*, 19. 2.; 15.

7. *C. G.*, 19. 4.

8. *C. G.*, 11. 5.

9. *C. G.*, 3. 2.

10. *C. G.*, 32. 2.

11. *C. G.*, 11. 1.

12. Herbert H. Farmer, *Revelation and Religion* (London: Nisbet and Co., 1954), p. 52.

13. *C. G.*, 4. 4.
14. *C. G.*, 4. 4.
15. *C. G.*, 128 ff.
16. *C. G.*, 3.
17. *Insichbleiben* and *Aussichheraustreten.*
18. *C. G.*, 3. 3.
19. Paul Tillich, *Systematic Theology* (University of Chicago Press, 1951), I, pp. 41–42. Quotations from *Systematic Theology,* Vol. I, are used by permission of the publisher.
20. Cf.: *ibid.*, pp. 8–12, 41–42; Barth, *Die protestantische Theologie im 19. Jahrhundert,* pp. 386 ff. It should be remembered that the German word for "immediate" is *unmittelbar.*
21. *Ein Sichselbstsetzen* and *ein Sichselbstnichtsogesetzhaben* or *ein Sein* and *ein Irgendwiegewordensein.*
22. *Das schlechthinige Abhängigkeitsgefühl.*
23. *C. G.*, 30. 1.
24. *C. G.*, 6.
25. *C. G.*, 14. *Zusaz.*
26. *C. G.*, 4.
27. *C. G.*, 9. 1; 63. 1–2.
28. *C. G.*, 9. 1.
29. *Eigenthümliche Wesen.*
30. *Erlösung.*
31. *C. G.*, 10.
32. *C. G.*, 11. 2.
33. *C. G.*, 10. 1.
34. *Unmittelbar. C. G.*, 128. 2.
35. Sören Kierkegaard, *Philosophical Fragments* (Princeton University Press, 1944), pp. 74 ff. Quotations from this work are used by permission of the publisher.
36. *C. G.*, 91. 1.
37. *C. G.*, 91. 1.
38. *C. G.*, 11. 4.
39. *Gottvergessenheit. C. G.*, 11. 2.; 70–74. Cf. Luther: "What then does it mean to be 'in death and hell'? First of all, forgetfulness of God." *W. A.*, V, p. 209.
40. *C. G.*, 100.
41. *C. G.*, 62. 3.

42. *C. G.*, 74. 3.
43. *C. G.*, 11. 3.
44. *C. G.*, 11. 4.
45. *C. G.*, 11. 3.
46. *C. G.*, 14.; 128.
47. *C. G.*, 129.
48. *C. G.*, 27. 3.
49. *C. G.*, 27.
50. Sabatier, *Religions of Authority*, p. 261.
51. *Ibid.*, p. vii.
52. *Ibid.*, p. 283.
53. *Ibid.*, p. 164.
54. *Ibid.*, pp. 153, 155.
55. *Ibid.*, p. 252.
56. *Ibid.*, p. 176.
57. *Ibid.*, p. 186.
58. *Ibid.*, p. 209.
59. *Ibid.*, pp. 209, 212.
60. *Ibid.*, p. 205.
61. *Ibid.*, p. 349.
62. Auguste Sabatier, *Outlines of a Philosophy of Religion Based on Psychology and History* (James Pott and Co., 1897).
63. *Religions of Authority*, p. 349.
64. *Ibid.*, p. 271.
65. *Ibid.*, p. ix.
66. *Ibid.*, pp. 281, 257.
67. *Ibid.*, p. 347.
68. *Ibid.*
69. *Ibid.*, p. 365.
70. *Ibid.*, pp. 348–349.
71. *C. G., zweiter Theil.*
72. *Religions of Authority*, pp. 366–367.
73. *Ibid.*, p. 369.
74. *Ibid.*, p. 374.
75. *Ibid.*, p. 368.
76. *Ibid.*, p. 365.
77. *Ibid.*, p. 372.

78. *Ibid.*, p. 341.

79. James Martineau, *The Seat of Authority in Religion* (London: Longmans, Green & Co., Inc., 1890), pp. 157, 172.

80. *Ibid.*, p. 290.

81. *Ibid.*, p. 302.

82. *Ibid.*, p. 304.

83. *Ibid.*, p. 305.

84. *Ibid.*, pp. 305–306, 320.

85. William Temple, *Nature, Man and God* (The Macmillan Company, 1949), p. 322.

86. Martineau, *op. cit.*, pp. 321–322.

87. *Ibid.*, p. 322.

88. *Ibid.*, pp. 46, 76.

89. *Ibid.*, pp. 461, 71.

90. *Ibid.*, p. 288.

91. *Ibid.*, p. 129.

92. *Ibid.*, pp. 173, 311.

93. *Ibid.*, p. 356.

94. *Ibid.*, p. 331. Cf.: C. C. McCown, *The Search for the Real Jesus* (Charles Scribner's Sons, 1940); Maurice Goguel, *Jesus the Nazarene — Myth or History?* (Appleton-Century-Crofts, Inc., 1926), pp. 1–25; Albert Schweitzer, *The Quest of the Historical Jesus* (The Macmillan Company, 1948), pp. 1–222.

95. Henry J. Cadbury, *The Peril of Modernizing Jesus* (The Macmillan Company, 1937), pp. 15–16.

96. D. M. Baillie, *God Was in Christ* (Charles Scribner's Sons, 1951), p. 32.

97. Emil Brunner, *The Mediator* (The Westminster Press, 1947), pp. 56–71. Barth, *K. D.*, I, 1, p. 293 (*C. D.*, I, 1, pp. 317–318).

98. Cf. Paul Ramsey, ed., *Faith and Ethics* (Harper & Brothers, 1957), p. 23.

99. Martineau, *op. cit.*, pp. 356, 515.

CHAPTER IV. *Prophetic Reaction*

1. *The Principle of Authority* (London: Independent Press, Ltd., 1913), p. 347.

2. Sabatier, *Religions of Authority,* p. 347.

3. Sören Kierkegaard, *The Point of View* (London: Oxford University Press, 1950), p. 42.

4. *Ibid.*, p. 59.

5. Cf. Arthur C. Cochrane, *The Existentialists and God* (The Westminster Press, 1956), p. 25.

6. Sören Kierkegaard, *The Journals of Sören Kierkegaard* (London: Oxford University Press, 1951), 1025.

7. Sören Kierkegaard, *Philosophical Fragments,* p. iii, and *Concluding Unscientific Postscript* (Princeton University Press, 1944), pp. 18, 323 ff.

8. G. E. Lessing, *Lessing's Theological Writings,* ed., Henry Chadwick (London: Adam and Charles Black, 1956), pp. 51-55.

9. *Postscript,* p. 25.

10. G. W. F. Hegel, *The Philosophy of History* (Willey Book Company, 1944), p. 9.

11. *Fragments,* p. 48.

12. *Postscript,* p. 47.

13. *Ibid.,* p. 48.

14. *Fragments,* p. 87.

15. *Ibid.,* p. 52.

16. *Postscript,* p. 216.

17. *Fragments,* p. 32.

18. *Ibid.*

19. Sören Kierkegaard, *On Authority and Revelation* (Princeton University Press, 1955).

20. *Postscript,* p. 182.

21. *On Authority and Revelation,* p. 26.

22. *Fragments,* p. 37.

23. Karl Barth, *Der Römerbrief* (6th ed.; Munich: Chr. Kaiser, 1926), p. xiii.

24. *Fragments,* pp. 24-43.

25. *Postscript,* p. 116.

26. Sören Kierkegaard, *Fear and Trembling* (Princeton University Press, 1945), pp. 50 ff.

27. *Journals,* 809.

28. *Postscript,* p. 35.

29. *Ibid.,* pp. 23-44.

30. *Journals*, 1340.

31. *Journals*, 847.

32. *The Principle of Authority*, pp. 49 ff., 74 ff.

33. *Ibid.*, p. 10.

34. Cf.: R. J. Campbell, *The New Theology* (London: The Macmillan Company, 1907); J. S. Lawton, *Conflict in Christology* (London: S.P.C.K., 1947), Ch. 8.

35. *The Principle of Authority*, p. 20.

36. P. T. Forsyth, "The Evangelical Principle of Authority," *Proceedings of the Second International Council*, 1899, pp. 57–63. *The Principle of Authority*, pp. 39, 72, 184, 365, 401, 419.

37. H. Richard Niebuhr, *The Meaning of Revelation* (The Macmillan Company, 1946), p. 37.

38. *The Principle of Authority*, p. 300.

39. Cf.: *ibid.*, p. 149; Barth, *K. D.*, II, 1, pp. 1 ff. (*C. D.*, II, 1, pp. 3 ff.).

40. *The Principle of Authority*, p. 149. Cf. Martin Buber, *I and Thou* (Charles Scribner's Sons, 1958), pp. 134–137.

41. *Ibid.*, p. 11.

42. *The Principle of Authority*, p. 400.

43. Cf. Albrecht Ritschl, *The Christian Doctrine of Justification and Reconciliation* (Charles Scribner's Sons, 1900), pp. 8–26, 203 ff.

44. E.g., *The Principle of Authority*, p. 389.

45. E.g.: W. L. Bradley, *P. T. Forsyth, The Man and His Work* (London: Independent Press, Ltd., 1952), p. 106; Robert McAfee Brown, *P. T. Forsyth: Prophet for Today* (The Westminster Press, 1952), p. 31.

46. *The Principle of Authority*, p. 4.

47. Cf.: Immanuel Kant, *Critique of Practical Reason* (London: Longmans, Green & Co., 1948), p. 9; Forsyth, *The Principle of Authority*, pp. 201, 308–309.

48. *The Principle of Authority*, p. 5.

49. *Ibid.*, p. 6.

50. *Ibid.*, p. 366.

51. *Ibid.*, pp. 43, 164.

52. *Ibid.*, p. 7. Cf. P. T. Forsyth, *The Church and the Sacraments* (London: Independent Press, Ltd., 1949), p. xv.

53. *The Principle of Authority,* p. 172.

54. Forsyth seems to have been the first English-speaking theologian to use the word " existential," and he uses it in this sense and for this purpose. *Ibid.,* p. 192.

55. *Ibid.,* pp. 112–114.

56. *Ibid.,* p. 63.

57. *Ibid.,* p. 59.

58. *Ibid.,* p. 58. Cf. pp. 6, 37, 46, 116, 169, 299, 309, 401.

59. *Ibid.,* pp. 146, 300.

60. *Ibid.* p. 154.

Chapter V. *The Contextual Approach*

1. *Sytematic Theology,* I, p. 52.

2. *S. T.,* I, pp. 47 ff.

3. *S. T.,* I, p. 8.

4. Paul Tillich, " The Problem of Theological Method," *The Journal of Religion,* Vol. XXVI (January, 1947), pp. 18–19; *S. T.,* I, pp. 8–11, 40–41.

5. *S. T.,* I, pp. 3–4.

6. *S. T.,* II, pp. 5–10.

7. John Baillie, ed., *Natural Theology* (London: Geoffrey Bles, 1946); Barth, *K. D.,* I, 1, pp. 24–35, 251–252.

8. *S. T.,* I, pp. 3–8, 64–65; II, p. 14.

9. *S. T.,* I, pp. 30, 204–210; II, p. 14.

10. *S. T.,* I, p. 65.

11. *S. T.,* I, p. 64; II, pp. 15–16.

12. " Reply to Interpretation and Criticism," Charles W. Kegley and Robert W. Bretall, eds., *The Theology of Paul Tillich* (The Macmillan Company, 1952), p. 330. Cf. *S. T.,* I, pp. 53–54.

13. *S. T.,* II, p. 13; I, pp. 62–64.

14. *S. T.,* I, p. 63.

15. *S. T.,* II, p. 13 (italics mine).

16. *S. T.,* I, p. 61.

17. Kegley and Bretall, *op. cit.,* p. 330.

18. *S. T.,* II, p. 13.

19. *S. T.,* I, pp. 8–11.

20. *S. T.,* II, pp. 14–15.

21. *S. T.,* II, p. 15.

22. *S. T.,* I, pp. 8–11.

23. *S. T.,* I, pp. 202–204, 254–256; II, pp. 29–45.

24. Chapter III.

25. Cf.: Schleiermacher, *C. G.,* 3. 2; *S. T.,* I, p. 9, and II, pp. 10–12.

26. *S. T.,* I, pp. 46–49.

27. *S. T.,* I, p. 166.

28. *S. T.,* II, pp. 44–78.

29. *S. T.,* II, p. 35.

30. Kegley and Bretall, *op. cit.,* pp. 219–222. Tillich's contention is that the "transcendent fall" is "hidden behind" the Genesis story, and thus is indirectly Biblical. *S. T.,* II, pp. 37–38.

31. *S. T.,* II, p. 29.

32. *S. T.,* II, p. 37.

33. *Biblical Religion and the Search for Ultimate Reality* (University of Chicago Press, 1955), p. 42.

34. *S. T.,* II, p. 56.

35. *The Shaking of the Foundations* (Charles Scribner's Sons, 1948), p. 154.

36. Cf. Sören Kierkegaard, *The Concept of Dread* (Princeton University Press, 1944), pp. 27–32.

37. *C. R.,* II, pp. 31–32 (*Inst.,* I. i. 1–2). Cf. *S. T.,* I, p. 63.

38. *W. A.,* XL, 1, p. 481.

39. *S. T.,* I, pp. 11–15.

40. *S. T.,* I, pp. 11, 49.

41. *S. T.,* I, pp. 18, 23.

42. *S. T.,* I, p. 18. Cf. *Biblical Religion and the Search for Ultimate Reality,* pp. 5–14.

43. "The Problem of Theological Method," pp. 17–18. *S. T.,* I, p. 9.

44. "The Problem of Theological Method," pp. 16–18.

45. *S. T.,* I, p. 23.

46. *The Protestant Era* (University of Chicago Press, 1948), p. 87.

47. *S. T.,* II, p. 11 (italics mine).

48. *S. T.,* I, p. 21.

49. "The Problem of Theological Method," p. 17.

50. *S. T.,* II, pp. 30–31.

51. *The Protestant Era,* p. 89.

52. *S. T.,* I, pp. 24–25; II, pp. 26, 30.

53. *The Protestant Era,* pp. 88–89.

54. Kegley and Bretall, *op. cit.,* p. 337.

55. *S. T.,* II, p. 30. Kegley and Bretall, *op. cit.,* p. 336.

56. *S. T.,* I, pp. 71–81.

57. Hendrik Kraemer, *Religion and the Christian Faith* (The Westminster Press, 1956), p. 421.

58. *The Protestant Era,* p. 86.

59. Kegley and Bretall, *op. cit.,* p. 336.

60. *S. T.,* II, pp. 5 ff.

61. *Biblical Religion and the Search for Ultimate Reality,* pp. 81–85.

62. Hendrik Kraemer, *op. cit.,* p. 428.

63. E.g., *Das System der Wissenschaften* (Göttingen: Vandenhoeck and Ruprecht, 1923).

64. "Faith is the state of being ultimately concerned: the dynamics of faith are the dynamics of man's ultimate concern." Paul Tillich, *Dynamics of Faith* (Harper & Brothers, 1957), p. 1. Cf. *Biblical Religion and the Search for Ultimate Reality,* pp. 58–59.

65. *S. T.,* I, pp. 11, 88–90.

66. *S. T.,* I, p. 90.

67. Cf. Edward A. Dowey, Jr., "Tillich, Barth, and the Criteria of Theology," *Theology Today,* Vol. XV, No. 1 (April, 1958), pp. 43–58.

68. Paul Tillich, *A History of Christian Thought,* an unpublished, stenographic transcription of lectures delivered in 1953, p. 229.

69. *S. T.,* I, p. 47.

70. *S. T.,* I, p. 48.

71. *S. T.,* I, pp. 47–48; II, pp. 165–166.

72. *S. T.,* I, p. 48.

73. *S. T.,* I, p. 49.

74. "The Problem of Theological Method," pp. 16–17, 22–23. Cf. Kegley and Bretall, *op. cit.,* p. 331.

75. *S. T.,* I, pp. 76, 92–93. Cf. "Existential Philosophy," *Journal of the History of Ideas,* Vol. V (January, 1944), pp. 44–70.

76. "The Problem of Theological Method," p. 22.

77. *S. T.,* I, pp. 40–45.

78. *S. T.,* I, pp. 126–128.

79. *S. T.,* I, p. 46.

80. "The Problem of Theological Method," pp. 17, 20. "The Bible and Systematic Theology," unpublished paper, 1947, pp. 5–6. *S. T.,* I, pp. 50–52.

81. *S. T.,* I, p. 55; II, p. 10.

82. *S. T.,* I, p. 49.

83. *S. T.,* II, pp. 94, 119; *The Protestant Era,* pp. 204–205; *The New Being,* p. 22.

84. *S. T.,* I, pp. 132–137; II, pp. 118–138. Cf. " A Reinterpretation of the Doctrine of the Incarnation," *The Church Quarterly Review,* Vol. CXLVII (January–March, 1949), pp. 133–148.

85. *The Interpretation of History* (Charles Scribner's Sons, 1936), p. 33.

86. *S. T.,* I, p. 151 (italics mine).

87. *S. T.,* II, pp. 105, 113–117. *The Interpretation of History,* p. 34.

88. *The New Being,* pp. 22, 44–45, 98 (italics mine); *S. T.,* I, p. 151, and II, p. 114.

89. In an article, " The Jesus of History and the Christ of Faith," *Theology Today,* Vol. X, No. 2 (July, 1953), pp. 170–184. Cf. James M. Robinson, *A New Quest of the Historical Jesus* (S. C. M. Press, Ltd., 1959).

90. *Op. cit.,* p. 146.

91. Kegley and Bretall, *op. cit.,* p. 330.

CHAPTER VI. *The Scientific and Normative Approaches*

1. Immanuel Kant, *Critique of Pure Reason* (Willey Book Company, 1943), pp. xvii, 359.

2. *Critique of Practical Reason,* pp. 220–229.

3. *Critique of Pure Reason,* p. 357.

4. *Anschauungen.*

5. Anders Nygren, *Religiöst a priori,* p. 238, quoted from Nels F. S. Ferré, *Swedish Contributions to Modern Theology* (Harper & Brothers, 1939), p. 45.

6. *Ibid.*

7. Gustaf Aulén, *The Faith of the Christian Church* (Muhlenberg Press, 1948), p. 1.

8. Gustaf Wingren, *Theology in Conflict* (Muhlenberg Press, 1958), p. 85.

9. Aulén, *op. cit.*, p. 1.

10. *Ibid.* (italics mine).

11. *Ibid.*, p. 21.

12. Wingren, *op. cit.*, p. 9.

13. Anders Nygren, *Agape and Eros* (The Westminster Press, 1953), pp. 38, 39.

14. Aulén, *op. cit.*, pp. 3–7.

15. *Ibid.*, p. 12.

16. *Ibid.*, pp. 5, 35.

17. *Ibid.*, pp. 3, 6.

18. Gustaf Aulén, *Christus Victor* (London: S.P.C.K., 1931), pp. 28, 175–176.

19. Edmund Husserl, *Ideas* (London: George Allen and Unwin, Ltd., 1931).

20. *K. D.*, I, 2, p. 920 (*C. D.*, I, 2, p. 823).

21. Ferré, *op. cit.*, p. 60. Cf. Husserl, *op. cit.*, pp. 11–30.

22. Aulén, *The Faith of the Christian Church*, pp. 3–4, 18.

23. *Ibid.*, p. 18.

24. Cf. Ferré, *op. cit.*, p. 23.

25. *S. T.*, I, p. 8.

26. Wingren, *op. cit.*, p. 89.

27. Ferré, *op. cit.*, pp. 219–222. *The Christian Fellowship* (Harper & Brothers, 1940), pp. 70–82.

28. *Swedish Contributions to Modern Theology*, pp. 229 ff.

29. *Ibid.*, p. 231.

30. Nels F. S. Ferré, *Return to Christianity* (Harper & Brothers, 1943), pp. 5–6.

31. Nels F. S. Ferré, *Faith and Reason* (Harper & Brothers, 1946), pp. 156–157; *Evil and the Christian Faith* (Harper & Brothers, 1947), p. 1.

32. *Faith and Reason*, pp. 159–197.

33. *Ibid.*, p. 198.

34. *Swedish Contributions to Modern Theology,* pp. 209–210. *The Christian Fellowship,* pp. 1–31.

35. *Swedish Contributions to Modern Theology,* pp. 212–213. *The Christian Fellowship, passim.*

36. Cf. *The Christian Faith* and *Faith and Reason.*

37. *Ibid.,* pp. 2, 72, 209. *Christianity and Society* (Harper & Brothers, 1950), pp. 20–28.

38. *The Christian Fellowship,* p. 52. Cf. *The Sun and the Umbrella* (Harper & Brothers, 1953), p. 34.

39. *The Christian Fellowship,* p. 52.

40. *Ibid.,* p. 49.

41. *Ibid.,* pp. 48–49. *The Christian Faith,* p. 37.

42. Cf. *Return to Christianity,* p. 17.

43. *The Christian Fellowship,* p. 48. *Evil and the Christian Faith,* p. 140.

44. *Christianity and Society,* pp. 22–24.

45. *The Christian Fellowship,* p. 53.

46. *Evil and the Christian Faith,* p. 169. *The Sun and the Umbrella,* p. 107.

47. Nels F. S. Ferré, *Pillars of Faith* (Harper & Brothers, 1948), p. 84.

48. *Faith and Reason,* p. 207.

49. *Pillars of Faith,* p. 96.

50. *Ibid.,* p. 87.

51. *Agape and Eros,* pp. 30–48.

52. Cf., e.g.: *Swedish Contributions to Modern Theology,* pp. 226 ff., 238–239; *The Christian Fellowship,* pp. 87 ff., 105, 107; *Christianity and Society,* pp. 45–46, 50.

CHAPTER VII. *The Confessional Approach*

1. *Types of Modern Theology* (London: James Nisbet and Co., Ltd., 1937), p. 314.

2. Karl Barth, *Der Römerbrief,* pp. v, x–xvi.

3. *Ibid.,* pp. v, xii, xix–xxiii. Cf. *K. D.,* I, 2, pp. 516–517, 545–548, 591–593 (*C. D.,* I, 2, pp. 466–468, 492–495, 532–534). The passages quoted from Barth's *Die kirchliche Dogmatik* are in most instances from the original, in order that the American idiom rather than the

British may predominate. Where corresponding references in the English editions are available, they have been noted parenthetically for convenience.

4. *K. D.,* I, 1, pp. 42–43 (*C. D.,* I, 1, pp. 46–47).

5. *K. D.,* I, 1, pp. 1–3; I, 2, pp. 831–848 (*C. D.,* I, 1, pp. 1–3; I, 2, pp. 743–758).

6. *K. D.,* IV, 1, p. 382 (*C. D.,* IV, 1, p. 346).

7. Cf. *K. D.,* I, 1, p. viii (*C. D.,* I, 1, p. ix).

8. *K. D,* IV, 2, p. 741.

9. *K. D.,* I, 1, pp. 3–10 (*C. D.,* I, 1, pp. 3–11).

10. *K. D.,* I, 1, p. 1; I, 2, pp. 857–859 (*C. D.,* I, 1, p. 1; 2, pp. 766–768).

11. *K. D.,* I, 1, pp. 91–92; I, 2, pp. 894–895, 954–955 (*C. D.,* I, 1, pp. 84–85; I, 2, pp. 800–801, 853–854).

12. *K. D.,* I, 1, p. 83 (*C. D.,* I, 1, p. 91).

13. *K. D.,* I, 1, p. 84 (*C. D.,* I, 1, p. 92).

14. *K. D.,* I, 2, p. 858 (*C. D.,* I, 2, p. 767).

15. *K. D.,* I, 2, p. 871 (*C. D.,* I, 2, p. 778).

16. *K. D.,* I, 2, p. 874 (*C. D.,* I, 2, p. 781). Cf. I, 2, pp. 970–971 (*C. D.,* I, 2, p. 868).

17. *K. D.,* I, 1, p. 14; II, 1, pp. 1–287 *passim* (*C. D.,* I, 1, p. 16; II, 1, pp. 3–254).

18. E.g., in varying contexts: *K. D.,* I, 1, pp. 18, 21, 89–90, 94, 112–113, 118–119, 121, 142, *et al.* (*C. D.,* I, 1, pp. 19, 23, 98, 103, 123–124, 129–131, 133, 156).

19. *K. D.,* I, 2, p. 956 (*C. D.,* I, 2, p. 855). In his later writings Barth has tended to use the word " miracle " more, and the categories " act " and " event " less, within this context, but with no perceptible change in the actualistic meaning that has been intended throughout.

20. *K. D.,* I, 1, pp. 40–43 (*C. D.,* I, 1, pp. 43–46).

21. *K. D.,* I, 2, p. 859 (*C. D.,* I, 2, p. 768).

22. *K. D.,* I, 2, pp. 848–874 (*C. D.,* I, 2, pp. 758–782).

23. *K. D.,* I, 1, pp. 16–23; I, 2, pp. 848–874 (*C. D.,* I, 1, pp. 17–25; I, 2, pp. 758–782).

24. See, e.g., the epistemological passage in *K. D.,* II, 1, pp. 1–287 (*C. D.,* II, 1, pp. 3–254), which from a noetic point of view could prove to be the most important section in the entire *Dogmatik.* And

is this not the decisive factor in the arrangement of the " three forms of the Word of God," where the form that is materially the first form, and is subsequently referred to as the first form, is placed last rather than first?

25. *Die protestantische Theologie im 19. Jahrhundert,* p. 410.

26. *K. D.,* I, 1, p. 20 (C. D., I, 1, p. 22).

27. *K. D.,* II, 1, p. 228 (*C. D.,* II, 1, p. 203).

28. *K. D.,* I, 2, pp. 897–900 (*C. D.,* I, 2, pp. 802–806).

29. *K. D.,* I, 1, p. 188; I, 2, pp. 816–818 (*C. D.,* I, 1, p. 171; I, 2, pp. 727–730).

30. The word "adapts" is used advisedly both because Barth makes no pretense of simply reproducing Luther's thought at this point, and because Luther did not use the *larva* concept exclusively or even primarily within the context of the epistemological problem. Luther referred to the whole of creation and its *ordinationes,* parents, princes, magistrates, etc., as *larvae* of God, thus embracing an assumption from which Barth draws back. Cf. *K. D.,* III, 3, p. 540: " The acts of God never take place ' in and under ' but always above and in contraposition to, although with, human action."

31. *W. A.,* XL, 1, p. 174.

32. *W. A.,* XL, 1, p. 361.

33. *W. A.,* XVIII, p. 633.

34. *K. D.,* I, 1, p. 172 (*C. D.,* I, 1, p. 189). Cf. John Dillenberger, *God Hidden and Revealed* (Muhlenberg Press, 1953), pp. 117–143.

35. *K. D.,* II, 1, p. 215 (*C. D.,* II, 1, p. 192).

36. *K. D.,* II, 1, pp. 15–21 (*C. D.,* II, 1, pp. 16–21).

37. *K. D.,* I, 2, pp. 815–818; II, 1, pp. 238–240, 764–765 (*C. D.,* I, 2, pp. 727–730; II, 1, pp. 212–213, 682–683).

38. *K. D.,* II, 1, p. 68 (*C. D.,* II, 1, p. 63).

39. *K. D.,* II, 1, pp. 2–3 (*C. D.,* II, 1, pp. 4–5).

40. *K. D.,* II, 1, p. 68 (*C. D.,* II, 1, p. 63).

41. *K. D.,* II, 1, p. 261 (*C. D.,* II, 1, p. 233).

42. *C. R.,* II, pp. 54–55 (Inst., I. vi. 2).

43. *K. D.,* I, 2, p. 829 (*C. D.,* I, 2, p. 739). Cf. *K. D.,* I, 2, pp. 913–915 (*C. D.,* I, 2, pp. 817–819).

44. *K. D.,* IV, 1, pp. 382–383 (*C. D.,* IV, 1, p. 346).

45. *K. D.,* I, 2, p. 818 (*C. D.,* I, 2, p. 730).

46. *K. D.*, I, 2, pp. 802–809 (*C. D.*, I, 2, pp. 715–722).

47. *K. D.*, I, 2, pp. 819–825, 865–866 (*C. D.*, I, 2, pp. 730–736, 774–775).

48. *K. D.*, I, 1, pp. 89–128 (*C. D.*, I, 1, pp. 98–140).

49. *K. D.*, I, 2, pp. 505, 602 (*C. D.*, I, 2, pp. 457, 540–542).

50. *K. D.*, I, 2, pp. 505, 551–554 (*C. D.*, I, 2, pp. 457, 497–499).

51. *K. D.*, I, 1, pp. 120, 125 (*C. D.*, I, 1, pp. 131, 136). Cf. *K. D.*, I, 2, p. 896 (*C. D.*, I, 2, p. 802).

52. *K. D.*, II, 1, p. 291 (*C. D.*, II, 1, p. 260).

53. *K. D.*, II, 1, p. 293 (*C. D.*, II, 1, p. 261). Cf. A. C. Cochrane, *op. cit.*, pp. 113–132.

54. *K. D.*, I, 1, p. 112 (*C. D.*, I, 1, p. 123).

55. *K. D.*, I, 2, p. 595 (*C. D.*, I, 2, p. 535).

56. *K. D.*, I, 2, p. 597 (*C. D.*, I, 2, p. 537).

57. *K. D.*, I, 2, pp. 557–558, 568–571 (*C. D.*, I, 2, pp. 502–503, 512–514).

58. *K. D.*, I, 1, p. 113 (*C. D.*, I, 1, p. 124).

59. *K. D.*, I, 2, p. 569 (*C. D.*, I, 2, p. 513).

60. *K. D.*, I, 2, p. 511 (*C. D.*, I, 2, p. 462).

61. *K. D.*, I, 2, pp. 505–507, 587–588, 603–605 (*C. D.*, I, 2, pp. 457–459, 528–530, 542–544).

62. *K. D.*, I, 1, p. 116 (*C. D.*, I, 1, p. 127).

63. *K. D.*, I, 2, pp. 548–556, 587–588 (*C. D.*, I, 2, pp. 497–502, 542–544).

64. *K. D.*, I, 2, p. 545 (*C. D.*, I, 2, p. 492).

65. *K. D.*, I, 2, pp. 538–545, 647–652 (*C. D.*, I, 2, pp. 486–492, 581–585).

66. *K. D.*, I, 2, p. 512 (*C. D.*, I, 2, p. 463).

67. *K. D.*, I, 2, pp. 912–919 (*C. D.*, I, 2, pp. 816–822).

Index